DATE			

Actors Are Madmen

Sheng and ch'ou actors on stage

ACTORS
ARE
MADMEN

Notebook of a Theatregoer in China

A. C. SCOTT

The University of Wisconsin Press

Published 1982

The University of Wisconsin Press
114 North Murray Street
Madison, Wisconsin 53715

The University of Wisconsin Press, Ltd.
1 Gower Street
London WC1E 6HA, England

First printing

Printed in the United States of America

For LC CIP information see the colophon

ISBN 0-299-08860-X

"Actors are madmen, the playgoers are fools"

CONTENTS

PREFACE

THE FIRST IMPRESSIONS of any traveller in an unfamiliar country are usually formed from sights, sounds, and smells which, however inconsequential at the time, can evoke recollections in the mind long after their world has disappeared into the past. The ambience of a winter evening in Nanking some thirty years ago is forever associated for me with a visit to the theatre which had unforeseen repercussions, as I have set out to suggest in these pages. The idea for this book grew out of a lunchtime conversation with the director of the University of Wisconsin Press, through whose initiative some of my translations of traditional Chinese plays had been published. Discussion at the table had turned on the possibility of writing about an area as removed from everyday Western experience as the theatre in China, without talking above people's heads and yet remaining informative. Because of my particular acquaintance with the Chinese stage world in the years before 1949, it was suggested that an informal account of the theatre and the environment in which it flourished then, written from the viewpoint of one who was there, might interest people today.

It was soon after this luncheon that China cautiously opened her doors to the outside world again, arousing a predictable curiosity among a general public thirsting for information and an equally predictable willingness to satisfy that curiosity by "those who look at the flowers while riding on horseback," as the Chinese so nicely describe immediate commentators. No area is so attractive to such observation as the theatre, which for obvious reasons is accessible to enthusiastic sightseers and special pleaders alike. I felt the time was appropriate to begin the narrative that follows in the way that had been suggested at our luncheon. It can best be read as a notebook in which a traveller has confided his impressions—a traveller who became involved with the ephemeral world of theatre to the exclusion of much else, perhaps, but who was fortunate in being able to linger long enough on his journey to experience at firsthand the flux of everyday life among the Chinese.

Two years spent in Nanking allowed me to become familiar with stage forms and techniques, thanks to the many backstage acquaintances I made in that city as well as in Peking and Shanghai. Beyond the world of theatre, however, political events were moving relentlessly towards a revolution which profoundly altered the nature of Chinese society and relegated for good the stage community among which I had spent so much time. There followed a long period of further involvement with theatre in Hongkong, particularly with a group of leading northern Chinese actors who had temporarily settled there with their troupes, and afterwards I was led to Japan, where for three years I became as deeply immersed in the kabuki theatre as I had been in that of Peking. A climax was reached in this theatrical wandering when in 1956 I returned to China to meet theatre people I had known and discover what was happening to them under the communist government.

Those days seem far away now, and there have been sweeping changes in the lives of Chinese people, not the least in their theatregoing habits. Their traditional entertainments have been subjected to a long period of doctrinal repression from which they are only now beginning to emerge. It seems unlikely, in my opinion, that the old theatre can ever revert to its former place in Chinese life, if only for the reason that continuity has been severed in a tradition of performance dependent on actors who were the children of continuity — while the audiences of old have given way to a new generation with very different standards of appreciation and understanding of dramatic form and content. Moreover, it is only necessary to consider the about-faces concerning theatre since the downfall of Mao's widow to perceive the dubious premises on which apologists — both inside and outside China — base their claims for the derivative forms passing for the new revolutionary art directly inspired by Soviet influence and teaching.

It is true that since the so-called "Gang of Four" have become nationally discredited as the source of all cultural evil, a general artistic thaw has set in and even traditional drama is being revived and performed once again. No one can quarrel with that in principle, nor with the fact that instruction and participation in the performing arts is now everyone's privilege from kindergarten onwards. However, it is less easy for some of us to accept the fact that an art which has been so selectively reconstituted as the traditional theatre can be restored as a living form through political expediency. We wonder about the thinking that decrees whole areas of a traditional culture to be denigrated, relegated, and rehabilitated according to doctrinal calculation, or that children's imaginations should be politically coerced through artistic education.

In speaking of the Chinese theatre world as I intensely experienced it, there is no intent to seem a partisan in the vexed argument of tradition versus innovation. No one familiar with China would argue that tradition and innovation are incompatible forces or that new artistic developments are not the concomitant expression of human continuity. It is the way that traditional culture has been subverted in the name of political beliefs that has been uncomfortably suggestive of totalitarianism of the mind in contemporary China.

Theatre people there have again been granted freedom of expression, it seems, but find themselves ill-equipped to move forward. Intellectually and artistically "cabined, cribbed, and confined," as they have been for more than a decade, they must revert to where they left off and take up the threads again. As yet they are sustained by the questionable but very deep-seated influences of Soviet "social realism" of the 1950s and a prejudiced concept of their traditional forms which seem vitiated by "Westernisation" conceived as political expediency in the first place. The long years of isolation have been corrosive. The hope must be that in the theatre, as in all the arts, the creative transformation of traditional cultural concepts may yet prove a stronger force than totalitarian transplantation.

The China in which I lived for a time was a country demoralised by a long war, economic chaos, and ineffectual government. People had been brought to a desperate plight. It is hard to know how the conclusion to it all could have been different, given the reigning anarchy of existence, but at least the people were not yet anesthetised by dogma and the suppression of all critical thinking. I have no regrets that I lived among the Chinese then. They were a complicated but warm and tolerant people, from whose inexhaustible humanism there was a great deal to learn — not the least in following their example by going to the theatre to see the actors.

Actors Are Madmen

INTRODUCTION

THE CHINESE HAVE A PROVERB to the effect that "actors are mad-men, the playgoers are fools," an apt description of the world of theatre in which all who do not share the fanaticism of its vota-ries are tolerated as outsiders. In China the theatre addict is known as a *hsi-mi*, meaning one who is bewitched or infatuated by the stage. Do we ourselves not say that someone is "stage struck" or "mad about theatre"? Wherever the subject is raised, be it East or West, the suggestion of passions bordering on lunacy seems common.

The Chinese among whom I spent my days in Nanking were quick to diagnose the familiar symptoms of a *hsi-mi* upon seeing my reactions to their theatre. With a benevolence born of a natu-ral tolerance for human susceptibilities, they accepted the in-evitable and in their sagacity prescribed indulgence as the only remedy for bewitchment. Where that indulgence led me is the subject of this book. First, however, it seems wise to offer some background information for those who are as innocent about the Chinese theatre as I once was and who have perhaps never kept company with "fools."

The old Chinese theatre functioned on the well-tried principle that the actor must be a past master of his craft or else get short shrift from his audience. He was trained in a tradition whereby the essential skills to make things work on the stage had been transmitted from generation to generation. If he had failed to profit from that legacy, the audience had little use for him. Pe-king plays were devised to give full scope to the prized virtuosity which wrung from the audience staccato shouts of *hao, hao,* "good, oh very good," when the performer met his obligations to the spectators. And if he failed them, he was quickly showered with cries of *t'ung, t'ung, t'ung,* a verdict on a par with the cries of "off, off, off," with which the gallery hurled down disapproval on the Victorian actor.

3

The Peking audiences of other days were uninhibited, autocratic in their expectations, and single-minded in their assessments. They went to the theatre to savor the interpretations of their stage favorites; the true connoisseur of form would often leave the theatre after seeing a well-loved passage rendered to his satisfaction. Yet it would be foolish to suppose that every Peking playgoer was bound by similar standards. Indeed, although the Chinese man in the street was second to none in expecting full value for his money, he would hardly have curtailed an outing to the theatre on such precious grounds. The fact that such purists existed at all, however, suggests the nature of the entertainment, and even the humblest playgoer expressed his appreciation through an inherited sense of form.

That is not to say that the ordinary Chinese playgoer remained emotionally detached. Often in the theatre one would see a slow tear roll down the cheek of the old lady sitting in the next seat or hear sniffling from the row behind, as an actor developed a familiar harrowing scene in a way that would have left the average realistically minded Western theatregoer coldly unmoved.

Going to the theatre was a high social occasion for the Chinese audience, to be indulged in with gusto and unconcern for the proprieties of Western audiences. On any festive occasion in China, there was always a sense of bustle, a seething undercurrent of irrepressible energy, a pulse in the rhythms of a life force emanating from a race whose continuity over centuries seemed highlighted by the surge of sound and movement enveloping any crowd gathered together for celebration. Nowhere could this be more acutely sensed than at theatrical performances, which more than any other gatherings expressed the solidarity of the great Chinese family.

People arrived and departed during a performance as fancy took them, drank tea, cracked melon seeds, or moved over to chat with an acquaintance suddenly spotted across the aisles. Babies slumbered in family servants' arms, since everyone went along to see the show — or maybe a group of wondering children gathered to stare at two irate adults holding tickets for the same seat. Through it all the clang and clash of the percussion in the stage orchestra added to the general hubbub, while the actors made their entrances and exits across the uncurtained stage like figures set in motion to continue imperturbably throughout time.

4

The actors' family members, friends, and friends of friends often crowded the wings to watch the proceedings at first hand, not infrequently overflowing onto the stage area, where they stood gazing on the world at large. Audience participation, which has fascinated our dramatic theorists in recent times, was all in a day's work on the Chinese stage.

However, to suppose that commotion reigned supreme in the Chinese theatre would be an error. When the occasion arose there was no more attentive or critical body than a Chinese audience because if the play was not the thing, the players most certainly were. Every word and every gesture of the actors was submitted for the approval of the spectators as a performance unfolded in all its panache. In spite of seeming anarchy, there arrived the moment in every play when the audience suddenly fell silent and there was a hush throughout the theatre focusing sudden attention as an actor began to perform some well-loved scene.

The old-fashioned theatre habitué had an intimate knowledge of the actor's craft. Frequently he was an amateur performer himself, for the Chinese theatre has always boasted an enthusiastic corps of amateur actors. In earlier days they came mostly from the ranks of government officials or better-off families, some even from the Imperial Palace itself — in any case, men with the leisure and means to employ professional actors as tutors. Government officials in Imperial China were recruited through a grinding series of competitive literary examinations, which required candidates to be steeped in the Confucian classics and philosophical works as well as having an absolute mastery of literary compositional skills. Only thus, it was reasoned, could men of the right wisdom to govern be found. In theory the famous examinations were open to all commoners who could qualify.

"All walks of life are lowly, only the scholar stands high," went the proverb, expressing a belief that has always lain deep in Chinese minds. No sacrifice was too great for any family, however humble, to support a son year after year if he aspired to enter government service.

Everybody who went through the traditional educational mill in China gained a ready familiarity with metaphor, proverbs, and literary allusions, which were readily assimilated in every-

5

day usage. Chinese officials were well-schooled in the subtle art of verbal imagery, avoiding a direct statement whenever a suitable metaphor was available, and it usually was. It goes without saying that in a land whose people absorbed figurative language with their mother's milk, as it were, and where every conceivable human activity was covered by some ready aphorism, the theatre was both a fertile source and subject. Peking theatregoers took keen delight in savoring the verbal juggling and play on sounds invoked through the vocal skills of actors, whose accomplishments in such matters was mandatory. In former days, apprentice actors were taught that the four cardinal elements of vocal training were laughter, weeping, speech, and singing—to be mastered in that order. Though the priorities became less rigidly specified in practice, this suggests the importance attached to having a quick ear for the nuances of sound.

Spoken Chinese has a superabundance of homonyms. It therefore relies on a built-in system of pitch variations to establish the particular sense of words having identical sounds but different meanings. The written language has no alphabet, a single printed character being the equivalent of a single spoken syllable. Moreover, single characters are often used with a second character in order to qualify meaning, thus producing a two-syllable compound. Many such compounds are derived from classical sources, and their true implication can only be grasped by familiarity with their origins. Therein lie pitfalls for unwary Western students of the language. There can be no more comforting sight for them than the little pantomime performed when two native speakers, perplexed by some verbal ambiguity, are compelled to trace out an offending character on the palm of a hand while their vociferous discussion proceeds. In its own way, this common little scene is an intimation of the indivisibility of sight and sound as they function on the Chinese stage. A balanced syllabic arrangement was the stuff of the actor's lines, correlated with a splendid precision of gesture and timed movement to achieve that immediacy of the theatrical moment dear to Chinese sensibility.

Because the traditional Chinese actor sings a great deal on stage, the easy comparison with opera has long been made in the West. The validity of this is questionable to my mind. I once accompanied a Chinese acquaintance to his first opera, a performance of Verdi's *Otello* given in a leading European opera house. My companion was a great admirer of his own theatre and anxious to see and hear this much talked-about Western form of entertainment whose name had been bestowed upon the Peking theatre. He did his concentrated best to follow the stage action, but he was finally defeated by the climactic scene of Desdemona's violent death. The role was played by an operatic star of generous girth, and the flamboyant portrayal of her being suffocated, coupled with her physical bulk, was too much for my companion's trained sense of dramatic distancing. He needed no further convincing that opera and Chinese theatre were two quite different propositions.

Perhaps the most pointed indicator of the great difference between the two is the long, arduous training which every traditional Chinese actor must undergo. It is comparable in the strictness of its principles to the training of the classical ballet dancer in Russia and Europe. There was little glamour about becoming an actor in old China. Students worked to an iron discipline under relentless teachers who were not above the harsh punishment of any laggards. Their aim was to ensure that acting apprentices became absolute masters of their craft, and those who stayed the course and entered the profession usually justified their teachers.

Because of the ingrown nature of theatrical society, acting tended to be a family profession handed on from father to son. However, family background was not the only way of entering the theatre under the old apprenticeship system prevalent until the beginning of this century. Under this method boys were apprenticed between the ages of seven and eleven for a normal term of seven years. During his apprenticeship the pupil was under the sole jurisdiction of the master of the troupe, most often a retired actor — although working actors ran their own training troupes as well. The system was open to many abuses, and if a boy wanted to leave a troupe he had to be bought out. Yet the teachers were not all evil men and closely followed the traditions of their day, making it their business to see that apprentices were trained to earn a living on the stage, precarious though that living often was. The greatest evil was the lack of formal education the boys received, resulting in a widespread illiteracy in the acting profession.

A new era in theatrical training began with the opening of a school in 1903 that became a model of its kind and endured until the end of the 1937–45 war. Pupils were admitted between the ages of seven and twelve for a course of training lasting seven years. During that time they were fed, housed, and clothed by the school; no student was allowed to withdraw unless the school decided he was an undesirable character. The selection process was therefore strict, and the personal supervision and training of the students was equally so. The working day began at 7 A.M. and finished around 11 P.M. In the fifth year every student's progress was reviewed, and if it was seen that he was not likely to succeed in the highly competitive world of acting, he was put to learning some aspect of theatre technology which would ensure his being able to earn a living. Training meant not only hard work in the classroom, where all the teachers were working actors, but a baptism in the real theatre for the senior apprentices. It was the custom for theatre managements in Peking to offer parts to the most promising students in the school, which welcomed this source of income, particularly since no tuition fees were paid by students. Theatres opened at 12:30 P.M. and closed at 6 P.M. It was a familiar sight in Peking to see the acting apprentices in formal dress being led in a single file through the city streets as they made their way to and from the theatres where they were to perform. The Fu Lien Ch'eng, as the school was known in its later years, produced many of the great actors of the present century.

In 1930 came another important new step in training school reforms when the Chinese Theatrical Training Academy was opened in Peking under the direction of a famous traditional-style actor who had visited Europe for a year to survey methods there. It was the first institution of its kind to become co-educational, accepting both boys and girls for professional training and also providing them with a sound general education, revolutionary moves from both points of view. The school had to close with the outbreak of the Japanese war, but it served as a prototype for the future, not the least in its acceptance of the actress long ostracized in the theatre.

During the eighteenth and nineteenth centuries, Imperial decrees had been issued which forbade women to perform in public on the grounds of moral conduct. These sanctions encouraged the artistic dominance of the female impersonator and drove the actress underground to the licensed quarters. Deprived of male cooperation, actresses were forced to rely on their own resources and all-women theatre groups soon sprang up within the licensed quarters. In Confucian China brothel areas, licensed by law, provided a social milieu where men did their personal entertaining and went to be entertained. The women of these quarters had their own hierarchy, many among them trained musicians and accomplished entertainers who graced the banquets indispensable to Chinese ways of life. No man incurred the opprobrium of his fellows by frequenting the licensed quarters; rather, it was an accepted thing to do. Rising actresses were impelled by purely pragmatic considerations when they sought to gain recognition in such an environment. It was not until 1912 that the ban against actresses was openly lifted, and even then women's troupes were only able to appear in designated theatres. Men and women did not appear together on the traditional stage until a decade later. A number of clever actresses had emerged by then; interestingly enough, several of them made their mark as male impersonators.

In contrast, Mei Lan-fang, the most celebrated actor in China before 1949, played only women's roles. His name was a household word among his own people until his death in 1961, and he was the first Chinese actor to gain an international reputation following visits to Japan, Russia, and America in the 1920s and 1930s. With his death some last links with the older acting traditions were broken.

Mei was the third member of his family to specialise in women's roles, and one may be sure that before that decision was made there was the most ruthless assessment of his capabilities for undergoing the necessary training. Once his fate was decided, there was no turning back for a youngster in the theatre if there was to be any future for him at all. None knew better what was entailed than members of a theatrical family, who combined the functions of parents, teachers, advisers, and professional performers rolled into one.

Mei Lan-fang grew up at a time when actors were still regarded as the riffraff of Confucian society, members of a class subject to government decrees which forbade them or their descendants to sit for the revered Imperial examinations for the civil service, supposedly open to all men. Actors were thought to be people who lived an abnormal existence in a world apart, immoral devi-

9

ates and wanderers with no social affiliations. It used to be said in China that to have an actor for a son was worse than having no son at all — a parental sentiment that has not been confined to that country.

Mei not only earned the respect of his countrymen for the perfection of his stage artistry but also for his high personal standards and integrity, which brought a new dignity to the once despised status of the actor. He upheld the artistic precepts of his forefathers and took them to new levels of achievement; at the same time he broke down some of the old social taboos and did a great deal to ensure public acceptance of women on the traditional stage. During the twenties he began to accept women pupils, an unheard-of situation in the closed world of theatre then, and together with a few other brave spirits helped prepare the way for the rise of the actress. It was not a speedy process, prejudice dying hard, but a starting point was established from which there was no retreat.

Transvestism and the professional theatre have always been related. Female impersonation in China attained a high point of dramatic skill based on evocation and stylisation, and the ordinary theatregoer had no problems with a willing suspension of disbelief. However, throughout the history of theatre, the practice has been associated with sexual perversion, or at best considered to be the prerogative of stage buffoons. The subject has always raised questions which are not easily dispelled by artistic rationalisation and have constantly bedeviled the theatre.

And yet female impersonation has a long history reaching back into classical times, and it was probably associated with the beginnings of all theatre. It was accepted practice in the Greek and Roman theatres; the introduction of mime actresses and courtesans into popular spectacles during the Roman decline may well have set one precedent for the double standards which have since prevailed. On the other hand, for centuries female impersonation was at the core of all serious theatre in Europe, as witnessed by the training and use of boys in Shakespearian performances.

Female impersonation as practised by a great exponent like Mei Lan-fang was based on principles of selection and elimination which fascinated Bertolt Brecht, the politically inspired provoker of much that has affected our own contemporary stage

10

practices. On a never-to-be-forgotten occasion, he saw Mei, still dressed in formal Western evening clothes, give an acting demonstration at a diplomatic reception held by the Chinese embassy in Moscow. Brecht was impressed by the actor's detachment and yet complete metamorphosis, which inspired some new thinking about his own work for the stage. There is something theatrically apposite in the fact that a prophet of revolutionary methods in the Western theatre was given new insight through the venerable craft of the Chinese female impersonator.

There were other matters for wonder on the Peking stage besides female impersonation. The Chinese are endowed with superb acrobatic skills, which have provided entertainment for street crowds and palace audiences as well since ancient times. Acrobatics have been developed to an incredible degree of perfection on the traditional Peking stage to provide some of the most visually exciting theatrical moments seen anywhere. Certain actors are especially trained in this genre and perform nothing else. With their high-diving somersaults, fantastic cartwheels, and sense of hairbreadth timing, they seem to subdue space in a joyous abandon of every known law of human gravity, leaving any audience marvelling in its seats.

The simian mime and acrobatic antics of Sun Wu-k'ung, the Monkey King, endeared him to everybody. There were actors who made a lifelong speciality of this role, which demanded physical talents of a high order. Those Western spectators unfamiliar with some of the more esoteric aspects of Chinese theatre had no problems of appreciation with the Monkey King. He still has a prominent place in the traditional shows that have toured abroad in recent years, although some unnecessary Western-style knockabout has been introduced into his miming.

The Monkey King is a figure direct from literary legend who has been familiar to Chinese readers, young and old alike, for generation after generation. Among numerous pranks, he was reputed to be able to cover six thousand miles with a single somersault. "Monkey Sun turning somersaults in uninterrupted succession," was a saying commonly heard at one time as a description for Chinese politicians who were credited with a capacity for changing sides in ways that even the Vicar of Bray might have envied.

The tempestuous performances of the actors playing the

11

painted face roles, with their bizarre make-up, bombastic prancing on high-soled boots, and booming voices, provided choreographic excitement of a different kind. These fantastic characters were like visitations from another world as they whirled about the stage, locked in combat with a balletic wielding of swirling weapons in a furor of controlled sound beaten out by the gongs and cymbals of the stage orchestra.

Nor were the women's roles devoid of stirring performance demonstrating combative grace and speed. A stage combat between two actresses, or actors playing amazon roles, often climaxed in an airy tossing of a double set of long spears through space — to be caught and returned with faultless judgement and an instantaneous riposte across the stage, until the air became alive with weapons hurtling at dizzying speed and the audience shouted *hao, hao* and *hao* again.

Yet among this wealth of colourful acting and dazzling display, there was probably nothing that drew the seasoned playgoer more than the moment when an actor playing the scholar-official role entered the stage. Moving with measured step and feet lifted high with an oblique thrust, he took up his stance center stage, caressing his beard with a downward sweep of his hand before getting into position. The flicking of the long, flowing, white silk cuffs attached to the voluminous sleeves of his robe provided a visual echo to his singing, as he poured out the emotions of the character he was portraying in a soaring lilt of measured sound that set heads nodding to the beat. Peking people used to call going to the theatre *t'ing hsi*, "listening to the play." I can think of no more perfect symbol of happy abandon than the sight of a Peking playgoer of the old school sitting back lost to the world as he listened to the singing of a favorite actor in one of the city theatres.

It is hard for anyone who has not lived in China prior to 1949 to imagine how intensely devoted to their old theatre ordinary people were. No social or festive occasion, whether in town or countryside, was complete without a theatrical performance. A stage and actors were the first condition for a celebration of any kind. Neither Confucian prudery nor government controls were ever proof in the long run against the resilience of theatre or the deep attachment of its supporters. Among those none were more passionately concerned than the amateur performers who have been such a feature of the theatrical world in China.

The Chinese name for an amateur is *p'iao-yu,* literally a "ticket fellow." Although today the term is applied in the broadest sense, it originally meant an amateur actor only and is still most commonly used in this sense. According to all I was told, it was coined in nineteenth-century Peking at a time when the many distinguished actors who graced the city's stages inspired an enthusiastic amateur following. So great was this interest that groups were formed and acquired their own premises where they could meet, rehearse, and generally promote their activities. The members were drawn at first from social circles that included younger members of the Imperial family and sons of high officials, men who could afford to pay well-known actors as tutors and to hire musicians. A number of them took their hobby very seriously; for others it was simply a fashionable craze enabling them to show off before friends.

Another class of amateurs came from wealthy homes where since childhood they had been accustomed to private performances given by professionals engaged for these family occasions. Many such amateurs took lessons from an early age, developed as experienced performers, and earned a reputation among their own circles.

When an amateur gave a performance, he had personally to defray all expenses for musicians, stage hands, and supporting players but was forbidden to accept payment for himself. If he broke this rule, it was said that he had "seized the black pestle" and after that was ostracised by all his associates. When an amateur turned professional, as occasionally happened, the Chinese with their talent for the apt metaphor described it as "diving into the sea." However, this irrevocable step could not be taken without the sanction of the professional world. When the time came to change his status, the hopeful amateur held a banquet and under the eyes of his master teacher and professional guests performed a ritual in homage to the God of Theatre. After his acceptance into the professional world, there was no turning back. Having dived into the sea, he had to sink or swim. Only truly talented people ever reached this point, yet in the early years of the century there were several well-known actors on the Peking stage who had begun their careers in this way.

Amateur performers have continued to flourish through the years, since the traditional theatre has remained dear to the Chinese in exile; wherever they have gone in the world, there have always been those who had the fever within them and would form a group and begin to perform. The long, hard physical training in movement and acrobatics were beyond the scope of most amateurs, for obvious reasons, although many worked hard to attain greater proficiency under professional tuition. In general, however, the amateur Chinese actor tends to concentrate on the sung forms, and many people took lessons for the sheer pleasure of practising their hobby in their homes, where friends might often join them in a recital. At restaurant parties one constantly met someone who had learned pieces from well-known plays, with which he entertained the guests over their wine.

Everywhere in China I used to meet amateurs who proudly claimed to be students of this or that celebrated actor, when what they actually meant was that they had taken lessons from a disciple of the actor concerned. In a tradition that decreed mastery of a particular skill was only acquired through transmission from master to pupil, it was in the nature of things that people liked to bask in the reflected glory of a great actor's name. I sometimes used to think that if every eager amateur I met who claimed Mei Lan-fang as his teacher were to be taken literally, that distinguished actor would have been hard pressed for time to go on stage at all.

It would be unthinkable to end these introductory notes without any comment on Peking, by long tradition the heart of the theatre world described in this book. Peking was a city with a magnetic charm which acted upon Western senses like vintage wine, or as the cynics might aver, a soporific. The mere thought of the capital's tiled roofs, their muted yellows, greens, or blues glistening with diamond points of reflected sunshine above the city walls, was enough to stir emotions of initiates responsive to the romance and mystery with which Imperial Peking has been invested since the days of Marco Polo.

The Peking I first encountered, however, was no longer the serene capital aloof from the modern world as the guardian of a traditional past. The fascination of the old city still existed in the bustling streets, crowded theatres, and noisy restaurants, even though the clash of old and new produced some jarring contrasts. But Peking, no less than the rest of China, revealed the effects of a long war, ineffective government, and economic chaos. People seemed anxious, bereft of hope, and the atmosphere was heavy with the sense of waiting for something to happen. On my first visit to the fabulous Forbidden City, the willing flights of imagination few of us can resist in such historic settings were deflected by the air of decay which hung over the great courtyards, where grass and weeds sprouted from the crevices of paved terraces and between roof tiles. A sough of wind stirred eddies of dust against the doors of empty pavilions, whose echoes were disturbed only by the twittering sparrows, ubiquitous invaders of past glories.

Outside the Forbidden City, neglect was again evident in the broken plaster of the high persimmon-colored walls, now daubed with political slogans. Once the residential quarters for the princes and high court officials, their palaces and courtyards had long since been taken over for a multitude of plebian purposes. Beyond this lay the Tartar City, the outermost of the three walled areas built one within the other to form the main architectural layout of Peking. The Tartar walls were forty feet high, crenelated, buttressed, and pierced by nine gates. Over each of these towered a three-storied guardhouse. It was said that these were built not to exceed ninety feet in height, because the geomancers ruled that the Beneficent Spirits prevailed at one hundred feet and were not to be disturbed by interfering architecture. But once more sprouting weeds, broken plaster, and shabby piles of rubble seemed to imply that the Beneficent Spirits had long since fled in disarray before the creeping menace of civil war.

Yet in the restless city streets, life seemingly pursued its normal course with a fierce vitality, of which the incessant tide of sound flowing from every crowded thoroughfare was a potent expression. The wailing cries of street peddlers and the clack of their wooden castanets rose sharply above the general hubbub. This was offset by the strident blare of radio loudspeakers and everlasting tintinnabulation of scores of bicycle bells as the cyclists wove in and out among the streams of pedicabs, the human propelled, three-wheeled "taxis" whose sweating drivers toiled like draft horses.

From the great principal streets with their carved and gilded frontages, one could wander on through a spreading maze of narrow, twisting lanes, among which lay the residential heart of

Peking. These huddled byways were mostly unpaved, thick with mud in winter and in summer covered by a yellow dust over which trickles of sprinkled water trailed away in cloudy globules. To a casual stroller the lanes presented a vista of blank grey walls broken at intervals by a studded red door, which accentuated a sense of *no prying, please*. Behind such doors lay the gracious Peking houses, each built around a series of courtyards set among gardens and trees. They provided an atmosphere of serenity and domestic secrecy typical of Chinese concepts of living.

In the poorer areas the narrow lanes echoed to the shouts and laughter of swarms of playing children, the bare bottoms of the smallest ones visible through the slitted rear of their cotton trousers that Chinese pragmatism deemed best for juvenile convenience. Aged grandparents sat basking in the clear sunshine before the low, dark entrances of their small houses with latticed windows of oiled paper. Dogs barked, bicycle bells kept up their incessant tingle, and above the clamor there drifted the occasional rancid whiff from a bad drain or the more pervading stink of nightsoil — as much a part of the Chinese scene as more fragrant odors. Among it all trotted the peddlers and itinerant food-sellers, the air shrill with the different cries peculiar to their several wares.

The ordinary people of Peking were mostly a community of merchants, traders, and shopkeepers whose principal business lay in catering to the material needs of their fellow citizens, their own interests jealously guarded by the many trade and craft guilds. The larger of these had their own premises, providing a social center for members and sometimes incorporating a large hall that could be used as a theatre. Until the early years of this century, the guilds were great patrons of the theatre, and the performances they sponsored at the New Year Festival were eagerly awaited events. The New Year was the most important holiday season of all for the Chinese. It was the occasion when families gathered together, paid respects to their elders and ancestors, and in doing so celebrated the solidarity of the clan, the continuity of life, and its renewal for the year ahead. On New Year's Eve all business accounts were settled, shops and offices were boarded up for days on end, people put on new clothes, and once the family rituals had been observed everyone settled down to a long period of relaxation and enjoyment, everyone, that is, except the actors. This was the busiest time of the year for theatre people. Leading actors were often called to take parts in the guild shows, where the audiences were noted for their critical acumen. In addition, it was a long-established custom for wealthier households to organise private performances at the New Year, for which they liked to book the most popular actors. Mei Lan-fang has described in his memoirs what a hectic time he had rushing from house to theatre to guild-hall all over the city in an effort to meet all the engagements offered to him during the holiday season. No one could afford to turn these engagements down, since they were a welcome source of extra income against leaner times never far around the corner for actors.

According to Mei's accounts, the Peking theatres early in this century opened from 9 A.M. to 3 P.M. on New Year's Day, but the actors played to very poor houses, as people were so busy visiting their relatives on that day. Apparently the hours were an old theatre ritual honored by actors as a token of good faith to their public for the year ahead. Every troupe of standing observed the custom, and it was mandatory for all actors to appear on the stage. They were not paid for this ritual occasion, but whatever his ranking every actor received a small red paper envelope containing an equal number of token copper coins.

The private performances keeping actors on the run at the New Year were called *t'ang-hui*, a clumsy approximation of which would be "a gathering held in the rooms of a private residence." Guests at these performances were always offered a list of plays written on red paper, the color for festivities, and from this were asked to make their choice for the actors to perform. This old custom persisted up until 1949, although on a declining scale, yet another instance of how closely their theatre was related to the everyday life of the Chinese.

There were no evening performances in the old days; except for the early closing at New Year, all theatres shut down around 5 P.M. It was not until 1914, when a big modern-style theatre with the proud name of The First Stage — meaning of them all — that evening performances were first given.

Most of the older Peking theatres were situated in an outer area of a city gate called Ch'ien Men and were scattered through the neighborhoods of what had once been the fish and meat markets — to which the Manchu authorities had originally condemned them, all theatres being forbidden within the Imperial precincts. In spite of this, the area became one of the most popular entertainment quarters in the city, bustling testimony to the fact that authorities' attempts to diminish theatre were bound to be ignored.

The theatres I visited in Peking were crowded, noisy places, seething with an unquenchable vitality, frigid in winter, lacking effective ventilation, heavy with tobacco smoke and the odors of closely confined humanity. These were no deterrents at all to the committed spectators, for whom their theatre was a supreme ultimate in entertainment and Peking the centre of its universe.

After the performance was over, it was customary to make for one of the score of excellent restaurants which abounded in the theatre quarter, there to discuss the acting with fellow connoisseurs. Social custom decreed that men never entertained in their homes but invited guests to a restaurant, whether to make a business deal, hold professional discussions, or merely relax among kindred spirits.

The Chinese respect for eating and drinking as a fine art essential to the better conduct of civilised man has only been paralleled by the French in the deference paid to flavors, quality of ingredients, relationship of dishes, and the cardinal virtue of simplicity. Indeed, Peking often invited comparison with Paris not only because of a mutual respect for what the French term *dégustation* in matters of food and wine but because of the aura that has surrounded both cities, where the past has been indissolubly fused with the living present to confer upon two capitals an intellectual and artistic supremacy embodying the essence of their national cultural attitudes.

One Chinese acquaintance of mine used to take a mischievous delight in baiting foreigners who rhapsodised about his native city. "Everything about Peking is *chia-ti*," "counterfeit," he would say with the scorn that only Chinese can muster in uttering this word, cutting short some Western visitor's panegyric. The food which excited foreign palates came from everywhere but Peking, he jibed. *K'ao yang-jou*, the savory mutton grilled over charcoal, came from Mongolia. The yellow rice wine, *huang-chiu*, drunk everywhere in the city, came from Shao-hsing in central China. The celebrated Peking duck came from Soochow, as attested by the name of the most famous duck shop in the capital, Ku Su

(Ancient Soochow); so too did the pretty girls, a reference to the fact that the women entertainers who graced the scholar-officials' banquets in former times were supplied from that city. The redwood tables and chairs came from Canton, he continued, and even the Emperor was a Manchu. As for the Peking theatre, he concluded with a sly glance at me, everyone knew there was no such thing — which was true to a point, since the Peking drama was a synthesis of several regional styles. On the basis of this Chinese leg-pulling, one might say that there was no such place as Peking, the capital of a nation which has been the great cultural assimilator for many centuries.

After first arriving in China, and before the blank screen of consciousness had absorbed the images and impressions recorded here, I have to confess that there were moments when the mere mention of Peking raised a feeling of irritation. "What, you've not been to Peking yet?" someone would incredulously ask in conversation. It became a tediously repetitive query, implying the pitying superiority of the initiated. After a more than usually starry-eyed example of this special pleading by the wife of one old China resident, I suggested that Peking was more than likely to prove very disappointing if one listened to the constant eulogies it provoked. There was a pause, then: "The man's a barbarian," said my hostess, addressing others present with a dismissive side glance at me. "A complete barbarian!"

It was one way of crushing detractors of the Peking cult, certainly, but then all foreigners had been so classified in the past. When the British signed a treaty with the Chinese in 1858, it was agreed that the character *yi*, meaning "barbarian," would be struck from all future documents describing foreign visitors. Since throughout their long history the Chinese had been troubled by a succession of strangers who overstayed their welcome, the term had been useful to provide them with a common means of identification — particularly since the strangers shared a predilection for armed followers on land and sea. But of course Western dignity was affronted and the Chinese, secure in possessing an immense vocabulary of expressive ambiguities to meet any situation, condescended to delete the term barbarian. In conversation among themselves, it was replaced by such descriptive alternatives as *mao-tzu*, "hairy ones," *ta pi-tzu*, "big noses," or simply *fan kuei-tzu*, "foreign devils." Once the hirsute limbs, jutting chins and noses, and extrovert behavior of the foreigner were familiar to the Chinese, there was less need for particularities and the all embracing term *wai kuo-jen,* "people from countries outside," or *wai-jen,* "outsiders" pure and simple, passed into common usage and have remained as testimony to a fine sense of cultural exclusiveness unsurpassed in its dismissive finality.

Some time after the cycle of events related in the following chapters, I took my wrist watch to be repaired by a Chinese firm in Hongkong. In the flush of early sinological accomplishment, I wrote my name in Chinese characters on the slip the Cantonese shop assistant behind the counter handed me. He took it to the rear of the shop with my watch and returned to hand me a receipt, which I glanced at as I passed into the noisy bustle of the street. In the space for the customer's name were pencilled in the characters for *wai-jen.*

1

ONE AUTUMN MORNING in 1946, I stood before a discreet white door in the London headquarters of The British Council for Cultural Relations, a new recruit making myself known to departmental chiefs on the eve of my sailing for Shanghai. The nameplate on the door confirmed that this was indeed the office of the Director of Drama whom I sought, so I knocked and entered at the call of invitation from inside. The director was seated behind a wide desk on which stood framed photographs of Gielgud and Olivier, and she waved me to a chair while sitting back in her own.

"Well, well, well, so we're going to China," she began, pointing to a large map of the world on an adjacent wall. "Do show me where you are going to be based," she continued, "I like to flag all our overseas centers. It's so interesting keeping track of them." I walked over with her to the map and pointed out Nanking. She gazed at the spot for a moment before turning to exclaim, "Such a long way . . . *such* a long way." I agreed that it was.

Remoteness is a quality which has always been associated in the Western mind with China; probably no other country has fascinated the occidental world more from a distance or provided a subject for so much bizarre misconception. The shedding of preconceived notions about China begins fairly quickly for most travelers, however, tempered by a sense of discovery for some, disillusion for others, with probably a mixture of the two for a majority. By "travelers" I do not mean the package tourists of the jet age, for whom the propaganda of preconceived ideas is a mandatory sop, capitalized upon by East and West alike, but those who through deeper experience learn to resist the deceptive comparisons and generalizations which can spring so readily to the mind when confronted with an unfamiliar culture. That leaves out of account the "old China hands," of course, far duller than their fictional prototypes, at least as we first encountered them on the R.M.S. *Strathmore,* a P. and O. liner still converted as a troopcarrier which sailed out of Southampton on a wet February day in 1947. She was bound for Shanghai with two thousand souls who for a variety of reasons considered China their rightful home or temporary home-to-be.

The ship was one of the first to repatriate China residents after the war, and the passenger list was swollen far beyond normal capacity. There were the missionaries and their wives and children in abundance, the businessmen and traders from Hongkong and Shanghai, colonial police officers and their wives, a scattering of Chinese students and diplomats returning from wartime exile, and finally a handful of extras like my wife and myself. Strangers to China, we were relegated to a kind of no man's land where we became the objects of much good advice, anxiety for our spiritual welfare, or simply a puzzled regard for our presence at all — outcasts from the privileged majority of passengers who "knew their China."

The days passed; embarkation was a thing of the distant past and disembarkation a remote adventure that did not yet obtrude itself on the mind. Time related only to the microcosm of the ship as day succeeded day with a by then all-too-familiar pattern of faces. It was hard to remember there *had* been a time when we were not on board the *Strathmore,* whose entity blotted out the past and constituted all the present — while who could visualise the future? Only the old China hands, yet even they had become fixtures in the enclosed world in which we were captive.

The ship sailed on and on. Far out a school of dolphins hurled themselves from the water, the sun glinting on their wet curves as they dived and reappeared and dived again. Flying fish skimmed away from the ship's path, to regain the water with a feathery splash which broke into a pattern of spreading circles. Large jellyfish drifted below the swell of the waves, a tangle of evanescent purple discs and long, beaded coils. The shadowy mass of a shoal of small fish twisted and turned in the depths for an instant and was gone. Darkness came suddenly with no twilight, and a bright moon was reflected in a rippling sheen across the water. From the deck rail phosphorescent bursts could be seen glittering in the foam creaming away from the ship's side.

Then one evening as the sun dropped rapidly through a fiery sky, we steamed into the Malacca Straits, and it was as though an unseen tocsin sounded along the crowded decks. Singapore was on the horizon, the gateway for that long-anticipated return to labors on behalf of both God and Mammon which beckoned a majority on board.

We docked at Singapore next morning. Soon after breakfast some of the Chinese with whom we had made a warm acquaintance on the voyage appeared one by one and with nervous gestures and polite apologies excused themselves for being unable to go ashore with us, then vanished as quickly as they had appeared. China was getting near, and the family door was already being held ajar by that apparently inexhaustible supply of cousins with whom every Chinese seems blessed, to welcome the wanderers home.

We went ashore by ourselves. As my wife was curious to see the Raffles Hotel of literary legend, we took a pedicab straight there, only to find the shabby and nondescript interior bare of all romance. Instead of Maughamesque planters flirting with their paramours over gin slings, we found only a succession of dull little men with rubicund complexions and waistlines bulging above navy blue shorts and white-stockinged hairy legs, suitably complemented by the freckled forearms and generous bosoms of their suburban-looking wives.

The heat had become oppressive even under the draft from the whirring ceiling fans. Thunder rumbled intermittently outside until suddenly the tropical storm broke with huge flashes of lightning, and the rain dropped in vertical torrents which hissed and rebounded from the ground, flooding gutters and spurting from overflow pipes in miniature cascades. The weather at least did not belie the novelists we had read. The storm died away; the air for a time seemed fresh and cool, filled with the sounds of drips from overhanging palms and the gurgling from some cracked spout. We finished our drinks and set off to return to the ship.

During the next two days there was an air of bustle and preparation on deck, since large numbers of our passengers were leaving the ship at Hongkong. The evening before we docked there was a rowdy celebration at the bar, where the secular portion of the old hands celebrated their return with a whisky-laden "Auld Lang Syne." As we sailed through the Lymeum Pass next morning, the missionaries gave thanks for *their* impending arrival on familiar ground with hymn-singing from the promenade deck.

23

The *Strathmore* seemed blessedly empty that evening as we sailed out of Hongkong, a myriad lights twinkling over the dark land mass. The dining saloon was now dotted with empty tables, islands of white napery above which the fixed patterns of remembered faces still lingered in the mind's eye.

The next morning China was actually in sight on our port side, her mountain ranges hazy as we steamed up the coast. At night there were fleets of fishing junks, black silhouettes against the glimmer of the waters below, the faint lanterns at their mastheads like half-extinguished stars. Daylight came once more, and although far at sea we could still see China.

Sailing on, we began to pass through mile after mile of ocean stained a filthy brown. This was the result of silt and filth from the great Yangtze River, its mouth fed by the Whangpoo up which we now steamed through a landscape of smoking factory chimneys, shipbuilding yards, cotton mills, and oil tanks which might have belonged to any European or American industrial port. And then we were anchored below the famous Shanghai Bund, viewing a skyline familiar from a hundred photographs, with its tree-shaded waterfront and the high buildings of the Customs House, Jardine and Matheson, dubbed the "uncrowned kings of commerce," and the Hongkong and Shanghai Bank, three nerve centers of Shanghai, a city mentioned in the same breath as London and New York. The newcomer was left dazed on a first immersion in its seething streets with their dizzy flow of buses, cars, taxis, trolly cars, pedicabs, and bicycles.

Groups of sweating stevedores hauled grotesquely overloaded handcarts drawn by stout ropes at which they strained like draft horses, while coolies carrying heavy bales slung from either end of a bamboo pole held across the shoulders padded backwards and forwards in a steady rhythmic job to an interminable chant of *hai yo, hai yo, hai yo,* which rose and fell above the hubbub with breathless monotony.

For our brief stopover in Shanghai, we were taken to the Palace Hotel on the corner of the Nanking Road where it intersected the Bund at its busiest point. There we were left, after being provided with a supply of what was euphemistically described as small change, meaning a wad of notes in which the lowest denomination was five hundred yüan. This seemed a contradictory expression of the diminutive until we learned that the nightly charge for our room was one hundred and twenty thousand yüan.

At the entrance to the hotel, pleading beggars with babies in their arms clutched at our sleeves or followed us down the street demanding *cumshaw,* a present of money. For a moment we were being given a glimpse of the writing on the wall, which as quickly faded in the atmosphere of the Palace Hotel. There the thick carpets, dark woodwork, steam heating, and hovering odor from the Grill Room were reminiscent of the hotels which grace the railway terminuses of every large English city. Apart from the Chinese faces of the white-coated hotel staff, the ten thousand miles separating us from the quayside at Southampton might never have existed.

Since the next two days were spent chiefly in briefings at the British Council office in the towering Sassoon Building overlooking the Bund, there was little time to explore the Shanghai which lay beyond the Nanking Road.

When darkness fell and the shapes of banks, shipping offices, and department stores were blurred beneath the glitter of the lighted streets, and multi-colored neon signs cast a hard glare on the faces of a restless crowd drawn from a score of nationalities, a different Shanghai came to life. Through the bars, brothels, dance halls, and cabarets, a throng of pleasure-seekers pursued a nightly quest unequalled in its feverish energies among the cities of the world.

It was a different evening scene when we set out by train a couple of days later, en route for Nanking and our new life. The night express for China's capital was already drawn up at the long platform as we arrived at Shanghai North Station accompanied by Mr. Yung, the head clerk of the Council office—who looked rather like a jovial lohan behind his gold-rimmed spectacles—and the Council director himself, come to send us on our way. People were scurrying up and down the platform in several directions at once, chattering excitedly and carrying umbrellas, enamel basins wrapped in towels, bedrolls, and string bags holding everything from oranges to whole roast ducks. Every man, woman, and child seemed to clutch a thermos flask—not the puny little specimen of the Western picnic basket but a positive giant of a flask, its gaudy enamel surface decorated with stencilled patterns of dragons or goldfish. There is little that is reminiscent of the delicate crafts of old China in the ubiquitous thermos flask, but it is "a jade worth several cities," a priceless article in the everyday life of modern China. In hotel room, office, or study, the thermos flask stands guard. On a visit to friends it is always present, thanks to the ancient custom of tea drinking. Tea is the symbol of hospitality, the indispensable attribute of any labor — mental or physical — the companion of leisure, deterrent of dysentery, and soother of feelings. Every meal begins and ends with tea; it cools in summer and warms in winter; it is indispensable to theatregoing. It is sipped from morning to night, whether the clear green tea of the north, the acrid red tea of the south, or the fragrant jasmine tea of social occasions. And the thermos flask of hot water is essential to keep the pot replenished or, if not the pot, the lidded glass tumbler into which a pinch of fresh tea leaves has been dropped. It goes without saying that on a railway journey the thermos flask is no less important than the engine driver.

The third-class coaches on the train were a tumultuous jumble of people trying to crowd through the doors at either end or heaving bundles through the open windows to their companions, who by some miraculous process had managed to board and, true to family solidarity, hauled their less aggressive kin through the windows. It seemed that the coaches could never contain all the passengers who continued to stream in. Each window revealed huddled groups sitting and furiously cooling themselves with wicker fans or arranging their bundles against the restless blur of figures struggling down the center aisles of the coaches.

A privileged calm, however, pervaded the sleeping coaches to which we were led. Here every berth was reserved against a numbered ticket, which the uniformed attendant took from passengers together with the ticket of destination and retained until the end of the journey. The coach was divided into compartments, each of which contained four berths arranged in twos at either side — an upper and a lower — which were not screened off in any way. Inside our compartment a Chinese businessman and his plump little wife were settling down for the night. We were about to be ushered in when two more Chinese passengers arrived on the scene. Consternation followed. Ticket numbers were examined, and a long discussion ensued between the coach attendant, Mr. Yung, and the two newcomers. The attendant returned to his cubbyhole at the end of the coach and came back with the tickets of the businessman and his wife. There was a minute comparison of all our tickets, leading to a lively discussion in which first the attendant and then the two newcomers and finally Mr. Yung took the lead. Next came a great deal of theatrical gesticulation, in the middle of which Mr. Yung paused for a moment to convey to us the by now obvious fact that two sets of tickets had been issued for the same berths and the newcomers refused to relinquish their rights. The discussion continued, and the director looked agitated.

"Well, what are they going to do about it?" he reiterated to Mr. Yung, who was too deeply involved in the contest of words to notice such trite interruptions. We foreigners stood by helplessly, and it began to seem as though we should not be traveling to Nanking that night. Suddenly there was a lull in the seemingly interminable flow of argument. The two newcomers began to pick up their bags. Mr. Yung turned and explained to us that there were two empty berths in a compartment at the other end of the coach and the other two passengers had agreed to transfer.

"Well, why on earth didn't he say so in the first place?" asked the director a little wearily, as we began to move inside. "But the tickets were numbered for these berths," replied Mr. Yung. "Yes, I know, but — oh well, never mind . . ."

A whistle blew. We all shook hands; then came a sudden jolt and creaking of wheels, and we began to pull out of the station. There were the vague forms of people waving, and the station faded from view. We were on our way at last to our destination.

The plump little Chinese woman opposite us had already settled down on her bunk to sleep. Wearing the neat Cantonese-style trousers and tunic which served admirably for pajamas on extempore occasions, she was lying on her side with her back towards us and the form of her round bottom symbolized repose by its very immobility. On the top bunk her husband was sitting up, taking off his shirt and then by a skillful wriggling process, his trousers as well. He emerged like a caterpillar from a chrysalis, clad in a single-piece woolen garment of the kind we used to call "combinations" in England. His complete unconcern with us and concentration on the business at hand was typical of Chinese practicality in these matters. One imagined the effect on that almost pathological Anglo-Saxon attitude toward respectability if

27

a middle-aged couple in England had been asked to share their compartment with two foreign visitors in the same way.

There was a small portable ladder fixed to the lower side of the bunks. Climbing aloft, I left my wife installed in the lower berth. I began wriggling out of my clothes, giving my head a sharp crack in the course of my gymnastics, still a novice in these matters. I leaned over the side to see my wife was rolled up in her quilt and switched off the overhead light. The monotonous clatter of the wheels rattling over the rails formed a steady rhythm far below: "Nanking, Nanking, Nan, Nan, Nanking, Nan, Nana, Nanking, Nan . . ."

I was startled into wakefulness by the wild screech of an engine whistle as a second express passed us on the down line in a roaring vortex of sound, which as suddenly relapsed into the steady rattle of our own wheels. I dozed fitfully, only to wake up with a start and the realisation that the train was not moving. It was 3:30 A.M. by the luminous dial of my watch. There was a hiss of escaping steam far down the line and the ring of metal against metal sounding nearer and nearer as a wheel-tester passed along the exterior of the coaches with his hammer. Occasionally came the sound of a voice in an unfamiliar language; then I heard the clashing of buffers in a series of jerky reverberations as we got up steam once more. From the bunk opposite my Chinese fellow passenger was snoring with the gentle rhythms of a drowsy bee.

When I awoke again it was daylight, and the conductor was sliding back the compartment door to tell us we should be in Nanking in two hours time. A white-jacketed attendant followed him, carrying an enormous long-spouted brass kettle from which he poured hot water on the green tea leaves in the glasses standing on the small shelf beneath each window of the compartment. With what amounted almost to a feat of juggling, the attendant whipped off the lids of the glasses as he filled them and as swiftly fixed small paper receipts to the knobs of the lids. The conductor had drawn up the blinds, and the morning sunlight streamed through the compartment; there was a freshness in the air which contrasted with the city closeness we had left in Shanghai. I wriggled into trousers and shirt and clambered down the ladder to slip on the rattan mules which stood neatly on the floor in pairs. My wife was stirring, and her Chinese counterpart was sitting up combing her hair with the help of a small hand mirror. Her hus-

28

band had already disappeared; when I arrived at the toilet down the corridor, he was immersed in a vigorous clearing of the throat which I quickly came to associate with morning ablutions in China.

The train had slowed down to a leisurely speed. From the windows on either side, open country could be seen, green fields stretching away into equally green, humped hills with mountain ranges beyond. Then we saw mile after mile of paddy fields and across them farmers in wide-brimmed straw hats standing knee-deep in the flooded squares of rice shoots or plodding along behind water buffaloes, whose grey hides matched the mud they trampled down. Next came a village, a cluster of grey-tiled roofs with curving gables surrounded by a high wall, behind which rose thin spirals of smoke. There followed a winding river, more mountains, then paddy fields again.

Suddenly there was a shrill blast from our engine's whistle, and we began to pick up speed once more. Houses and roads were seen in greater profusion; we passed a group of children all clad in blue cotton, crop-headed boys and girls with plaits waving to us as we rattled over a level crossing. Soon there was a vista of a long, grey castellated wall twisting sharply away above a lotus-covered moat, which gave way to houses and more houses and mud-walled shacks clustered around a large pond.

We passed dense areas of nondescript architecture, a spreading mass of grey brick walls and slate-tiled roofs, with occasional glimpses of the curved eaves and thick walls of a past age — the last remnants of old Nanking, the Southern Capital, in Chinese legend the capital of dying regimes. The ill-fated Ming dynasty had begun their reign there but later deserted it for Peking, although Nanking remained a city within whose walls the ambience of a long-cherished social order lingered on. During the nineteenth century the Taiping rebels held it under siege for eleven years as their headquarters, and in 1911 revolutionary forces seized it to make it the capital of the provisional Republican government. Chiang Kai-shek had designated it the new Nationalist capital in 1928; then during the war years it had become the seat of a puppet government. Now it was once more the setting for a regime entering on the last phase of its political collapse — although at the time of our arrival that would have been a foresight to which we had no pretensions as newcomers. We

Nanking street scene, 1948

were pulling into Nanking, the capital of postwar China, and our senses were eagerly alerted for every minute vibration attendant upon the traveller entering new places.

To step from the train was to become enveloped in that stir of sound which defies description, surging above the crowded streets of every Chinese city, a manifestation of energy throbbing like an electric current beneath a plurality of noises. These included the quacking of great flocks of white ducks swimming on a wide stretch of water as we passed into open country from the station. They were destined, we later learned, to be dried, salted, and flattened into skewered shapes — resembling small boys' kites rather than the carcasses of ducks — and then suspended in the windows of the city shops and restaurants, to be used for soup-making and other cooking purposes for which Nanking ducks are regarded as supreme in the Chinese kitchen.

There was a view of green countryside and stretches of the city wall, behind whose crumbling, castellated heights encircling the city for twenty-two miles one imagined a romantic architectural setting. Yet the great stone arch of the city gate through which we drove, while recalling past splendors, revealed only an urban vista of nondescript dullness. A crazy network of telephone wires and overhead power cables looped and sagged on drunken-looking poles which lined the main streets. The important thoroughfares of the city radiated from a traffic circle in the middle of which stood a statue of Dr. Sun Yat-sen wearing a frock coat, his pedestal surrounded by a plot of dusty-looking shrubs, providing a depressing air of Victorian urbanism. A redeeming feature was the famous Purple Mountain, which dominated the ragged skyline of the town and became an unexpected backdrop to the perspective of many a narrow lane or back alley.

Modern Nanking had begun as a planned city to be worthy of the bureaucratic needs of a new Nationalist government, with all the amenities that Western city planners considered progressive in the 1930s. A six-year program was initiated in 1929, but its ambitious design was never fully realised due to the advent of the Sino-Japanese War. At a first appearance the city gave every indication of something half-begun and abandoned to wartime neglect, not at all enhanced by a new kind of shoddiness imposed by the postwar building speculators.

Nanking stood in a beautiful natural setting that fortunately remained comparatively unspoiled, but the urban area was a mixture of densely populated districts and narrow streets typical of old Chinese cities, interspersed with large areas of still open country dotted with farms. Many of the official buildings standing as testimony to the prewar planners' dreams were in the so-called new "national" style, American-inspired and recognizable through the traditional Chinese design details on buildings which were essentially Western in conception. The style began with attempts to impose local color on the schools and universities built by missionary organizations and then was further developed by American-trained Chinese architects who returned to their country hoping to restore the great traditions of their past by adapting them to modern buildings. But the reality of architectural style results from structural values, not surface embellishment, and the new national style resulted in little more than chinoiserie grafted onto stereotyped Western structures. An example was the Nanking Ministry of Railways building, which like others of its kind rose in dingy isolation above a mass of two-storied blocks of indeterminate office buildings, open-fronted shops, restaurants, and a cinema or two. Here and there a more genuine monument to tradition was visible, such as the ancient Drum Tower situated at the northern end of one of the city's main thor-

31

oughfares, built in 1092 and rebuilt in the fourteenth century by the first Ming emperor.

Speeding along in the official car sent to meet us, my wife and I gazed with eager curiosity on the passing scene. Suddenly we turned off the main road to drive down a lane lined on one side with small plaster-walled hovels and on the other by an evil-smelling ditch covered with turbid green slime. Then, turning right, we passed through a high wooden gate and stopped before a newly built, Western-style house, its freshly painted stucco walls gleaming against a wilderness of tall grass heaped with builders' bamboo scaffolding, facing across open country to the distant Purple Mountain gloriously dominating the skyline. The house was divided into two apartments, of which we had been allotted the top one. The newly polished woodwork, French windows, and plastered walls appeared elegantly modern in style until closer inspection revealed the defects of bad workmanship and poor materials. Within six months the walls would be cracking, ceilings leaking, and the fittings of doors and windows refusing to function, while the iron stoves which stood in the center of each room periodically smoked us out. But this was to be our home for the next two years, and that was all that concerned us for the moment. Considering the accommodation of a majority of the Chinese we were soon to meet, it was luxury beyond compare and at a price beyond belief. For the house was only one of scores springing up mushroom-like all over the suburbs, built by the speculators rushing in to profit from the boom caused by the postwar influx of embassies, relief organisations, cultural missions, and press agencies — all scrambling to find housing in the wake of the American military advisers who dominated the scene with their lavish resources. These groups added their own fillip to the rise of rents and caused official missions to conduct their activities in buildings having all the appearances of a mislaid English garden suburb.

Mr. Wu, the contractor who was responsible for our particular dwelling, probably saw himself as a benefactor to the foreign community for making official accommodation available at all in a situation where the Nanking government preferred to remain unhelpful. With his trilby hat, large cigar, and long fur-collared coat, our contractor was the personification of the saying that truth is stranger than fiction, for he might have stepped straight

32

off a stage after playing the heavy villain, the wicked landlord who has such archetypal importance in the theatre of communist China.

To show his faith in his role of public benefactor, Mr. Wu invited the whole office staff to a Chinese banquet at Nanking's most expensive restaurant the day after the contract for our house was signed on behalf of the London office. The hospitality was lavish and the food was superb. A cynic might have observed that Mr. Wu had possibly made a better bargain than even he had planned, but the more philosophic-minded would have agreed that at least it was a tactful way of acknowledging it.

The Chinese are punctilious in observing social etiquette; foreigners arriving to work in their country were always welcomed with a dinner party and another when they left it. Traditional hospitality demanded that these parties be lavish and formally arranged according to unswerving rules of procedure.

Soon after arrival in Nanking, therefore, our Chinese office staff invited us to a popular restaurant in the Fu Tzu Miao entertainment district. The restaurant was entered through a wide, stone-flagged passage, indifferently lit and lined with sacks of rice and cans of cooking oil. It was presided over by the stout proprietor, informally dressed in wide black silk trousers and white cotton singlet, who sat busily doing his accounts on a clicking abacus. The senior office staff member, Mr. Chang, was waiting to receive us and led us down a corridor compartmented into small private rooms, each of which was entered through a swinging double half-door. We were shown into an end room, where the assembled Chinese staff rose from their seats to greet us as we entered. The women were transformed in their high-collared, long slit gowns of glistening silks and satins; the men were more soberly dressed in Western-style suits.

After being introduced to everyone in turn, we were seated at the round table in the middle of the room set with bowls, chopsticks, and cups for wine and tea. A large circular platter containing thin strips of cooked ham, morsels of smoked fish, pickled white cabbage, and quarters of the famous preserved eggs — all arranged in symmetrical layers — made a centerpiece on the table called the "four cold dishes."

As guests of honor, we sat at the "north" side, the head of the table facing the entrance, according to Chinese custom. Directly opposite at the "south" side were the senior staff member and his wife, our hosts on behalf of the rest, who were placed on both sides of us—the next in seniority to our left, the next to our right, and so on. There were ten of us altogether, the customary number at a formal dinner of this kind, where hallowed ritual was scrupulously followed. The dishes were chosen beforehand to conform with what the Chinese called *cheng-cho*, "established order"; that is to say, the correct number and kinds of dishes in sequence of serving.

A formal dinner in those days usually consisted of the so-called "eight large, eight small dishes," excluding the rice and extras like fruit and sweets served after soup and fish which usually concluded the main sequence of dishes. Within such a formidable meal, the skilled host sought to preserve a harmonious balance between vegetable and meat dishes and those in which rice and flour were used.

All food in China is cut up into small portions and mixed in different ways, with great care given to flavors by the flexible use of ingredients which provide great variety to the dishes. The prized "rare" steak of the Western dinner table is regarded among Chinese as a barbarous form of eating, and I must admit to sharing the prejudice. The passion for numbered categories of food to be served represents a different attitude to quantity from our own. It is true that the well-to-do in China have been addicted to extravagant banqueting, an example followed by the not so well-to-do on all occasions for celebration; however, the Chinese eat frugally in everyday life. Culinary inventiveness and a judicious use of ingredients, in which absolutely nothing is wasted, have made frugality not only a virtue but a studied art.

The poor have always comprised the majority of China's vast population, the hundreds of thousands who work only to share the common lot. War, natural disasters, exploitation of labor, and absence of social welfare have inflicted dire want and misery on them in the past. But given these distressing realities, it could be said that inherent resourcefulness and attitudes in the matter of food have enabled the *lao pai hsing*, the "common people," to live better than most of their kind in other countries throughout their long history.

The sensory pleasures of dining have been accorded unique respect by the Chinese, whose culinary sophistication has become legendary. Yet the significance of eating extends far beyond the quality of the cooking and preparation of food, crucial as these are, for the ritual of dining has been central to the everyday conduct of living at all levels of society in China. Whether it was the peasant in the fields, the actor on the stage, or the official in the capital, a dinner party was the symbol celebrating the enduring strength of the family, the cohesion of the clan, and the power of political persuasion. Dining out was an essential ritual honoring the correct relationships and obligations which ran like binding threads through every social activity, providing the means for getting along with one's fellow men as well as outmaneuvering them.

Some of the precise details of our first formal Chinese dinner party have faded a little with the passing of time, but discounting a mellow inexactness induced by the wine-drinking, the general conception of that convivial Nanking evening remains forever in the memory. We had practised assiduously with chopsticks in a London Chinese restaurant before sailing for the East and had become tolerably competent. There were still those agonising moments struggling with some slithery morsel in a main dish when it was triumphantly seized and held between the chopsticks, only to fall with a plop on the wasteland between the center of the table and one's rice bowl. However, there was little need to worry on this occasion, for our Chinese hosts plied us assiduously, leaning over the table every few minutes to place some fresh tidbit in our bowls, until we might in parody have cried, "And still we ate and still the wonder grew that one small bowl had so much work to do." It began with a waiter filling our minute porcelain cups with warm yellow rice wine from a long-spouted pewter beaker. Our host raised his cup saying, *ch'ing,* "please," to which the assembled group similarly replied before taking a drink of the warm rice wine that tingled on the palate and seemed deceptively innocuous at a first sip. We then began with the four cold dishes, which are the equivalent of a Western hors d'oeuvre. Next came the first of the main dishes, each of them served separately by the waiter. To each as it was placed on the table, the host raised his cup of wine with the cry *kan pei,* "dry cup," meaning the wine had to be drained at a single gulp, a procedure which everyone in theory was supposed to emulate. In practice, I much later discovered, this was avoided by some —

particularly the women, who filled their cups with tea or else simply replied with *sui pien*, meaning "please oneself," which entitled one to forego the "dry cup."

The first dish was the famous sharks fin, which the Chinese regarded as a rare delicacy offered only to the most important guests, a category in which foreigners were automatically included, either from innate courtesy or political expediency. The slivers of shark fin are served in a thick, clear, slightly glutinous sauce cooked to such a high temperature as to burn the mouth of the unsuspecting guest. I always thought that sharks fin was a much overrated delicacy and suspect it was the prestige value of this expensive dish which led the Chinese to list it so high on their banquet menus, rather than for any special effect upon the palate.

The sharks fin was followed by small pieces of braised chicken cooked with walnuts in a sour sweet sauce, which was duly toasted with more "dry cups." Then came bean curd and shredded seaweed fried with bamboo shoots, preceded by yet another toast. After this appeared the celebrated Peking duck, the pride of every formal dinner party. It is difficult to describe unless one has eaten it. There are tender morsels of duck and flakes of crackling skin roasted in molasses, together with wafer-thin flour pancakes into which the fragments of duck meat dipped in a thick brown plum sauce are wrapped with a scrap of scallion. The result is a savory roll guaranteed to tempt the most abstemious diner.

More dishes and toasts followed in profusion, but the exact details are by now a little vague, for by then I had begun to realise that a Chinese banquet demands a certain kind of endurance. I had been told that it was discourteous to refuse the host's cup, so that when the senior staff member Mr. Chang offered me his personal toast, I once more poured the warm wine down my gullet to run burning into depths below and life suddenly seemed to be accelerating. I sat back breathlessly and was a little startled when almost immediately I was called upon to repeat the process with Mr. Yang, another member of the company, followed in quick succession by yet another, Mr. Li. Then, perfidy upon perfidy, I was called upon to drink a toast on behalf of my wife, who had long since claimed her feminine privilege in company with the Chinese wives. I dug my heels in beneath my chair and steadied myself with a firm grip on the edge of the table. I remember thinking I had somehow to see it through and let neither my hosts nor my wife down. The faces of the men I noticed were suffused with that dull crimson flush characteristic of the Chinese countenance after drinking wine, which fades like a midsummer sunset only long after the last wine cup has been drained. "As soon as the wine is in, restraint is out," the Chinese say and frequently take a mischievous delight in putting their foreign guests to the test as proof of the maxim.

Drinking in China is a gregarious habit indulged only over a meal and in the company of others. Solitary drinking and the cocktail habit are completely alien to most Chinese. Drinking is a token of good fellowship and hospitality between hosts and guests, whether they be friends or relatives, professional acquaintances, or business associates. A wine-drinking party attains a noisy exuberance while it lasts, but once the party has run through the prescribed number of dishes, the merriment subsides. The wine is finished and the evening is over; the guests depart for home in high good humor as evidenced by their red faces, but no one dreams of prolonging the party. Enough is as good as a feast, and Chinese hospitality functions on the decorous principle that the well-bred guest knows when the feast is enough.

At a somewhat different level, of course, the Chinese wine cup is a subtle symbol of political tactics emanating from centuries of experience in rendering the "barbarian" ineffective through hospitality which disarms. The image of the consummate strategist Chou En-lai toasting the vain and devious Nixon at a nine-course banquet in Peking in 1972 evoked comparison with a scene from the Chinese stage, where drinking scenes served their own special theatrical purpose. It was no coincidence that the old Peking playgoers had a particular relish for certain stage characters who constantly got the better of their enemies and rivals by a ruse rather than direct confrontation.

There was a famous cycle of plays called *The Meeting of Many Heroes* which abounded with the exploits of strategists and plotters. One in particular concerned Chiang Kan, a talkative, scheming emissary of the State of Wei sent across the river to visit Chou Yü, a brilliant military strategist of the rival State of Wu. The latter immediately saw through his visitor. He therefore prepared a forged letter implicating two high commanders of Wei as traitors and hid it in an obvious place to be found by Chiang

Kan. The emissary from Wei was then invited to a banquet at which both men toasted each other in cup after cup, secretly emptying them beneath the table. Feigning intoxication, Chou Yü retired to pretended sleep while keeping one eye on the duped Chiang Kan busily going through his host's dossiers by candlelight, where he quickly found the forged document and disappeared triumphantly into the night with his prize. The document was duly delivered, resulting in the execution of the two falsely accused men. When the forgery was discovered, the head of the State of Wei was in a terrible rage, Chiang Kan discredited, and Chou Yü continued his further intrigues — to the greater advantage of the Peking stage repertoire.

The analogies are there for all who care to see them, and the shocked Western admirers of Mao Tse-tung might indeed have profited from a deeper acquaintance with the Chinese theatre when the Supreme Leader openly demonstrated his preference for the synthetic Nixon as deuteragonist.

Naturally, no such reflections entered my mind at that first formal dinner party in Nanking. Even had it been possible to forestall events in that way, I was much too preoccupied trying to sustain myself under the seemingly endless reiterations for a "dry cup" now reaching me from every side. I began to wonder how I should last out. As far as I could tell, I was still reasonably firm in my seat, but the wine was certainly having its effect and I hoped I did not appear as light-headed as I seemed to be. I made one more determined effort to respond to Chang — or was it Li or Yang — until finally Li and Chang — or was it Yang — rose in their seats like shooting stars to toast each other. And then, oh blessed relief, the trial by ordeal had ended, and Chang, Yang, and Li had closed the proceedings. The table appeared to have distanced itself somewhat, and people's voices "passed over the ears like an autumn wind," as they say, but Chinese hospitality had been vindicated. As we were driven home in the office jeep, the night air rushing past my heated face was merciful in its soporific release.

I arrived at the office next morning with a bad head, feeling anything but a hardened diner-out in the Chinese tradition and fairly convinced that I had made a rather poor showing the night before. This was in spite of my wife's reassurance that I had retained a stoic demeanour until reaching home, and only then had things fallen apart. To my surprise, I found the Chinese had admitted me to the ranks as a "strong" drinker, although never did a title sit more uneasily on the head (and stomach) than mine at the time. But thus are heroes made. Having been bestowed, the title would be passed along through concentric processes which would transmit each minute detail about my personal character and circumstances, as well as those of every other member of the foreign staff, through wider Chinese circles. How this happened was beyond the ability of any of us to know. There was a term "bamboo wireless" used to describe the effortless system that enabled the Chinese staff and their friends, and friends of friends, to know everything about the foreigners within their gates. It was not malicious prying; there was no surreptitious reading of letters or listening at keyholes. Information was disseminated discreetly, quietly, and invisibly through appropriately descending and ascending levels. It came from nowhere and went everywhere — not in the interests of mere idle curiosity but for the welfare of a harmonious society in which all persons were able to know their rightful place. The unassuming nature of this process was only equalled by the speed of which it functioned, enabling the Chinese staff to know everything about the "tide in the affairs of men" well in advance.

Having been initiated into dinner party customs, a next step for every foreigner who took up official residence in China was to be given a Chinese name. The main reason for this was to provide a phonetic approximation which could be conveniently rendered in Chinese written characters for documentary and literary purposes. A name usually consists of three characters, sometimes two. The first character is always a surname from a collection called the Hundred Family Names, which includes in fact not one but four hundred of the most common family names used in China. The other two characters represent one's personal name. Finding a suitable Chinese name for a foreigner was a task of some complexity and deliberation. This was because not only that in many cases a foreign name presented difficulty in itself but also that great importance was attached to the Chinese characters used for the purpose. They had to be selected from the group legitimately used for nomenclature by the Chinese themselves, while those meant for the personal name were required to have a polite and formally dignified implication as well.

The Chinese name given to me, for example, Shih Kao-te,

sounds something like "Shih Gao-de" in phonetic transliteration. The first word is a Chinese family name, and there are thousands of people with this particular one. Yet apart from its function as a family name, this character can also mean "to bestow," "to grant" — or to act or do. The two words Kao-te literally mean "high virtue," and when the three characters Shih Kao-te are elided in pronouncing them, the result is the nearest possible phonetic equivalent to Scott. Chinese itself is not a phonetic language, of course, which is why romanization systems have been devised to cope with this problem. I was always referred to as Shih Hsien-sheng, "Mr. Shih," in conversation, the personal name only being used by the most intimate friends and relatives in Chinese custom.

Among themselves the Chinese sought relief from the rigid dictates of courtesy by giving every foreigner a nickname, so that instead of "High Virtue," I would be identified among the staff by a more colorful if less courteous description. It says much for native discretion that I have never discovered to this day what my nickname was.

For a week there were prolonged deliberations among the Chinese staff in devising names for us. Five different people gave their daily individual attention to the knotty problem under consideration. One morning one of them would lay before me a slip bearing three characters upon which it had almost been decided my name should be based. I was asked how I felt about it. My feelings were obviously academic at that point, but I was prepared to accept their decision. Then a little later someone else would come along and discreetly ask if they might have the slip back. The choice had been judged all right as a name, but on deeper consideration it was believed to be perhaps not quite suitable. There was some doubt as to the relationship of the last character with the middle one, since it was open to the wrong kind of interpretation. I agreed this might be unfortunate and handed the slip back. The name-choosers finally returned a week later with a version they assured me was now free of any literary misconception. I was Shih Kao-te, and so I remained.

Having acquired a Chinese name, the next step was to get visiting cards printed. The visiting card in those days was indispensable to everyone in any walk of life in China. In a country where in the course of a day one might meet a dozen people with the same phonetically sounding name but whose written characters were anything but the same, it obviously served a very practical purpose to have a printed confirmation of the variations. Moreover, if the cards were arranged neatly under the sheet of glass which customarily covered the desk of any office or study in China, they provided a kind of address book visible at a glance. There was always the snag that for those who knew no Chinese characters a visiting card meant little; however, most professional and business people had their names in Chinese characters on one side and English on the other.

Quite apart from these practical considerations was a deep social significance, for to be able to flourish a visiting card confirmed that one had achieved a place in society. And by having the name of some organization printed after the personal name and a telephone number — even if only sharing a neighbor's — it showed that one belonged. The humblest coolie employed in the British Embassy inscribed his card with the stately title, even though he only swept the floors. Whatever one did in China, it was important that one's name be followed by that of an institution of some kind.

It was unthinkable to assert a position as an individual without the necessary ties, however tenuous, that marked one as a unit of society. Only actors flaunted their names alone on their cards, usually in handwritten characters often bold in their printed form, but then actors were notorious individualists and were expected to maintain their public image with appropriate symbolism and studied concern for all the accessory details.

This was particularly true with the top-ranking artists, who like their kind everywhere revealed a certain panache of dress and personal appearance in everyday life. Essentially creatures of tradition by training and environment, they remained faithful to the long, high-collared Chinese gown, always made from the finest materials and smartly tailored to the point of dandyism. At the same time they were always abreast of fashionable progress and were to be seen in Western-style dress on occasion, which they obviously enjoyed wearing as only actors can enjoy such social "dressing up." A look at the photographic records of Mei Lan-fang throughout his career reveals him at various times in tweeds, formal morning coat and top hat, tails, dinner jacket, lounge suit, and stiff collar — to say nothing of dapper tropical sharkskin — all worn with an elegance and style revealing the actor's sense for personal appearance and stage presence wherever he went. Mei, of course, had more opportunities than many of his colleagues to appear in Western panoply because of his foreign travels and close connections with Shanghai, China's most Westernised city. Shanghai actors were probably more addicted to flirting with Western fashions than their Peking colleagues, conservative representatives of a conservative city. During the thirties many of the Shanghai actors favored the style of hat called a fedora in America, an appropriate theatrical derivation from Sardou's play of that name. The Chinese simply called it "American hat," *mei-shih mao,* and the actors wore it at a jaunty angle with their traditional gowns.

The actresses, on the other hand, after desultory experiments with Western fashion found nothing to outdo the glamour of their own close-fitting, high-collared gowns with side splits — the *ch'i-p'ao.* These were cunningly tailored to meet the inexorable vagaries of fashion from which even the enduring unity of Chinese clothing styles was not immune, as evidenced in the lengthening — or shortening — of hemlines, slits, and collars according to the trend of the day.

It was the film stars rather than the stage actresses who set the fashion in these matters, however. In general, the ordinary stage actress, hard working and usually meagerly paid, tended to dress as simply off-stage as did women in less colorful vocations. At any rate, this was the case in the Nanking theatre world of the late 1940s with which I was first acquainted. In spite of being the capital, Nanking was a far more provincial city than Shanghai, where people combined a shrewd eye for the main chance with a taste for smart dress and good tailoring and where the silk shops were calculated to fill any woman with envy. More to the point, Shanghai was the center of the Chinese film industry, whose popular actresses lived and worked in a constant aura of romantic publicity redolent of their Hollywood counterparts.

The Chinese were ardent filmgoers in the big cities, where the rising popularity of the cinema in the twenties and thirties — "electric shadows," as they were named in Chinese — revolutionized ideas of public entertainment among a theatre-conscious people and offered visual revelations of lifestyles and social behavior radically different from their own conservative ways and frequently downright offensive at first acquaintance.

42

It should be no surprise, however, that the popularity of Charlie Chaplin in China almost outdid his vogue in the West; his film *City Lights* proved to be one of the biggest draws in the country's entertainments before the war, when his name passed into current usage. Audiences instinctively reacted to his mimicry, drawn by the perfection of his style, his brilliant mime, and the interplay of illusion with reality, fundamental qualities of their own theatrical precepts given cinematic credibility through the integrity of Chaplin's art. The irony was that in their transition to film making, the Chinese seemed unable to rely upon the values of their own theatrical philosophy as a basis for new visual creativity. They seemed mesmerised by a stilted naturalism which was a legacy from their uneasy experiments with a Western-inspired theatre style after the founding of the Republic in 1911.

Some of the pioneers of the Shanghai film world were veterans of this early theatre movement, whose largely amateur actors seem to have been more remarkable for their good intentions and social zeal than for any significant creative advance. As claimants for public attention, they scarcely presented any real challenge to the old theatre, where in the words of the famous Russian director Meyerhold, "the actor proclaimed the self-sufficiency of the acting craft." Whatever the old theatre lacked in relevance to the new climate of social reform and the contemporary world, it retained the affections of a wider public as a familiar entertainment, beside whose highly trained professionals the new-style actors seemed the groping novices they largely were.

In the intellectual ferment which swept China after 1919, following widespread national resentment against her unequal treatment at the Paris Peace Conference, Western drama was intently studied for its portrayal of social problems. Ibsen, for one, awakened many responsive echoes in China at a time when a new generation was particularly concerned about arranged marriages and the social segregation of females, so that many a young woman sought to emulate Nora of *The Doll's House* — in thought and intention, if not always in deed.

Nevertheless, the attempts to create a new theatre were seriously lacking in practical understanding of naturalistic acting and stage procedures. In their haste to banish the past, the reformers forgot that the visual coherence of their old theatre, and its handling of rhythm, space, and timing, were invaluable assets in devising new naturalistic styles of acting. It was a problem which the film makers in turn failed to resolve. In their concern with surface imitation, they too overlooked the lessons to be learned from applying their own aesthetic principles to new methods of visual narration.

Chinese films tended to be long, tearful, and sentimental, even when they broke away from the seemingly stock formula of all Shanghai producers: the eternally faithful and virtuous wife, the erring husband, and the staunch old mother-in-law as witness to the omnipresence of the family. I saw my first Chinese film in Shanghai in 1947; entitled *Spring River Flows East*, it was so long that it had to be shown in two parts. At the end of the afternoon matinee, we adjourned to a neighboring restaurant for an hour and ate a welcome meal of fried noodles. We then returned fortified to sit through the second half of the long sequence of events, which to my then unpracticed eyes and ears seemed most remarkable for the reciprocal and copious flow of tears between the characters on the screen and the audience around us.

The film was newly released and the critics considered it a breakthrough commendable for its honest realism and avoidance of the customary sentimentality, although I wonder about that when I remember all the sniffling that ensued at the Shanghai premiere.

The central characters in the film were a husband and wife who had become separated by the eight years of war, from which in 1947 China was still emerging, and the theme played upon the hardships, hopes, and disillusions of the long struggle. Corrupted by the venal society of Chungking, the wartime capital, the husband proved unfaithful to his loyal and suffering wife alone in Shanghai with her small child and an ailing mother-in-law. The war ended, the philanderer returned to Shanghai with his new love, and we concluded with a harrowing confrontation when the deserted wife — by then a waitress — arrived to serve at a cocktail party held in the husband's ostentatious new home.

As was the custom, several subsidiary issues were woven into the main theme of the film for good measure. The agonies of the Chinese under Japanese military repression, an obsessive requirement for so many films of that period, were given full treatment. And as I recall at this distance of time, the husband's sliding into the moral abyss was given extensive visual emphasis. The part of the wife, however, played by the famous screen actress Pai Yang, seems to have been devised along well-worn lines, suggesting an ingrained reluctance to abandon hallowed concepts.

In film-making the Chinese appeared completely inhibited by the restrictive nature of the archetypal roles favored by the old theatre. The passion for stock characterisations in so many Chinese films amounted to a vice which at times almost seemed to be a matter of taking the old stage characters and merely giving them a new look, so to speak. For example, the distraught grandmother or mother-in-law, as the case might be, with lined face, tear-filled eyes, and tremulous voice — expressing herself in no uncertain terms nevertheless — was a perennial figure on the screen. This was a naturalistic transposition of the *lao-tan*, that matriarchal symbol of the Peking stage whose theatrical image enshrined the abiding spirit of the clan. But where the old lady on the stage was given dramatic life through structured rhythms of sound and gesture that provided a forceful theatrical device, her screen counterpart was dependent on the bathos of a contrived naturalism lacking all conviction.

So too with the virtuous wife, whose Confucian integrity sustained her throughout all her trials and tribulations on the Peking stage. Her melancholy personality drew the crowd's response by means of patterned forms of brittle delicacy; however, transferred to the screen, she became a stock contrivance diminished in dramatic credibility.

No such abstract speculations would have troubled the minds of the Chinese film audiences with whom I sometimes mingled in Nanking. Going to the cinema for them was a family occasion for everyone, from grandmother down to the youngest child. They had an insatiable visual curiosity and I believe would have watched anything for the sheer pleasure of being at a show. Getting into a Chinese film matinee was an adventure in itself. Long before the doors opened, the excited, chattering throng outside was ready for that great moment when it swept forward like a tidal wave. Respect for age prevailed, so that if grandmother got left in the rear, the family closed in protectively to form a battering ram which propelled her to the fore and enabled her to nip smartly down the aisles and commandeer a complete row of seats to be held triumphantly for her kin as the mad scramble for the most advantageous places broke out. Then a great chattering and

45

meeting of neighbors followed, as the problems of going to the cinema were recounted in detail while peanuts and melon seeds were purchased from the vendors in the aisles. At last the lights went down to excited applause, as everyone abandoned themselves to uninhibited involvement with the happenings on the screen. And how they cheered and clapped whenever the villain was outwitted — or the hero declaimed some noble sentiment to touch all hearts. There was never any question as to which side a Chinese audience was on, since the pointed comments at crucial moments, such as *t'a shih huai-jen*, "he's a bad lot," or *k'o-lien ah*, "pitiable, eh?" left nothing to speculation.

Film performances of a rather different genre were those I had to arrange for the various educational institutions in Nanking during the course of my official duties. We had a small library of highly technical films for showing to specialist audiences. Among them was one shot in a London hospital, showing the surgical removal of a patient's lung and the post-operational therapy that followed. It was arranged that we should screen the film at the Nanking Central Hospital one evening, and I was startled on arriving there with my Chinese assistant to find the audience of doctors and nurses complemented by dozens of the non-medical staff and their wives and children. They stood or sat in little groups inside the several entrances to the lecture hall, their eyes fixed expectantly on the blank screen. A show was a show, it seemed, and nobody was going to be denied the dubious pleasure of the occasion. I think it was on that evening that I first savoured the implication of those much-quoted lines: "What is this life if full of care we have no time to stand and stare?"

It is said that curiosity killed the cat, but it cannot have been in China, where curiosity is indulged as a fundamental right of every man, woman, and child. It was Chinese curiosity indeed that was ultimately responsible for my getting so deeply involved in the technical secrets of the Chinese stage. It came about in the following way. One evening a Chinese acquaintance asked me if I would like to pay my first visit to a teahouse theatre, an invitation which I enthusiastically accepted. I knew very little about Chinese theatre, but as a newcomer to the country I was ready to savor every new experience. Many years earlier I had seen the performance of *Lady Precious Stream* that had delighted London

46

Singing girl Fu Tzu-miao, Nanking

theatregoers, myself included, although I was soon to realise what a mere pleasing whimsy that performance had really been.

As we set off on our night out, the myriad stars glittered far above us and rime sparkled on the frozen mud surface of the road. Savory smells drifted across from wayside food stalls, where groups of customers, swaddled in long, blue-padded gowns were silhouetted in the harsh light from hissing acetylene lamps. The theatre to which we were going was situated in an old quarter of the city, reached by way of a narrow cobblestoned street. The street was lined with low-storied buildings surrounding an old Confucian temple set among a jumble of restaurants, storytelling halls, and teahouses. In the latter singsong girls performed to the strains of currently popular sentimental tunes. The area as a whole bordered a narrow, turgid river which gave off a rank whiff happily soon lost in the cooking smells from restaurants overlooking the dark waters.

The raucous shouts of diners playing the finger game over their wine sounded in crescendo through a restaurant door flung open to the night by a departing guest; the muffled clatter of mahjong pieces floated down from the shuttered window of an upstairs room. As we approached our destination, I felt that sense of pleasurable expectation of the traveller bent on new experiences.

We came to the theatre and passed through a low entrance leading to a narrow foyer, from beyond which echoed the percussive clash of gongs and cymbals. Entering a small auditorium hazy with tobacco smoke, we were met by an attendant wearing the inevitable long blue gown and a woolen stocking cap, who led us to our seat, a wooden bench placed at a small rectangular table near the front of the stage. This was a thrust platform about twenty feet square and three feet high, with curtained entries to the right and left of the rear stage area. It was empty of anything or anybody except a small, starkly bare wooden table with an equally bare wooden chair on either side of it at center rear stage, and five musicians — a combination of string and percussion players — seated downstage left. They were creating what to unaccustomed ears sounded a very tornado of sound which reverberated throughout the small theatre.

The attendant brought us two lidded glasses of tea, made by pouring hot water from the kettle he carried onto the scattering of green leaves in the bottom of each glass. He then collected our admission money and handed us two hot face towels. These preliminaries over, I was curious to take a closer look at our surroundings.

The single-storey auditorium held about two hundred people, predominantly men but with a scattering of women huddled in their padded winter clothes, looking rather like squat versions of the Michelin man in the unheated theatre. Playgoers in the rear of the house sat on rows of long benches, while those at the front occupied tables like our own, of which there were about a dozen. The concrete floor was littered with the husks of dried melon seeds, which people cracked between their teeth with squirrel-like dexterity. As he went his rounds, the attendant offered peanuts as alternative refreshment and replenished the tea glasses with hot water, while collecting used face towels and slinging them over one shoulder.

On reaching the front of the house, he turned and with sudden sleight of hand began hurling his used towels across the heads of a magnificently indifferent audience, to be as adroitly caught by a fellow attendant at the back of the auditorium. This nonchalant display of skill was only matched by apparently equally nonchalant happenings on stage, where the noise on that brightly lit platform had by now become climactic. The informal dress and attitudes of the musicians, who used no scores, suggested a complete unconcern with everything, as though they had simply wandered on to amuse themselves by letting go of all restraint. However, that illusion was dispelled when the opportunity for closer observation revealed a cunning control of timing and rhythm, as the musicians anticipated every minute move of the actors while their craftsmanship and precision imposed order on the stage action generally.

The cymbals and gongs had by now commenced a swift but powerfully measured beat that sent echoing waves of metallic sound across the theatre. One's senses were irritated but at the same time goaded on by the percussive clamor; cessation would have been sweet, yet expectancy lurked in continuance. Suddenly a resplendent figure strutted onto the bare stage, moving with a slow deliberate pace alternating right and left, feet lifted high with each forward step. Ornaments on the actor's headdress trembled and flickered in rhythmic echo of his delicately precise head movements. Dancelike motion alternated with pauses which contained action within inaction, as the actor adjusted his long, white silk cuffs, his beard, or the hooplike girdle round his waist, with lightly emphatic gestures reinforcing a subtle quality of line before he moved into a series of postures accenting a rhythmic play of hands, fingers, and eyes. The constricted stage area seemed to grow beneath the plasticity of the acting form which drew all space within it.

The appearance of an actress evinced a similarly magic command of space, as she created delicate sleeve patterns marked by an unbelievably graceful manipulation of hand gestures and supple fingers, underlining high-pitched vocal passages rising to drawn-out flights of sound, which then dropped through the air in melancholy cadences. My attention was held and imagination caught by the sheer theatrical magnetism of forms, which although imperfectly understood in their literal context, were intensely realised through my senses.

The spell was broken when a stagehand wearing a cotton undershirt and baggy-seated black cotton trousers strolled downstage to hand a small pot of tea to an actor in the middle of a sustained passage of song. Taking the pot, half-concealed by his voluminous white silk cuffs, the actor raised it to his lips and, tilting back his head, drank through the spout. Then handing back the pot to the waiting stagehand, he went on with his song as though nothing had occurred to divert him.

These were some of the impressions which lingered in my mind as we left the theatre on that faraway evening, vivid images compelling me to discover more. I wanted to ask my companion a host of questions. He led me to his favorite restaurant in the quarter, a house noted for its *chiao-tzu* — small, steamed, half-moon-shaped dumplings stuffed with chopped pork and herbs, served piping hot and eaten after dipping in rice-vinegar and soya sauce with accompanying warm, yellow rice wine. It was a favorite supper with Chinese playgoers, and even now the very name *chiao-tzu* recalls for me nights at the theatre.

The restaurant itself, like the theatre we had just left, was a nondescript little place. It had bare, whitewashed walls, a concrete floor, and was furnished with shabby wooden settles partitioning off the scrubbed wooden tables. However, the atmosphere was vibrant with shouted orders of the waiters, who hurried between tables carrying long-spouted pewter beakers of warm rice wine while balancing tiers of cylindrical wooden boxes containing the portions of hot dumplings. Ceremony or elegance of any kind was completely absent, but the food and wine were superb and the simplicity of conception outdid the most elaborate banquet. As we ate and drank, I was struck by the fact that unpretentious surroundings concealing sensory sophistication seemed to be a common factor of theatregoing and dining out. Such philosophic reflections undoubtedly resulted from good food and wine as, warmed by both, we set out for home.

From then on I became a regular visitor to that small theatre; scarcely a day passed without my spending some part of the evening watching the performers and familiarising myself little by little with the stage action. It was not great theatre, as my Chinese acquaintances were constantly at pains to remind me while being puzzled by my obsession, but as a novice I was fascinated by what it had to teach me. Better still, it was always there, a permanent source for the asking at a most modest cost. The theatre people themselves, half amused, half flattered by my constant presence, went out of their way to help me to the point that whenever I appeared they had my vantage point near the stage reserved for me. It was what the Americans would have called a "good learning situation," enabling one to get a perspective on certain aspects of everyday Chinese life that would have been possible in no other way. The bigger theatre troupes from Peking and Shanghai only visited Nanking spasmodically for a few nights' stand, and with the black marketing that went on and the nepotism in high circles, it was difficult to get a seat at all for those events.

I started taking a sketch pad to the theatre to make quick notes of the movements and gestures of the players which had begun to absorb my attention. Sitting only a few feet away from the stage, I had often been aware of long and curious stares from that direction until one evening when I suppose I was concentrating a little more intently than usual on my sketching and became conscious, as one sometimes does, that I was being watched. I looked up to find the action on stage had paused for a moment and the two actresses there appeared to throw an almost anguished glance as if to say, "We can't bear it any longer," before making their final exit.

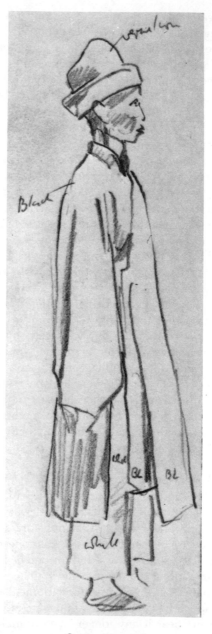

Supernumerary

The next evening I asked my Chinese assistant to go to the theatre with me, thus providing the actresses with a sign that their curiosity could be satisfied and that I was interested in meeting them — social prejudices and gossip notwithstanding. The signal was received, and during the course of the evening an attendant came with a request that the foreign gentleman come backstage after the performance and show them what he had been doing.

We sought out the two actresses in their cramped, badly lit dressing room that was little more than a small attic reached by a rickety staircase from the dingy backstage area. No performer would have tolerated such dreadful working conditions in the West. Since these were the star attractions of that small theatre, whose names drew in the audiences, it was a forceful reminder of the lack of human concern for stage people that still prevailed in China.

The two of them turned out to be modest but spirited and frank young women, with great strength of character. Like young actresses everywhere, East or West, they were anxious to be given their chance to prove themselves on the strength of their talents and those alone. The elder of them had a sister who had left the theatre for films, and she herself was ambitious to follow in those footsteps to what she felt was a freer, better-paid profession with greater opportunities. That evening's encounter was the beginning of a passing but informative and enlightening acquaintanceship. The two actresses, Wang Hsi-yün and Wang Hui-chüan — the same surname but no relationship — were modest about themselves and yet obviously pleased by the interest shown in their work. They immediately made me free of the backstage at any time I wanted to ask questions or watch technical procedures. They demonstrated their acting techniques, posed for sketches, and loaned some of their costumes to study in detail. In truth, they did everything possible within their power to advance my knowledge about their craft.

They used to visit our house and came to dinner with us several times. My wife and I had cause to remember the first occasion because another Chinese acquaintance we had invited to the dinner party declined the invitation, since it meant sitting down at a table with actresses. It shocked our Western minds, but I have to say that our other Chinese guests on that occasion were at ease and seemed to enjoy the novelty of the company.

Wang Hsi-yün as Ying Ying, Chun Lo Theatre, Fu Tzu-miao, June, 1948

It was clear from the conversations we had with the two actresses that they had to work hard for their living and that the theatre owners who employed them were not the most generous or considerate of men. However, both young women gave the impression of being able to take care of themselves in presenting a united front to the management. They were, I suppose, neither better nor worse off than many others of their kind; their chief desire seemed to be to move on to better things. Like everyone else in China, they were anxious about the future and what might become of them under communist control. As with so many of their profession, they came from humble families and their lives centered upon the introverted world of the theatre. Shanghai was for them a beckoning city of wealth and sophistication, with the added attraction of being the center of the Chinese film industry, where a number of actresses trained in the traditional theatre had risen to fame and fortune and set an example many aspired to follow.

It was hinted by many Chinese I knew that the theatres were only able to operate through the connivance of the Shanghai underworld and the levying of protection money on theatre owners, who in Nanking were well within the orbit of this vaguely sensed society within society. This was completely outside the naive conceptions of people like ourselves, innocents at large in the idealistic pastures of cultural relations. Such murky undercurrents were never mentioned by the actresses, in whose profession the accepted Chinese attitude that if one takes care of one's own business, one's neighbor's will take care of itself had its own connotations. This is understandable, since the tortuous ramifications of the Chinese underworld could have impinged upon their professional survival and possibly their personal safety.

The two young women retained their natural ebullience nonetheless, although this was tempered by a decorum stamped upon them through centuries of Confucian upbringing and marked the restraint of their general deportment towards guests and strangers no less than did the behavior of their more "respectable" peers. Modest practitioners though the two young actresses were by Chinese critical standards, they nevertheless were trained in a great tradition of which at that point I was beginning to get an inkling. The sheer intensity of their expressive performance gave me the feeling of a profound unity of disciplines which had endured through time; it was as though the craft of acting was laid bare at its source. From constantly watching those two Nanking performers, I learned a great deal which advanced my understanding of Chinese stage techniques and revealed some fundamental precepts of theatre in a new light for me.

2

THE PERFORMANCES at that first small teahouse theatre led me on to explore the stage world further, so that I began to attend the larger city theatres when they were occasionally visited by touring companies from Peking and Shanghai. Anything so simple as purchasing tickets outright for such events, however, was well-nigh impossible in postwar Nanking. Houses were invariably "sold out" as soon as they opened, the better to accommodate government and military personnel who claimed right of privilege as was the custom. An alternative was to go to the ticket scalpers who infested the entertainment world in that era when everyday life functioned through the black market. It was better by far to trust in the magic words *yu fa-tzu*, "there's a way," which when uttered by some helpful member of our local office staff indicated setting in motion those quietly circuitous processes that, through long familiarity, the Chinese have perfected as the fine art of accommodating everybody. The desired tickets then invariably arrived safely upon one's desk.

The most common visiting attractions in Nanking at that time were provided by well-known actresses leading their own troupes. Women by then were no longer regarded as intruders on the traditional stage except by the most hard-bitten conservatives. However, few actresses had reached the top without overcoming obstacles everpresent for their kind in the old theatre world, with its systems of private patronage and entrepreneurs — among whom warlords and tycoons had often flaunted their power in the past. All successful actresses had come up the hard, professional way, most frequently from modest family circumstances. They were usually the daughters of professionals in the theatre but in any case had all undergone an exacting training from their early years, under constant admonition from teachers and parents to work unsparingly in order to survive in a profession which had no mercy on those content to remain second best.

A life of rigid discipline and regimentation was the way to success in the theatre, and there were no short cuts for an actress, who had to work harder than most to make her way in a world that had not been particularly sympathetic to her cause in the past. The impression gained from watching all the old-style actresses at work was a sense of something done with total determination, a transmission of vibrant energy and unerring skills, an affirmation of indomitability which was confirmed in the spirit of their bearing when meeting them backstage.

Nanking theatre habitué

Before the first co-educational dramatic training school was opened in Peking in 1930, the only way for an actress to get her training was through private teaching. This meant finding professional actors who would accept her as a pupil, and then only after years of hard study would she be accepted into the "Pear Garden" by the theatrical hierarchy. The Pear Garden is the name by which Chinese theatre people designate their professional world. It refers to the fact that the Emperor Ming Huang (A.D. 712–756), founded the first training school for court performers, reputedly set up in the palace pear orchard.

It was very difficult for women to find good teachers of acting in the old days. They faced the paradoxical situation of having to learn the craft of playing the traditional women's roles from men, and many of the older actors who were the best teachers either refused or did not dare to pass on professional expertise outside the closed shop of orthodox theatrical circles. It was not until Mei Lan-fang and one of two other actors flouted conservative prejudices by taking women pupils in the 1920s that the ice was broken. The result was that a talented group of young actresses gained public recognition in Shanghai, where resistance was more easily overcome than in ultratraditional Peking. In 1928 two actresses, Hsüeh Yen-ch'in and Hsin Yen-ch'iu, both pupils of some of Peking's most famous actors and highly regarded for their talents, created a historical precedent by performing with actors in a Shanghai theatre. Both these women did much to enhance artistic recognition of the actress, and their names are important in the history of the Peking stage.

Hsin Yen-ch'iu, born around 1915 — actresses' ages were rarely revealed in China — died in tragic circumstances. She was performing before a full house in a Peking theatre in 1938 when an assassin tried to shoot the Chinese leader of the Peking puppet administration who was at the play. The attempt failed, and the assailant escaped over the stage, resulting in the Japanese police arresting the actress for cross-examination. When she pleaded ignorance, she was imprisoned and later died from the treatment she received for refusing to confess, a bitter fate for a talented artist in a profession which had tribulations enough for her sex.

Another important actress of this earlier period was Meng Hsiao-tung, the daughter of an acting family who became famous for her playing of male roles in which she was regarded by many critics as being superior in her interpretations to many male counterparts. However, in spite of her great popularity, her life seems to have been dogged by misfortune. During the twenties she was involved in an incident during a social gathering in the home of Mei Lan-fang, with whom her name was intimately associated, when an intruder shot a journalist dead. The facts of the affair have never been revealed, but they affected the actress to the point that she retired from stage life for several years. She made a brilliant comeback in the 1930s after studying under Yü Shu-yen, a distinguished interpreter of the scholar-official roles.

His actress pupil proved herself a most distinguished performer and made a tremendous reputation for herself until the close of the decade and the outbreak of war. After that her life seems to have moved into the shadows once again, and her name became linked with that of one of the most bizarre public figures in contemporary China, Tu Yueh-sheng.

Perhaps some facts about his life would throw light on some hidden aspects of the world of traditional theatre. Tu was born a village boy in the Shanghai area and, orphaned early, went to seek his fortune in the city. There he eventually became the protege of the police compradore of the French concession in the International Settlement. Compradores were men who served as local agents and go-betweens for the foreign businessmen and merchant adventurers who flocked to China in the nineteenth century, to whom compradores owed their rise as a social class. Usually they came from modest backgrounds and were shrewd and aggressive personalities. The nature of their employment and indispensability enabled them to amass considerable fortunes due to their privileged access to information. The compradores eventually became the nouveaux riches of China, and like their kind elsewhere they developed social aspirations and bought their way into the world of their superiors. The police compradore of the French concession was a powerful figure in the Shanghai underworld and a member of The Green Society — comparable only to the Mafia in its ramifications — through which he operated lucrative gambling and opium interests in addition to extending his activities to the entertainment world as a theatre owner.

Tu became a capable lieutenant to his master, amassed a fortune, and used his organizational talents and position in the underworld to play high politics and become an indispensable aid to the government. By the thirties Yueh-sheng had become one of the most respected and one of the most feared men in China, if such contradictory descriptions can be reconciled, and commanded the will of both Chinese and foreign communities alike through an ability to bend political, social, and financial resources to his desire — to say nothing of other people's lives when required. The underworld he controlled was run like a well-organized business. They used to tell us in Shanghai that before the war if one's watch was stolen in the morning, it could be retrieved by the evening from the relevant organisational section on payment of the appropriate fee. More vicious crimes like kidnapping and murder were said to be equally "correctly" controlled. Free lance activities were not tolerated. How apocryphal such stories may be is difficult to know, but of Tu's underground connections there was no question. Through these he was able to render services to the government during the war, from which he emerged with a patriot's halo.

In his heyday Tu was also a labor boss said to break strikes with a nod of his head as well as being a public figure with the highest credentials. These included directorships of banks, membership in the Chinese stock and cotton exchanges, presidencies of two hospitals, a supervisory membership of the Chamber of Commerce—besides owning a shipping company and paper mill and for good measure serving on the board of the Great China University. This was the public image of a man who controlled the dark forces of Chinese society to the extent that his powers of arbitration could apparently save the greatest in the land from the consequences of their own follies, just as easily as they could destroy them. Although the friend and manipulator of big business and corrupt politics, he was reputed to be generous towards distressed and needy persons for purely altruistic reasons, and his name was surrounded by the legend of good deeds during his lifetime.

At the summit of his rise to wealth, power, and respectability, Tu like every good Chinese decided to pay homage to his ancestors and ordered a family shrine to be built at his native village across the river. The whole of Shanghai went *en fête* for the occasion, upon which Tu was said to have lavished funds in the most prodigal way. Thousands of his underworld followers, high government officials, the mayor of the city, and members of the business community took part in the spectacle or sent their tributes in the form of congratulatory scrolls held aloft in long processions. A highlight of the celebrations was a series of theatrical performances which lasted for three days and in which the hierarchy of the Chinese stage took part. No artist of repute was missing from the festivities. It was a measure of the influence wielded by Tu as a patron of the arts and, according to all I was told in China, boss of the protectionist racket to which the world of theatre paid its dues. No actor or actress would have dared to refuse Tu's invitation, for his was the unseen power to which their livelihood was ransomed.

Chinese theatre proprietors were known as "those behind the stage" and were responsible for hiring a theatrical troupe for a stipulated period. The leader of the troupe, the principal actor, was known as *lao-pan*, "the boss" or *"le patron,"* and was responsible for making the contract on behalf of his company. The profits for a theatrical run were divided in the proportion of 30 and 50 percent between the theatre owners and the troupe leader, who was responsible for paying his actors. They received their portion according to their professional seniority and status. "Protectionist" controls applied to this system were obviously open to pressures. Being politically naive myself and involved with the stage world as an outside observer, it was some time before I began to get an inkling of these murkier issues. Although I never had any direct involvement with the world of Tu during my innocent days in the theatre, it was impossible not to become aware of its presence.

Tu himself was said to be fond of the theatre, and in 1947 his friends and associates honored his sixtieth birthday by organizing a ten days' theatrical performance in Shanghai — the proceeds being given to charity, presumably an intended allusion to his roles of public benefactor and patron of the Chinese arts. It was even claimed by some people that Tu liked to perform in a purely amateur capacity, preferring to play the painted face roles which used a predominantly black make-up, *hei-t'ou.* One of the best-known characters in this genre was the famous judge Pao Kung (999–1062 A.D.), renowned for his staunch integrity and devotion to public service. Tu's gaunt figure, narrow head, and emaciated countenance of the confirmed opium smoker were hardly reminiscent of the broad facial features and bulky form of the typical painted face actor, although a wish to identify with Pao Kung — if indeed Tu's acting was fact — seems in keeping with the pretensions of the man's public image in real life.

I only saw Tu once, voting for the Nanking National Assembly at a Shanghai polling booth, his stock by then no longer so high and his power on the wane. A year later he moved his large household to Hongkong, where he died in 1951. The large family who survived him included three concubines, one of whom was the actress Meng Hsiao-tung, previously mentioned as one of the most talented artists of her era. Her first professional appearance had been in 1925; in her later career she achieved acclaim for her interpretation of the male roles of the Peking repertoire, in particular the scholar-official characters, including the strategist Chu-ko Liang from the play cycle based on the historical novel *The Romance of the Three Kingdoms*. Chu-ko Liang was credited with being able to plot the interaction of heaven and earth, a talent evidenced on the stage by his ability to defeat superior forces through trickery, a quality already described as much admired in Chinese folklore.

At what point the actress entered Tu's household few can know, for these relationships were treated as strictly private in the old Chinese society, which was not monogamous. People told me that Tu took her under his protection after she fell upon hard times during the war. Whatever the facts, she moved to Hongkong with him and lived in seclusion there for a time after his death. When we resided in Hongkong during the 1950s, a Chinese woman librarian on my wife's staff in the university who was acquainted with Meng Hsiao-tung offered to try to arrange an interview with the actress. Apart from the natural curiosity which underlies meeting with any legendary figure, I hoped I might get some firsthand information about the professional life of a traditional actress during the early part of the century. This is an area of knowledge which by its nature remains obscure, inadequately documented, and upon which no one could offer better commentary than Meng Hsiao-tung.

Eventually word came back that she had agreed to my coming to her home with my sponsor for tea on a prearranged afternoon. The much anticipated day arrived, but an hour before we were due at her apartment there was a telephone message to say she was indisposed and could not see us that afternoon. My intermediary arranged a second appointment, which again ended in the same last-minute cancellation. When a third attempt was also called off, I withdrew disappointed but not surprised at this very Chinese way of saying no. I was all too aware that it had been a little naive to think it could have happened otherwise. After Tu's death the actress never returned to the stage out of respect for his memory, or so it was said in public. According to what I was told in Hongkong, however, it was a condition of Tu's will that she not do so. What lay behind this perhaps no one can know. The

63

Chinese concerned will never tell, and those "who sit on the wall and look on" and critics who write about the world of Chinese theatre are deft in saying everything about nothing. Meng Hsiao-tung eventually moved with Tu's family to Taiwan, where she led a secluded life and died in 1977. Two tape cassettes of her singing at private gatherings in the household were issued as a memorial tribute, inadequate reminders of an actress once high in her profession but with whom life dealt capriciously during a career in which artistic success was mingled with personal tragedy.

Not all the early actresses ended their lives in so sombre a way as the two described, but the names of those prominent in the twenties and thirties, or even the postwar years, are lost in the past and mean little or nothing to a new generation. They are remembered only in the intimate circles of today's dwindling body of old professionals, and seeking out reliable personal details about them can be an unrewarding task indeed.

It was not done for Chinese women to talk about themselves in the past; their modesty induced in them a keener sense of ambiguity than most, particularly in that universal human desire to conceal one's age. I often used to wonder when looking over applications for secretarial posts in our Nanking office at the attention given to making time stand still on paper, a need possibly aggravated by the fact that everyone in China was reckoned, somewhat logically, as being already a year old by the time of being delivered into the world.

The Chinese have been most indifferent recorders of their own theatre, for there has always been a social gulf between the world of traditional ethics and the greenroom, the latter considered unworthy of serious attention. Matters have been intensified by attitudes towards women on one hand and the paucity of objective writing about theatre as theatre on the other. Social prejudice, human vanity, and literary snobbism together have been unkind to the image of the actress on the Peking stage.

However, the leading actresses one saw at work in the troupes which visited Nanking were committed stage artists, every one of them, whose rare skills commanded a wide following and drew full houses wherever they appeared. Nevertheless, the theatregoing public still reserved admiration for the great female impersonators. Even the actresses would have conceded popularity there, for they never ceased to pay homage to their artistic progenitors, the masters of their genre — among whom Mei Lan-fang was regarded as the supreme exponent. When his last appearance before the communists seized power was announced, it was enough to create a near-riot outside the Shanghai theatre where he appeared; the black market traffic in tickets exceeded all precedents, even in the prevailing economic chaos. I was fortunate enough to be able to see this performance because a Chinese painter friend, by means best known only to himself, had succeeded in getting tickets. It was said that Mei had staged this event only to help his hard-pressed company, for whose support he was completely responsible according to old theatre practice. This for him, as for all stage people, had become an almost impossible task in the accelerating inflation beginning to reach insane proportions in 1948 when the performance took place. I still have in my possession a reservation slip for a Peking hotel in March of that year. The daily room rate is quoted as one million Chinese yüan with a heating charge of one hundred and sixty thousand yüan, so worthless had the national currency become.

We had tickets for a Friday evening, and it seemed that every theatregoer in China was by hook or by crook determined to be present at that performance. Getting into the theatre proved as formidable a task as the occasion was auspicious. The swelling crowds outside the foyer pushed and shoved like people deranged. If by some miracle a line of sorts began to form, it was immediately broken in the frenzied scrambling. The worst offenders were those in military uniform, who blustered and bullied their way through the mob, apparently considering it their inalienable right to thrust aside their fellows. In the end we simply abandoned ourselves to the mad surge, the breath being nearly squeezed out of our bodies until we were finally swept inside by the sheer momentum of the crowd. The theatre was one of Shanghai's largest Western-style auditoriums, with a proscenium stage. By some miracle we arrived at our seats breathless but intact without the necessity of disputing the validity of our tickets, an achievement in itself.

The play that evening was *Ssu Lang Visits His Mother*, a great favorite with Shanghai audiences. It was not a piece that I should have chosen to see Mei perform for the last time, since it does not best set off his particular talents. But I would not complain about an occasion that turned out to be the end of an era in theatre history, the last opportunity of seeing China's most highly regarded actor perform.

The play's theme is based on the exploits of the Yang family, patriotic warriors whose deeds during the tenth century A.D., when China was threatened by invasion, have gone down in legend. The action commences with General Yang's fourth son in captivity after a bloody battle in which his three older brothers were slain. Taken before the Empress Dowager who ruled his captors, he concealed his identity and so impressed the old lady that she gave him her princess daughter in marriage. The two lived in conjugal bliss and had a child, upon whom the old Empress doted. One day Ssu Lang heard that a Chinese expedition had launched an attack against his captors and his mother and sixth brother were with the advancing forces. Sitting and grieving over the fate which prevented a meeting with his mother, he was discovered by his wife, the Princess.

At this juncture the actors appeared on stage, first Ssu Lang, who after a prologue introducing himself and the events in which he had been involved, delivered in formal, heightened speech, seated himself and began to sing an air once familiar to every messenger boy on the streets:

> Yang Yen-hui sits in the palace
> And thinking to himself sighs
> While reflecting on events of years ago . . .

At these opening lines the audience settled back in their seats with anticipatory pleasure, heads nodding to the well-known rhythms.

The rest of the story of the play is soon told. After learning of her husband's secret sorrow, the Princess offered to help him meet with his mother on the condition he return to the palace before dawn. He agreed, and in order to get the arrow of command —the token of authority to allow him safe conduct through the military lines—she devised a strategy. Taking her baby son to see her mother in the council chamber, she pinched him to make him cry; when the alarmed dowager asked what ailed him, she was told he wanted the arrow of command to play with. The doting grandmother handed it over with the proviso it must be given back before dawn in time for the imperial audience. Armed with the precious token, Ssu Lang rode through the night to the enemy

Ssu-lang taken prisoner on his return

lines, where he was intercepted by a patrol led by his own nephew; the latter then took him before his father, Ssu Lang's sixth brother. When his identity was revealed, there was an emotional reunion between Ssu Lang and his mother as well as with his first wife, living in enforced widowhood since his disappearance. After his story was told, he insisted on keeping his promise and, following a tearful farewell, he rode back. But Ssu Lang's absence had been discovered; he was arrested and taken before the angry Empress Dowager, who ordered him executed. Following a fiery scene, she relented, softened by her daughter's pleas; the culprit was pardoned and ordered to a distant northern post.

It sounds like sorry stuff if judged by Western ideas of a playscript, but to criticise a theme like this in terms of the psychological depth, dramatic tension, and credibility which invest our own understanding of the theatre is to misunderstand the play's function. Credibility was the last thing sought by Chinese playgoers, for whom such elementary fables were simply convenient devices around which to develop theatrical conventions rejecting all scenic representation of time and space in favor of an uncompromisingly bare stage allowing full scope for the plasticity of movement within space. A total synthesis of vocal, musical, and gestural techniques was the basis for formally structured rhythmic patterns used in recurrent permutations and combinations. These were easily memorised by audiences brought up to learn by rote from childhood, and so the songs and dialogues of the Peking stage repertoire passed deep into the consciousness of the people. Playgoers followed the presentations of their favorite actors with a keen appraisal born of long familiarity with the conventions used and savored skills displayed for them in accordance with the dramatic rules.

One good reason for the immense popularity of *Ssu Lang Visits His Mother* was the scope offered within the compass of that single play for several of the important role genres of the Peking repertoire. With its nine principal and four supporting roles, the fans were offered an opportunity to enjoy a rich selection of acting styles interpreted by a galaxy of well-known artists on the stage together. This play has a long history of memorable performances, including the 1932 version when a pioneer actress Hu Pi-lan made history in the role of the Princess at a time when women performers were still frowned upon by the diehards. Mei's performance as the Princess on the night I saw the play was tumultuously received by the packed house, whose resounding applause marked an occasion which belongs to history. There were no curtain calls in traditional Chinese theatre; as soon as the actors were off the stage, there was a concerted rush for the exits and again it was every man, woman, and child for himself. When the play was over, it was over with a vengeance in China, and the pragmatic business of getting home overruled all else. We waited until the crowd had dispersed a little and then set off down the Nanking Road where the playhouse was situated, in search of an after-the-theatre supper in time-honored fashion.

The busy Nanking Road ran in a straight line from east to west with the Bund, or quayside, at one extremity and the other connecting with Bubbling Well Road. The latter skirted the famous racecourse to continue through an affluent area of tree-shaded streets, once the exclusive residence of the taipans. A convenient translation of this word, a corruption of the Chinese *ta pan*, would be "big stuff." As applied to foreign businessmen, it implied "boss of the firm," but household servants and employees used it indiscriminately to serve the flattery of rank which kept the wheels of Chinese social relationships smoothly turning. Therefore to the Chinese man in the street, *taipan* meant any foreigner, since it was assumed they were all there for the purpose of doing business and in any case regarded themselves as the boss whatever their occupation. In the old days children in the street used to shout *taipan* at every foreigner who passed by. Later this became *ying-kuo jen*, "Englishman," or -woman, which conjured up the supreme image of colonial authority in Chinese eyes. On the other hand, by the time we arrived in China the street urchins used to greet us with *mei-kuo jen*, "American," wherever we went, indicating a colloquial awareness of a changed balance of power but an unshaken conviction that foreigners were all the same only different. The fickleness of political change was further revealed in the cries of children who shouted *su-lien jen*, "Russians," at us every time we appeared during a 1956 visit to communist China. Becoming a little exasperated by the vehemence of one noisy group, my wife awed them into silence by asserting we were English, not Russian, and seized upon one startled crop-headed lad with the question, "Do you know where England is?" Back came the pat answer *pu chih tao*, "don't know." As Beckett's Estragon remarked, such is life.

To return to describing the Nanking Road, this bustling thoroughfare was the main shopping area for the foreign community, pampered with every known commodity for sale in shops that mingled the products of Bond Street, Fifth Avenue, and the Rue de la Paix in the luxury of their displays. Nanking Road was also the site of three large, six-storied department stores, named Sun Sun, Sincere, and Wing On, monuments to Chinese business enterprise and foresight. Each was topped by ornamental spires reminiscent of children's building blocks, bearing the firm's name in large Chinese characters which cast their neon glow high above the Shanghai night streets.

The pride of the Chinese, these popular stores combined all the facilities of their Western prototypes, ensuring that customers lacked nothing, Chinese or foreign, for their comfort and convenience. The Wing On building included a seven hundred-room Western-style hotel, billiard rooms, a restaurant, and a roof garden, which was a favorite meeting place after wandering through the bewildering floor displays. A visit to a department store constituted a day's outing for many a Chinese family, who were able to indulge a native passion for just gazing — and best of all, it was absolutely free.

Each of the stores was a permanent blaze of light reflected from every glass-topped counter and showcase, since Chinese merchants have developed an inordinate passion for fluorescent lighting. The shifting stream of shoppers on the crowded floors complemented the never-ending flow of passers-by in the street beyond the ornate copper and plate glass entry doors. Among it all a murmur ran through the stores like the distant twittering of a gigantic flock of birds, which rose and fell beneath the cacophony of loud speaker systems relaying the latest "yellow music" hits from every floor. The development of modern public address systems in China has encouraged an imperviousness to the hubbub of "canned" music in public places second to none in an age which seems to have forgotten the meaning of silence.

"Yellow music" was the name given to popular song pieces composed for the dance halls, cabarets, or films in China. The phonograph, the cinema, and the radio became powerful factors in popularising the rhythms and melodies of Western jazz and light music among a younger generation in the large cities, where the rise of ballroom dancing in the twenties and thirties first familiarised youth with such pastimes. However, ballroom dancing was constantly under attack by the Nanking government, who issued an edict in 1937 imposing a ban on public dancing with a proviso that all students discovered in dance halls would be expelled from their schools or universities, whatever the excellence of their academic records. Such campaigns continued sporadically, and when in 1947 the Chiang government again banned dance halls on the grounds of thrift, increased production, and so on, the two hundred thousand taxi dancers of Shanghai threatened to march on Nanking and lay their petition before the tomb of Sun Yat-sen, the father of modern China. Needless to say, the ban proved as ineffective as most other governmental regulations of the period; it required the communists to succeed in banishing ballroom dancing.

In assimilating the musical forms of the waltz, the fox trot, and the tango, the Chinese were quick to create their own popular sentimental melodies. Though derivative, ephemeral, and no less banal than their Western prototypes, these were far less nerve-racking in their aural impact. Yellow music had its own character, and though it was faithful to Western compositional methods, it became essentially Chinese in the quality of its sentimental transmutation and could never have been mistaken as occidental in origin.

The "king" of yellow music during its formative years was a song composer named Li Chin-hui, at the height of his fame during the 1930s. Like dancing, yellow music was the constant target of the reformers, and Li came in for much criticism in his day. He was stoutly defended by his admirers, who pointed out that although he used Western musical techniques, his tunes were essentially Chinese. In 1931 Li signed up a young musician called Nieh in his Bright Moon Variety Company. Nieh was later given a contract with one of the early Shanghai film companies, for whom he composed some of the more popular "hits" of the thirties. He met an early death in 1935 by drowning, but his name has been perpetuated. A theme song he wrote called "Children of the Storm" for a film began with the line, "Arise all you who refuse to be slaves"; it was proclaimed the new national anthem of China by the Maoist government in 1949. So out of yellow music greater things were born, after all.

Some of the tunes currently popular when we were in Nanking still echo in the mind and act as an impulse to those sudden moments when images of extraordinary intensity give way to subliminal recollection. There was one tune in particular called "Yeh Shanghai," "Shanghai Night," which goes round in my head still, so often was it trilled out from every loudspeaker and radio in town. As tin pan alley tunes do, it lodged in the consciousness, to be singled out as occasion willed from the mental rubbish heap of the past. The ghostly remembrance of its catchy rhythm still evokes with startling clarity the atmosphere and events of the China we knew thirty years ago. The words of the lyric were banal enough in their celebration of Shanghai's famous night life, but the repetitive alliteration of the linguistic devices to which the Chinese are ever-faithful, even in their yellow music, added a rhythmic pungency lost in the prosaic English translation, which begins:

> Shanghai is not a dark city at night.
> Only seeing her smiling face, who can be gloomy in heart.
> I would not exchange the new heaven on earth for any other place.

This was a declaration of belief which would have outraged the old priest who, when saying goodbye to an Italian acquaintance of mine leaving for China, warned him: "Don't go to Shanghai, my son. The devil lives there."

Nanking Road was crowded with a jostling mass of people moving in kaleidoscopic procession against the fluorescent glitter. The night sky was suffused with the spreading glow of the city, and the shadowed summits of the tallest buildings were delineated in a receding perspective by scores of winking neon signs in Chinese, adding a hieroglyphic attraction to their mundane messages.

Faces glimpsed in the orbit of exchanged glances across the human tide were as quickly superseded by more faces in the ceaseless parade, where masks were laid aside for the world of sought pleasures. The great banks, offices, and stores — daytime witnesses to commercial enterprise of unequivocal assurance — by night presided over the transactions of a new saturnalia, even then celebrating its own extinction. We turned from the Western

Singing girl going home — Shanghai

sophistication of Nanking Road, to enter a network of side streets and alleys. It was like crossing a frontier, so different and uniquely Chinese an atmosphere prevailed in a self-contained domain of shops dealing in tea, cotton goods, silks, native medicines, and rice wine. There were also jewelers, silversmiths, tailors' shops, and a score of other trades and crafts, including restaurants and food shops in plenty. A fortune teller sat at a small table illuminated by a dim oil lamp, strategically placed on the curbside adjoining the grilled frontage of a money changer. The seer was busy predicting the future for his clients, who had lost faith in the government's economic policies — if indeed they had ever possessed it — and preferred to rely on the age-old necromancy of their forefathers.

The inevitable odors from smouldering charcoal, dried fish, incense, sesame oil, fried noodles, and a variety of less tangible sources mingled in a grand emanation hovering above the still noisy and brightly lit streets. In the rear of many a shop, families sat around the household table eating their late evening meal or relaxing over a game of mahjong. Shutters were taken down early and put up late by Chinese tradesmen, whose shops were also their homes. There people ate, slept, and toiled on behalf of the family, that great bulwark in a fecund society where the gap between the necessities of life and want was a narrow one. The gap was bridged by industriousness, frugality, and the pressing need to take care of one's own, knowing that there was always someone eager to seize slender opportunity if others were improvident enough to let it slip by. And in the fluorescent-lit tailors' shops, wisps of young girls were bent over their needles and sewing machines, working far into the night making the traditional, high-collared, close-fitting dresses slit at the sides, which would be called for within a few hours by the servants of fashionable wives and daughters of the city. There was no early closing nor required days off for those in the tailors' shops. If the employees felt resentment against their sweatshop conditions, their passive faces gave no sign. And if the inordinate number of counter assistants in each silk store or cotton goods shop seemed to defeat all individual enterprise, again there was no outward indication, for such would ignore the social protection owed to every member of the family clan.

We finally reached the restaurant chosen by our friend for an after-the-theatre supper, a rather insignificant-looking little place that we were assured had the best *chia-chiang mien*, a special northern noodle dish, to be found in town. The noodles are dished up hot from the kitchen and covered with a thick sauce made from soybean paste, minced pork, and vegetable oil; the sauce is well-stirred into the noodles before eating. They are served in large individual bowls and accompanied by a plate of thin, fresh cucumber slices, making a meal of compact simplicity but flavored subtlety — a description which aptly defines the essence of culinary art in China. There noodles are eaten by lifting a portion to the mouth with chopsticks and allowing the bitten-off lengths to slither back into the bowl, or alternatively and more commonly, sucking the whole portion into the mouth with the help of the chopsticks. This is an aurally accepted solution attesting to the pragmatic function of chopsticks as against the butchery committed with knife and fork, which to the Chinese seems to be an unwarranted intrusion on the dining table of practices rightly belonging to the kitchen chopping block.

We drank warm rice wine with our noodles and chatted over the events of a memorable theatrical evening. Our friendly waiter, with the insatiable curiosity of his people and alerted by the name of Mei Lan-fang — the mere sound of which was enough to start anyone off in a Shanghai restaurant — began to question our Chinese host about his foreign guests, their antecedents, occupations, reasons for being in China, in Shanghai, in that particular restaurant, opinions on Chinese food, of course Mei Lan-fang, and whether we had visited The Great World. The Great World was the recreational venue of the Chinese public in Shanghai, being a department store of entertainments, so to speak, to which the crowds flocked daily in the thousands. In the early years of the century, an entrepreneur named Huang decided to provide the ordinary people of Shanghai with a modern amusement center, attuned to new concepts of entertainment in accordance with the Westernised spirit of the times. The result was for those days a tall building, given a Chinese name signifying "the paragon of all such edifices" and embodying a large theatre, open air cinema, and roof garden where people could sit and gossip over their tea. The venture was a resounding success, and Huang decided to sell out his interests to build a bigger and better center called The New World. This was again so successful that the Peking authorities decided they too would have a modern amusement center which they built in 1916 under the same name.

Meanwhile, in Shanghai the enterprising Huang ceded his New World shares to the widow of his former partner and decided to consolidate the proud boast of his first venture by building a new temple of pleasures to outdo all the rest. Completed in record time due to the large bonuses given the construction workers, it was opened on July 14, 1917, as The Great World.

It was a large, reinforced concrete complex laid out with courtyards, roof gardens, a cinema, shops, galleries, stalls — in truth, all the fun of the fair, not the least important feature being the several small theatres and storytellers' halls where performances from different regional areas were given regularly. These provided a cross section of local entertainments into which visitors could wander at any time and be sure of hearing their own dialect spoken. One novelty of The Great World was a skilled troupe of young boys and girls performing the plays of the classical repertoire of their native Peking. They were a standing attraction for the Chinese, who like most Asian peoples, have a taste for savouring virtuoso accomplishments in the very young. This is induced possibly by the fact that intensive training in all performing disciplines begins in childhood, thereby offering opportunities for early critical scrutiny and complemented by that deepseated familial pride which the Chinese extend to their own at all times and on all occasions.

I saw my first Shaohsing drama in The Great World. This particular style originated in Chekiang Province south of Shanghai, in an area famous for a rice wine regarded as supreme of its kind. Of comparatively recent development, the Shaohsing drama began as a rural ballad form which assimilated new dramatic content in the late nineteenth century and was introduced into Shanghai at the time The Great World was being planned. Its range of expression was widened under the influence of the Peking theatre and the realistic production methods of Western theatre, which led to the introduction of stage scenery among other things. During the early twenties, troupes of women performers playing both male and female roles made their debut, becoming so popular that they took over the Shaohsing theatre completely, a situation which has continued until present times.

The plays were romantic and highly sentimental to the point of being maudlin, concentrating as they did on tragic lovers, betrayed wives, and thwarted passions — portrayed on stage with the maximum of melodramatic effect and spectacular costumes, some of the more dazzling of their kind. Shaohsing drama was a particular favorite with women playgoers; whether they were middle-aged matrons, old grandmothers, simple servant girls, or shop assistants, one and all were assured of a deliciously harrowing hour or two and a colorful stage presentation whenever they went to the theatre.

They were certainly well catered for in the first Shaohsing performance I attended. In the final scene the audience was overcome by the agonies of the heroine dying from consumption, which was suddenly revealed by the tortured coughing-up of property blood staining her white silk handkerchief to the accompaniment of concerted sniffling throughout the auditorium.

The Shaohsing drama was not total bathos, however, and at its best had a lyrical grace and musical charm contributed by its women performers. Their art was given international acclaim in 1955 when a new Chinese film based on one of the most popular stories of the Shaohsing repertoire, one taken from classical legend, was widely shown in the Western world. In brief, the play told how the beautiful daughter of a merchant disguised herself as a young man in order to become a student in a famous academy, women being forbidden to attend such institutions at the time. Successful in her disguise, she was admitted to the academy, only to fall in love with a young colleague, who discovered her true identity. Visiting her home later to claim her for his bride, he was devastated to find her father had betrothed her to someone else. The grief-stricken young man pined away and died. Heartbroken, the girl threw herself upon his tomb, which miraculously opened to enclose the two lovers; their spirits then became transformed into two gaily colored butterflies fluttering above the tomb.

This visually impressive color film, called simply *Liang Shan-po and Chu Ying-tai* after the two lovers, successfully preserved the theatrical framework of the play and conveyed the lyrical delicacy of the vocal form and sensitivity of the formalised movement and gesture as performed by the completely female cast of China's leading Shaohsing drama troupe. The fact that despite its unfamiliar idiom the film made a deep impression on Western audiences by the unpretentious purity of its presentation and acting style testified to the quality of the actresses and to this indigenous dramatic genre. Seasoned Chinese playgoers frequently found new pungency in plays where the nuances of sexual identity were theatrically transposed and mirrored through the pleasing complexities of a woman playing a woman playing a man, on a stage where men had always played women.

The professional storytellers who held their Great World audiences transfixed needed neither costume nor make-up to make female impersonation credible. Theirs was a self-contained art totally sustained by their astonishing mimicry, which was enough to set an audience off as soon as a performer made his appearance. There were both men and women storytellers, and neither was confined to impersonating their own sex in their narratives; the traditional long Chinese gown was the customary professional dress for men and women alike. Sometimes they carried a folding fan or a handkerchief as accessories to their interpretations. At other times they accompanied themselves on stringed or percussive instruments, according to the particular style of storytelling, for there are dozens of different forms conditioned by the many regional dialects. The Yangtze Valley area around Shanghai was particularly rich in storytelling styles, and the visitor to The Great World was always sure of a laugh in his hometown idiom if he dropped in to one of the several halls on the second storey featuring that art.

In the past storytelling had been a more leisurely entertainment, in which a performer would continue his narrative over a period of several days in the interests of keeping his audience with him. In the pressured life of the modern city, however, it became the custom to break down the much-loved rambling tales from the traditional epics and romantic novels into single episodes that could be narrated separately or in sequence to make an integrated story.

Besides the old historical pieces, there were those in which no musical instruments were used and depended only on the performer's brilliant sense of characterisation, marking the essence of a style that was very popular in Shanghai. The house became vibrant as soon as such a storyteller appeared and, taking his seat, immediately launched into a patter developed through a sequence of soliloquies, dialogues with unseen individuals, and mischievous asides. These were interlarded with flashes of superbly timed wit and gentle insinuations which reduced his audience to uproarious laughter and a chuckling to themselves long after they had left the auditorium. Such was the essential craft of storytelling, as sublime a demonstration of the art of knowing what to leave out as could be found anywhere.

Having exhausted the topic of The Great World, our waiter inevitably digressed to the worsening political situation of the real world, the ever-present reality of which became too evident in his anxious face as he began a deep conversation with our host in Shanghai dialect we did not understand. Nevertheless, simply by watching him talk and from the fragments of his comments our host later passed on, one sensed anew a growing sense of desperation and mistrust of government among the ordinary Chinese people.

As we walked back through the brightly lit streets with their lines of traffic and pleasure-seeking night crowds, there was nothing to suggest that this incredible city with its huge cosmopolitan population including some sixty thousand Europeans and Americans, its ultramodern facilities and prosperous-looking shops, could remain anything other than the sophisticated urban citadel it outwardly appeared.

The Shanghai of the prewar years, with its spoilt foreign population protected by extraterritoriality and luxuriating in a halcyon world of colonial privilege and pleasure whose bulwarks were the vast enterprises of the China trade, was merely hearsay to newcomers like ourselves. Shanghai was now governed by a Chinese administration, and the fact that we were in the city at all was due to the new spirit of the times. The complacence and arrogance of the past were invited to give way to nonpolitical, noneconomic relations between peoples, relations affirming a common civilisation sharing the experiences and traditions of different cultures in the interests of a tolerable future for human society.

Admittedly, the outward symbols of foreign domination remained all around us in Shanghai, and we too benefited from materialistic comforts and conveniences provided as a result of colonial energy and commercial acumen. On the other hand, a sense of foreboding was aroused at sight of the beggars who waited in the streets to follow us. There were old men and women in tattered and stained blue cotton garments clutching at our elbows, dishevelled mothers holding up their crying babies in front of us, and ragged children with outstretched hands and a continuous wailing for *cumshaw, cumshaw.* This is a corruption of a word which in Amoy dialect originally meant "grateful thanks." It was now used to describe tips, bribes — presents with a purpose — and has been universally adopted as the beggar's cry for alms. As fast as a coin was doled out to one beggar, another pleader appeared. One had a sense of being caught in a vicious circle of circumstances completely beyond remedy and personal responsibility. Surrounded constantly by ragged people clutching viciously at our coat sleeves, it was difficult at times to suppress a feeling of resentment that uncharitably arose within one as a result of their persistent cries.

We had been told that in prewar Shanghai begging was an organised racket directed from the underworld and the piteous behavior and dreadful appearance of many a beggar a sham, but that even so one had to drop them coins as a safeguard against inconvenience which might be incurred by a failure to contribute to charity. We were in no position to doubt the old Shanghai hands in this matter, yet it was only too clear that the beggars who clamored around us were authentic enough. Shanghai undoubtedly had its own large quota of "professionals," but these were impossible to discern — the beggars' numbers grew daily with the continuing influx of refugees. They were for the most part country people made homeless by the fast-spreading civil war in the north, victims of the political strife rending the country, sending them in blind flight like hunted animals to seek shelter in a city that still retained the outward semblance of security. There they scavenged for food, importuned passers-by, and died in their scores on the streets.

In those days there was a popular Chinese strip cartoon called "The Wanderings of San Mao," published in a Shanghai daily and syndicated in Nanking. It depicted the adventures of an underfed urchin adrift on the city streets and his efforts to survive in the troubled era before the communists seized power. The mordant drawings of this cartoon series brilliantly caricatured the Shanghai social setting and revealed the anguish and resentment of ordinary people in the economic chaos and political corruption that prevailed.

San Mao, literally "Three Hairs," took his name from the fact that his otherwise hairless pate sprouted three wispy strands as an apology for a forelock. Chinese parents often identified their children in numerical order of their arrival in the world; for example, the eldest child would be called to table as number one, the next as number two, and so on, according to the size of the household. It was a custom calculated to emphasise the component strength of a family group and effectively deter creeping egotism.

The creator of San Mao was an artist called Chang Lo-p'ing, who had once known a poor family of seven children compelled to fend for themselves. An individualist, their father always addressed them as one hair, two hairs, three hairs — all the way down the line to seven hairs — thus providing the original idea for the famous San Mao.

One cartoon that stays in my memory began with San Mao rescuing another small boy from a pummeling inflicted by a street lout twice his size. With the bully vanquished, the rescuer and rescued set off down the road and, while passing a well-to-do residence, spied a bulky parcel lying on the ground. Eagerly unwrapping it, they were horrified to discover it contained a newborn baby abandoned to its fate, an all-too-common occurrence in that period. Gathering up the child, they went to knock at the door of the house, but the mistress shudderingly turned them away. Chastened, they sought out a day nursery, but there they were pursued by a truncheon-swinging policeman whose temper and rough behavior towards the unprivileged were typical of its kind. Escaping from their persecutor in despair, the two urchins fled after dumping the baby on the pavement in front of a shop window filled with a display of packaged Klim. This was a milk substitute shipped in bulk to China by international relief organizations. One of the major scandals of the postwar years was the manner in which supplies for the displaced and needy were sequestered for a thriving black market, to be sold only to those who could afford the inflated prices. As the well-known Chinese saying goes, "To see a thing once is better than hearing it a hundred times"; it was through the keen eye of a discerning cartoonist that the ills of a nation were revealed at a glance obviating all the political rhetoric in the world.

The inherent skill of Chinese artists with brush and ink suggests the potential for a vigorous and original school of pictorial commentators — although in fact achievements in this field have been comparatively limited and distinguished exponents few. Shanghai, needless to say, was the birthplace of a modern Chinese press which was always enterprising in adopting new ideas from the West to serve its Chinese purposes. Although other newspaper ventures had preceded it, the first truly important Chinese newspaper was the *Shun Pao*, founded by a British owner who delegated entire journalistic responsibility to the Chinese editors and staff, resulting in an essentially vernacular journal. At first catering to government officials by publishing imperial edicts and civil service appointments, it soon branched into local and provincial news with space given to crimes, disasters, and occult happenings, providing useful material for eager teahouse discussion and catering to that avidity for the sensational which is privy to the Chinese love of gossip. *Shun Pao* also published theatre announcements, shipping news, and market prices as well as a poetry section contributed by readers. The verse was eventually discontinued because, it is said, the poets began to intrude too alarmingly upon mundane affairs.

However, it was not until the late 1920s and early 1930s, when a number of new magazines and pictorial supplements began to appear, that the Chinese cartoonist was provided with real opportunities for publication. The first successful strip cartoon appeared during this period; it was called "Mr. Wang and Little Ch'en," Wang being the typical Shanghai middle-class citizen and Ch'en his foil. It was drawn by Yeh Ch'ien-yü, a clever draftsman with a fluid brush and pen line who became China's most distinguished cartoonist, although he eventually abandoned comic art for painting and illustration. Yeh's cartoon character Mr. Wang bore a distinct likeness to Chiang Kai-shek, although if anybody recognised the fact, they kept quiet about it — probably with good reason, for in the formidable social prejudices of his people the Chinese cartoonist faced his greatest occupational hazard. In a country where to lose face was social annihilation and where personal attitudes were so ordered as to avoid the slightest suggestion of this calamity at all costs, it was understandably a perilous occupation to deride people in high places with unflattering drawings in newspapers. David Low, the great Australian political cartoonist who produced his most brilliant work for the London press, once described how in prewar days he asked a leading Japanese cartoonist what would happen to him if he caricatured the Mikado. Said Low, "In reply he drew the edge of his hand across his throat and made a noise like sawing," an answer which would equally have applied in China. Had the creator of the San Mao cartoons dared to criticise the nation's leader personally in the same spirit of pictorial protest or derided the political operators behind the corruption so convincingly suggested in his cartoons, there would have been a summary end to the artist and his work. There is nothing more calculated to arouse the wrath of absolute authority than derisive laughter. As it was, the cartoonist, through his sharp observation captured the spirit of city life in a politically chaotic era by characterising the Shanghai waif as a dupe whose antics forcefully expressed the complaints of ordinary people against bungling officialdom.

The San Mao cartoons were so effective that a paperback collection of the urchin's adventures in misfortune were published in the early 1950s, by which time the idealized image of a different Mao dominated the newspaper columns. As a graphic reminder of the "bad old days," the San Mao cartoons were unique and lent color to the beliefs of a new regime that things were now all for the best under their care. For the outcasts personified in the cartoon figure of the Shanghai urchin this was demonstrably true, but San Mao had no successor to hold up the mirror to a new era, which had its own anomalies no less underscored by a gargantuan ethnocentrism resistant to the salutory effects of humor.

The cartoonist and the comic actor share a similar talent for inventing recognizable character types who reduce life to a common human level in the immediacy of the passing moment, while puncturing the self-esteem of authority. Debunking the mighty can bring retribution, and the cartoonist has possibly been most vulnerable to high displeasure because his pictorial jibes are published in print to remain as proof of his temerity. The comic actor, on the other hand — at least in the old days before radio and television — practised a much more ephemeral art and was only accountable for his mockery through hearsay. Nevertheless, he was by no means immune. There is a story handed down in Chinese theatrical circles, for example, about a famous nineteenth-century comic actor who was imprisoned, flogged, and later died for his improvisatory wit directed at the high dignitary Li Hung-chang and his handling of the Sino-Japanese War in 1895.

The Peking stage repertoire was particularly rich in its array of comic characters, among whom the servants, bumpkins, clerks, lechers, and shrews offered a gallery of archetypes we find present throughout the long history of the theatre everywhere. In any country the clown's instantaneous affinity with his audience depends upon such things as the saltiness of colloquial language, local customs, food, and social behavior. Familiarity with these sharpens perception and draws reactions to the timed jibe which goes home like a winged arrow and provides the exquisite moment of laughter that is the gift of the master actor. Nevertheless, the essence of the clown's skill lies in the sheer coruscating verve of his presence, and this in itself can transcend the elusiveness of a strange culture at times. The obsessive topics of the clown have persisted through centuries and remain fundamentally similar everywhere. To be attuned to them is really to be aware of the concerns and behavior of ordinary people who provide the very stuff from which the antics of the comic actor emerge. Even before I knew any Chinese, the stage clowns quite often drew my spontaneous laughter in those moments of comic truth when the barriers of nationality go down. Thus it is that Chaplin's silent clowning presented no problems of communication for Chinese audiences when they saw him for the first time.

In the Peking theatre the comic actor had his allotted place in serious drama much the same as the clown does in Shakespearian plays. His timed appearance at the appropriate juncture deflected emotions of the audience, lowered tensions, and returned everyone to the firm ground of everyday reality with a bang, rousing laughter that betokened a sense of solidarity with his routines. These reflected universal propensities of the clown for deflating bureaucratic arrogance, debunking the quacks, degrading the priesthood, and airing the vexations of all who served masters. In short, scope was given to the hidden grumblings of the multitude at those constantly on its back, the eternal protest against authority in all its guises.

Though the comic parts were placed last in the neat order of four principal role categories under which the Peking actor's techniques were always professionally listed, they were by no means least. Among the backstage superstitions prevailing in the old days, it was the custom before *k'ai lo,* the percussive tempest from gong and cymbals that heralded opening the performance, for the clown to apply the first daub of white to his face before any of the painted face actors were allowed to put on their make-up. Through what distance in time and to what early sources this once scrupulously observed custom could be traced was difficult to ascertain. It was usually explained to me as being out of respect for the long traditions of the role, and some ascribed it to the fact that Ming Huang, the eighth-century emperor who

founded the first training school described earlier, liked to play
the comic roles. This theory seemed always a little vague, although certainly there are good precedents in the history of theatre for rulers joining in their own court entertainments, and in
Asia generally the clown figure as the spirit of disorder was
sometimes equated with the gods.

It seems the white-daubed face has been the universal trademark of the clown, East and West, since remote times. In the Chinese theatre the comic make-up consisted of a white patch
painted over the nose, around the eyes, and part of the cheeks
only, its shape and proportion varying with the different roles.
This patch was usually embellished with red and black markings,
which again differed for each character. Despite all my question-
ing of people, it was impossible to discover how and why these

Clown

markings differed as they did; no one seemed really to know and certainly not the actors who used them. It mattered little, for the Chinese clown's make-up was unforgettable, providing the perfect focus for his sly glances aside and constant batting of the eyes with which he punctuated the quips and sallies directed at the audience from front stage. The gusty entrance of the clown stridently protesting or expostulating was a moment one learned to wait for in the old Peking theatre. The fleeting images of droll moments — a reproving finger here, an expression of pained surprise there — remain in the layers of memory as lasting testimony to the insinuatory force of the clown's physical presence.

On the Peking stage the comic actor was the one character who spoke in the ordinary language of the audience, who was able to make personal or topical allusions and in general "call a spade a spade." The Peking dialect has a resonant burr to it, and its deep-throated vowels and elision of the rolling r's were exploited to good purpose by the comic actor. At the same time he was bound by the conventions of usage and technical methods no less than his fellows in the other roles. In performance he frequently switched from ordinary speech to a rhymed monologue timed to the beat of wooden clappers wielded by the leader of the stage musicians, or relapsed into passages of heightened speech rhythmically modulated so that the voice rose or died away in climactic patterns of penetrating sound. Occasionally he burst into song, using traditional musical modes but retaining his colloquial enunciation, and the raucousness of his delivery added to the mockery.

There was a license to the comic role, a freedom to exaggerate and parody, so that much of the actor's technique simply became a more outrageous development of the classical formalism which imbued the orthodox Peking acting style. When the clown entered the stage, the atmosphere in the theatre perceptibly changed as the audience quickly came back to earth in their willing surrender to homespun reality. The varied cast of characters brought to life by his comic skills were ones whose personalities and predictable behavior have been fair game for the clown since time immemorial in his portrayal of the world upside-down. His methods were physical and situational, portraying people as they actually were and not what they would be. The Chinese comic actor came from a long storytelling tradition, and the obtuse officials, blockheads, mischief makers, profligates, and termagants he mustered came from a gallery of archetypes with whom storytellers have always delighted crowds.

One of the first performances I remember seeing in the Nanking teahouse theatre was a short piece called *Picking Up the Jade Bracelet,* a lighthearted example of consummate mime and laughable tomfoolery. In the play an old scold and professional marriage go-between, Mama Liu, became privy to a romantic flirtation between a young couple unaware that they had been seen making eyes at each other in the absence of a chaperon. Marital unions among the Chinese were formerly arranged solely to serve family continuity, respectability, and therefore financial security, so the professional matchmaker was kept busy attending to parental requirements for eligible offspring while maintaining a vocational disregard for anything so materialistically unrewarding as romantic love — although chance could sometimes be a good thing, as this play seemed to suggest.

It opened by showing an attractive young maiden busy with her domestic chores before a cottage door while her widowed mother was absent at the temple. A personable young man passed by and, being smitten by her charms, proceeded to make advances. Equally smitten yet affecting the embarrassment demanded by traditional etiquette at such male effrontery, she hurried inside and bolted the cottage door, which together with the cottage and everything else, was conjured up on the bare stage by the encompassing mime of the actors. To tempt her forth again, the young man left a jade bracelet lying on the ground and hid nearby. He confronted her, causing flustered agitation, when she ventured out of doors once more and was caught redhanded trying on the decoy bracelet.

On the prowl, the local matchmaker Mama Liu gleefully observed everything from a discreet distance. Deciding to profit from the occasion, she later called on the young woman and forced her to confess her amorous indiscretion through a loaded cross-examination. An exuberant scene followed when after a vehement denial the young woman admitted everything to the inquisitive matchmaker, who was always played by a comic actor. Through mime and gesture, the actor reenacted the circumstances of the temptation and fall with considerable verve, usually bringing the house down by a portrayal of the young woman's chagrin when caught in the act. Her stage part was imbued with all the precision, formalised grace, and delicate gesture of the coquette role as demanded by the Peking style. In contrast, Mama Liu was played with droll exaggeration in such a fashion that the traditional acting forms were parodied against themselves, as it were. High art was reduced to farce in amusing the crowd and the make-believe of theatre thereby called into account. This kind of fooling was common procedure with the Chinese stage clown, who invoked in this way his ancient prerogative of linking the commonplace with the elegant. It inevitably aroused a gale of laughter from the audience and in doing so disclosed the inanities within us all.

Some of the most mischievously convincing interpretations of the matchmaker I ever saw were those given by the "small comics," *hsiao-ch'ou;* that is to say, the actors who played servant boys, shopkeepers, boatmen, and the like, journeymen performers who were the mainstay of smaller troupes. Their versions of the cunning old dame with her sly innuendoes, raucous cackle, and shrewd eye for number one, belying any pretensions to romantic obligations, were tellingly depicted. They never failed to hit the mark with a delighted audience, for whom Mama Liu was a portrait drawn from the depths of the collective unconscious. *Picking Up the Jade Bracelet* was in fact only one scene from a much longer play set in the sixteenth century. Although hero and heroine were dressed in period according to stage conventions admittedly more theatrical than historical in realisation, the costume and make-up of Mama Liu was a replica of a style of dress commonly seen in north China until the early years of this century. Visually as well as psychologically, the personality of Mama Liu was one with which an older generation of playgoers were as familiar as their own grandmothers, perhaps even too convincingly so!

The juxtaposing of the farcical with the "straight" elements of female impersonation on the Peking stage, serving as it did the double purpose of parodying as well as symbolizing women's behavior, was a reminder of principles which have seemingly been at the heart of theatrical performance since very early times. The duality of female impersonation became a stage practice "as full of labor as a wise man's heart," perpetuated through sources like medieval miracle plays and Elizabethan entertainments until the

Wang Te-k'un, comic actor playing an old shrew

day when the Puritans succeeded in closing theatre down. When people were allowed back into the playhouses again, female impersonation was turned over to the transvestite skills of the comic player alone. The shrew, the mother-in-law, and the garrulous gossip were stock figures from theatre's beginning, but they were given new expression culminating in the kind of impersonations which delighted nineteenth-century English audiences and reached a high point of comic invention in the pantomime dames, with whom the wily Mama Liu had a certain artistic affinity. As a stage character, she owed her credibility to an acute perception of the behavior and vocabulary of the populace that has illuminated the talent of the skillful comic actor in all its manifestations. Yet this character went still further than that, for in Mama Liu's stage personality the reconciliation of unabashed pragmatism with more romantic aspects of life, so marked a characteristic of the Chinese temperament, was most craftily suggested. The old beldame was not just a funny character from a past age but the embodiment of a reality as present in the complex tissues of national character as it was a hundred years before — and therein lies the genius of the clown.

3

THE DAY CAME when a visit to Peking could no longer be post-
poned. Surrounded by communist-held territories as it was, the
old capital was only accessible by air, and no one could predict
for how long it would be accessible at all. Nevertheless, life still
went on there, and the only thing to do in those chaotic times was
to proceed with plans already made and let the morrow take care
of itself. Therefore, we found ourselves about to set off for Peking, I to set up a traveling exhibition of the life and work of William Blake that had taken six months to reach us from London,
my wife to advise on the library and reading room which was a
part of our Peking office. If this sounds a little like fiddling while
Rome burns, it is only because all of us in China at that time were
overtaken by the swift and destructive pace of the political debacle. Fresh from the disruptions of a long war ourselves, we were
still imbued with the optimism of survival and excitement of discovering an old culture in its contemporary manifestations,
meanwhile attempting to work for that reciprocity of "nonpolitical, noneconomic relations between peoples, the popular relations," which was the official reason for our being in China in the
first place.

The aftermath of war left Chinese universities deprived of
working facilities, their faculties and student bodies poverty-
stricken and desperate for intellectual replenishment against the
misery of their own living and teaching conditions. The Long
March of Mao and his followers to China's northwest in 1930 has
become a latter-day epic, thanks to the embellishing process of
legend and the power of propaganda. It is ironical, then, that few
today recall that other great saga of the 1937-38 winter when, in
the face of Japanese invasion, universities, schools, and acade-
mies trekked thousands of miles across China to the unoccupied
territory of the far west. It was a demonstration of belief in education and freedom of thought as the key to a great past and the

means to determine the future. It deserves to go on record equally with the Long March of Mao.

Chinese patriotism, rudimentary though it has sometimes appeared to Western minds as being primarily concerned with loyalty to the clan, was wedded to the confirmed belief that knowledge was sacrosanct and indispensable to society's well-being. However, the abolition of the old classical learning in favor of the utilitarian also provided means to promote a nationalistic patriotism, where before concern had been for ethics, and so bring about bureaucratic control with dictatorial rights over education. The older generation of intellectuals whose prestige and influence rated high fought to balance the two extremes and resist interference after the war. They sought government cooperation for educational and technological advancement in the nation and the fostering of international cultural relations but were rebuffed by an obstinate leadership, inefficient planning, and political corruption. The failure of the government to control inflation, civil discord, and bureaucratic repression of the worst kind—aided by a dreaded secret police—left the universities helpless under political jurisdiction. The liberal elements of the scholarly and scientific community were powerless, bitter, and eventually demoralized by the military and economic disasters of the postwar period. This is the picture of an age presented in hindsight; waiting to fly to Peking on that distant morning, we were too close to the situation and lacking in political perception to have realised these things except in a vague way.

The Nanking airport, like most of its kind in that era, was bleakly makeshift and a singularly poor example of so-called planning, adjoining as it did the city's largest hospital. The passengers scattered around the waiting area bore the expressions of long-suffering resignation that mark the air traveler the world over, although their hand baggage was distinctly individualistic. Weight restrictions in baggage were mandatory in those days but did not seem to worry the Chinese, who blandly ignored such interference with their personal affairs. There was one old woman moving towards her flight who carried a live duck in a wicker carrier, an oiled paper umbrella, of course a large thermos flask, and a cloth bundle half her size. None of it seemed to hinder her sprightly progress or that of fellow passengers trailing behind her, all loaded as though joining a caravan bound for the ends of the earth. Our pilot was Chinese — in race, if not appearance. His jauntily slouched cap, tight-seated trousers, and way of drawing his pack of cigarettes from his shirt breast pocket while he chewed gum and chatted to a girlfriend at the embarkation point, were transmutable signals from a new generation.

Our plane took off and Nanking, enclosed by its straggling wall, became a map traced out far below, with the wet paddy fields gleaming like blobs of quicksilver in the morning sunlight. Four hours later we landed in Peking, with little more to mark such a romantic transition than the nasal voice of the air steward offering his synthetic coffee in paper cups. It was early spring and we emerged from the plane into a crisp, clear atmosphere in which the distant landscape stood out in stereoscopic relief. The sky above was a luminous azure sweeping to infinity over brown fields and bare trees. The car taking us towards the city stirred up clouds of white dust along a road boarded at intervals with clusters of small, stone, grey brick houses with paper-paned, latticed windows. From shabby doorways fluttered the occasional strip of tattered crimson paper, lingering remnants of New Year celebrations. Approaching the outskirts of the city, we saw glimpses of the roofed vista that has fascinated generations of travelers, a vision sharply dispelled as acres of nondescript Western-style buildings and ill-kept streets came into view.

We were told that the month previously there had been a massive student demonstration outside Peking National University protesting the ineffective policies of the government and its repressive tactics. Still, Peking had always been a city of student protest, and to all appearances the universities had become calmer by the time we arrived. Life in the city carried on at a surprisingly unhurried pace, and the ordinary people went about their daily business as ordinary people do in troubled times which only later become invested with the portentous aura of history.

For the first few days, I was preoccupied with the William Blake exhibition. Its ceremonial opening was held in the National Library, followed by a talk from William Empson, the British poet and critic who held a chair of English at Peking National University. He was a character from the gallery of nonconformists who have always graced the scholarly-literary world; the Chinese were familiar with the tradition and wholly sympathetic towards him. Empson had a sharp, quizzical eye behind his thick-lensed spectacles, short grizzled hair, and a beard fringing his lower jawline. He chain-smoked cigarettes in a long holder, which he constantly tapped with his forefinger to scatter indiscriminate ash. He was the archetypal absent-minded intellectual, vague to the point of being oblivious to everything and everybody, seemingly mildly astonished at finding himself wherever he happened to be. At the Blake show he sat ringed by attentive Chinese students, delivering his talk with closed eyes and a gently continuous stroking of his beard to the end of his metaphysical discourse. He was the only foreigner to my knowledge permitted to leave communist China to lecture in America in the early 1950s and return to his post in Peking afterwards. I was in our Hongkong office by then and delegated to look after his affairs. Empson's passing in and out of China in such casual a fashion forcefully impressed me, simply because it reinforced a conviction that there were more powerful agents than the restrictive measures of political intransigence still at work.

The Blake exhibition remained on display for a week, but we were to stay a month, since there were personal contacts to be made and educational institutions to be visited. Moreover, in the city that was the heart of the traditional stage world, there were many performances to attend. The vibrant atmosphere of the theatres as I remember them from that visit seemed to convey the essential spirit of Peking life. Many would dispute that statement, but however disdainfully regarded today, the utter devotion of playgoers then to their popular theatre was remarkably deep-seated and expressed as nothing else could how aesthetically at ease the Chinese remained with it in their own minds.

Many elements contributed to the particular ambience of Peking, which all who have savored it find elusive of expression — whether they be the indiscriminate eulogists whom I have already cited or those of us classed as discriminate in lunacy. The grandeur of the city's unchanging architectural landscape, a sense of history, and the mere fact that it was implicitly regarded as the guardian of traditional Chinese life and culture produced a combination of intellectual pride, sensory appreciation, and sense of values. Peking embodied a heritage that was in some way transmitted through intellectual and pedicab driver alike. The course of human life itself is reflected in the rhythms of a great city. They

Peking grandmother

are both perceptible and beyond perception; they flow within everyone and are the incentive to communal behavior. The prevalent sense of rhythm shared by a people commands all that they say and do. Their speech, gesticulation, their characteristic emotional and intellectual reactions all provide constant rhythmic patterns which stem from the habits of a particular way of life. This is one reason why a people reveal themselves more sharply in their entertainments than in any other circumstances and why the distinctive nuances containing the essence of a national character are readily discernible in theatre. In nothing is this so implicit as the actions of everyday life—eating, drinking, different ways of conversing or greeting friends, the way people sit, stand, or walk in relation to the costumes they wear and the buildings they inhabit. And as stylized and contrived as the movements of the Peking actors on stage were, they presented an artistic transmutation of behavior whose form was shaped by such factors as the above. This is not to say that what happened on the Peking stage was in any way considered a replica of things as they really are. The abiding impression from nights spent in the Peking theatres was the exuberant strength of accord between actors and audience towards the expressive symbolism of the playacting. It was this that drew the vociferous approval of the crowd and disclosed the unanimity of the Chinese clan in their understanding of theatrical form.

The Peking theatres themselves were old, shabby, and for the most part suffered from the neglect which was all-pervasive in the time I first knew them. Nevertheless, there was always an aura of festivity about them, the sheer excitement of something going on impelled by the irrepressible energy of people enjoying themselves to the full. That was the first thing that struck one on penetrating the reverberant interiors of the packed houses. Inside them the air positively quivered with the swish of used hot towels flipped from one attendant to the other like soaring birds across the house, in seeming synchronization with the sharp shouts of approval from the audience to the actors. In the cold months people sat huddled in thick padded gowns, scarves, woolens of all kinds, their breaths vaporizing on the air of unheated auditoriums to which they seemed indifferent both from their enthusiasm and the utter practicality of their sartorial inelegance.

Judged by present-day standards, the old Peking theatres were comparatively small, usually being divided into two main seating areas — the ground floor and an upper balcony with open boxes. No curtains were used, and stages varied from the open style of the oldest playhouses to a semi-thrust or simple proscenium in the others. Compared to Western systems, Chinese stage lighting was rudimentary, the old-style footlights being used. However, the light deflected upwards from these was peculiarly effective with Chinese make-up; the reversal of light and shade and the softened contours this induced recalled simpler days in the theatre when this kind of illumination was a convention used to intensify the atmosphere of entrancing unreality surrounding the actors.

The ingeniously devised make-up used for the women characters on the Peking stage was unsurpassed in the sheer theatricality of its visual impact. The glow of the footlights gave this a special lustre, enhancing the rich texture of the costumes and the patina of the actress's face painted a matt white with the surrounding areas of the eyes heavily rouged and the sides of the nose and cheeks more lightly so. Arched crescent eyebrows were penciled in and the eyes, drawn upwards at the outer extremities, were boldly outlined in black. Flat coils of hair were symmetrically arranged around the brow, with two spears of hair defining the curve of the cheek at either side. A high, chignon-crowned hairdo completed the effect, one that in its way epitomized the cunning of all artifices devised to transform mundane realism into visual sorcery.

Early in the century, when all performances were given in daylight, the make-up used for the women characters was different from that just described, being a uniform white with the eyes and brows lightly accentuated and the mouth painted out with just a small dab of rouge on the center of the lower lip. It was almost anonymous in its effect, a token of an age of reticence and Confucian primness.

The introduction of electric light brought immense changes to the theatre, where the stirrings of a new age incited talented actors to redefine the image of women as expressed in costume and make-up. The new style was bolder, more decorative, and highly dramatic in its visual effect. It made a particularly deep impression on me the first time I ever saw it on stage, and in my mind it remains a supreme example of technical artistry of its kind. It could with justification be called an invention of the age of footlights. Although to suggest in our present technological age that the old-fashioned footlights created an atmosphere that cannot be recaptured today will be regarded by many as more lunacy, I would argue that the way light fell on an actor behind the footlights created a subtlety of texture missing from the contemporary Chinese stage.

In our contemporary theatre lighting has been carried to such sophisticated technical lengths that it often appears to supersede the presence of the actor, as the microphone does his voice. Technology can be too lavish and theatre too dependent on it. This is the impression I have received from such traditional Chinese theatre as we see performed today, either from the mainland or Taiwan, aided by all the gadgetry of modern lighting. There is a hard, even garish quality to some of it and a flatness of form induced by a surfeit of riches. The spell has been broken. The performances invested with a Degaslike chiaroscuro that I used to watch in the old Peking theatres have been replaced with the glitter of a new kind of "show biz." Traditional make-up has accordingly undergone a subtle change, and the cosmetic glamour of the Western fashion model and film star has induced standardization of a different kind.

The make-up for the women's roles required considerable time in preparation and application, although this was reduced to a fine art by the personal hairdressers whom every principal actor and actress employed prior to 1949. These men, *shu-t'ou erh* as they were called, were in constant attendance in the dressing rooms during a performance and always traveled with the troupe. They were skilled craftsmen who performed all kinds of other personal services for their particular charges. The hairdo for the female characters was not made in one piece like the ka-buki wig but had to be built up step by step with the many accessories devised for the process in order to give the required effect to an actor or actress. It was always an engrossing sight to watch the deft hands of the theatre hairdressers as they prepared the performers for their first entry with a precision and dexterity symptomatic of Chinese theatrical art as a whole. There was little these men did not know about the day-to-day work of the theatre, and I found them a mine of information on many technical matters. They were also useful go-betweens for visiting performers in their dressing-rooms; in consequence, I always made a point of getting on friendly terms with them.

Dressing room accommodation in the average Chinese theatre was in most cases inadequate and quite frequently very bad compared with even minimal facilities in the Western world or, for that matter, Japan. I was always amazed at the composure with which Chinese performers adapted to their cramped quarters considering the preparations they had to make. But the Chinese actor and actress were amazingly self-sufficient and self-contained, a result of their long and hard disciplined training.

The first theatre I ever visited in Peking was called the San-ch'ing, situated in the heart of the old entertainment quarter on the street named Ta Cha La. It was one of a group of famous theatres during the nineteenth century. Prior to the last war, it was very popular by virtue of the fact that it was used by the Fu-lien-cheng, Peking's best-known training school described earlier, for senior students making their professional debut. Because of this, admission prices were cheaper at the San-ch'ing than at other theatres. That was probably reason enough for full houses, but the San-ch'ing never lacked the patronage of discerning play-goers. The theatregoing public was always ready to follow the growth of new talent with an appreciative eye and kept a critical watch on those who would become the leading actors someday. Continuity was the watchword in Peking stage circles.

Coincidentally enough, the first play I saw performed at the San-ch'ing was *The Butterfly Dream*, also the first play I had seen at the Nanking teahouse theatre. However, it was extraordinarily popular with theatre audiences during my stay in China, and I saw it performed over and over again by many different actresses in Peking, Shanghai, and Nanking. Rare the day indeed when it was not being staged somewhere in one of those cities.

The text of the play, which I have translated elsewhere, was as far removed from being a literary masterpiece as the play itself was from portraying a "slice of life." It was a piece which made severe demands on the performers and required superb technical competence. For this reason it was regarded by many rising young actresses as an excellent medium through which to display their competence in the coquette role central to the theme. I used to admire the spirit and consistent standards of craftsmanship that marked the interpretations of the several actresses I saw per-form the role. They never faltered. The play concluded with a most powerfully sustained dance which was stunning in its im-pact; as much as anything I ever saw, it revealed the cleverness of Chinese performers in adapting themselves to constricted stage areas without in any way compromising the magic of their art. Their talent for converting some poky little stage into spatial in-finity was an aesthetically satisfying experience never failing in its appeal.

The Butterfly Dream opened with a speech of Chuang Tzu, a Taoist metaphysician returning home from a mountain retreat to answer his amorous wife's questions about his journey, which he described in the following way:

> When I reached the foot of the mountains and was traveling on my way, I came to a new grave on which the earth was not yet dry. By the side sat a young woman dressed in mourning, who whisked her paper fan over the mound without pausing. I went over and asked her who was buried there and why she was fanning the damp earth. The young woman replied that it was her husband, who had loved her dearly, and on his death-

bed he had asked her not to marry again before the earth on his grave was dry. This was the reason for her action she told me, and wept piteously. Moved by her tears, I took charge. And within three minutes dried the grave with my magic powers.

Chuang Tzu then explained that the young widow had given him her fan upon which she had inscribed a token of her gratitude. He handed it to his wife to read, and the storm burst when she recited these words aloud to herself:

> Taoist traveller who pitied me,
> When you return home tell your wife
> That she would be no more virtuous
> Than I have been.

From then on the audience was plunged into a series of bizarre events performed more in the spirit of the commedia dell'arte than a Grand Guignol horror story, and Chinese audiences loved it. The raging wife swore eternal fidelity before her completely unconvinced husband, who feigned sudden death through a mysterious illness in order to return from the "dead" to test her vows. Stricken with grief, the wife called her servant boy and sent him off to buy a coffin and two paper effigies—a boy and girl servant. Such effigies were set up beside the dead in old China as symbols of earthly status to bear them into the next world. The servant boy had quite a bargaining session with an unseen shopkeeper on the stage and finally purchased the male effigy for two hundred and fifty, *erh-pai wu*, copper coins. The effigy was thereupon dubbed with the name "Two hundred and fifty" in the subsequent events on stage, where he became central to the comic development of the plot. So well-known a figure did he become to Chinese playgoers that his name Erh-pai wu passed into common usage and was formerly often heard used in China as a term of ridicule for a stupid fellow.

In the midst of these preparations, a handsome young scholar arrived to pay homage to the "dead man," of whom in fact he was a reincarnation. He was accompanied by his servant, the paper boy effigy given life by Chuang Tzu's magic powers, which the disbelieving reader should bear constantly in mind. The "widow" immediately fell madly in love with the handsome stranger and arranged marriage with him on the spot, only to have him also stricken with a mysterious and fatal illness on the bridal night. In answer to her frantic queries as to what could restore her dead lover to life, she was informed by Two hundred and fifty that only an elixir culled from the brain of·a recently deceased man could achieve that miracle. Dominated by her passion, the widow turned a quizzical eye upon her own servant boy, who fled the house without more ado. Unable to restrain her desires, she seized an axe and after a highly emotional scene — portrayed through the already-mentioned dance — broke open the coffin, only to be confronted by the "dead" Chuang Tzu now very much alive. Defiantly she called upon him to prove his accusations, only to be confronted with the apparition of the handsome young stranger she had wed. Mortified, she killed herself on the spot with a single melodramatic gesture of the axe drawn across her throat as she fell to the ground. Then she leapt up immediately and quickly ran off-stage — a symbolic exit designed to emphasize that this was theatre only.

Inconsistent and improbable though this play might seem, the audience was not denied enjoyment on that score. People had paid to be entertained by good acting, and this they were given according to their expectations. *The Butterfly Dream* included some excellent mime, as when Chuang Tzu brought the funeral effigy of the paper boy to life and gave it speech in the classic tradition of all fairy tales. There was also some elemental but laughter-raising knockabout when the household servant was suddenly confronted with the live personage of the paper boy effigy at the front door when he had supposedly just left it inanimate in the funeral chamber. Returning quickly to the scene of mourning, he was even more astounded to find the paper boy motionless and rigidly in place, a situation characterized by some lightning changes and hilarious confrontations on the part of the two comic actors involved. An interlude between the two main scenes was enlivened with a dance by Two hundred and fifty moving like a puppet and endeavoring without success to catch a property butterfly manipulated on a long bamboo stick by a stagehand. The dance was performed on a darkened stage to a percussive accompaniment and provided a kinesthetic punning on the play's title. This was derived from the famous comment of the fourth-century philosopher after whom the play's Chuang Tzu was named. Once waking from a dream in which he had become a butterfly, the philosopher remarked that he did not know

A comic servant boy from "Butterfly Dream"

then whether he was a man who had dreamt he was a butterfly or a butterfly dreaming he was a man.

For a grand climax there was the dance of the widow as a prelude to breaking open the coffin, a choreographic masterpiece in which mounting agitation and suspense were beautifully suggested through forceful movement and expressive timing that excited the senses. Such was the play which started me off on a month-long exploration of the theatres in Peking. Among them was the Chi-hsiang; like the San Ch'ing, it had once been the host theatre for the students of a well-known training school, in this case The Theatre Training Academy, Hsi-chü Hsüeh-hsiao, which pioneered co-educational stage training. This school had the distinction of being built within the Inner City, as opposed to the other principal playhouses situated in the once-segregated area outside the walls of privilege. The Chi-hsiang also charged cheaper admission for student performances and never lacked audiences of devoted playgoers.

This theatre was situated just within the Tung An Market, a huge covered bazaar spread over ten acres in a labyrinth of alleyways lined with shops and stalls displaying merchandise of every kind. Curios, second-hand books, furniture, toys, confectionary, preserved fruits—everything one could imagine was offered. There great price-haggling went on, a game of skill conducted among the interweaving aisles where the crowds wandered incessantly, the hum of their myriad voices creating a constant tide of sound. Above it all rose the staccato click-click of the abacus, giving notice of bargains fought and won to the satisfaction of shopper and shopkeeper alike.

Standing also just inside the market and most conveniently placed for the theatre was the Tung Lai Shun, one of Peking's best-known restaurants. There the kitchen was built at the entrance so all who passed through were able to see with their own eyes the quality and skill of the cooking. Beyond this bustling area lay a large common dining hall, from which stairs led up to a series of private rooms on the galleried upper floors. In these the more elaborate meals called pa ta-wan, "eight courses," were served. Since the Tung Lai Shun was a Moslem restaurant, a special feature of the menu was the Mongolian dish k'ao-yang-jou, the basic ingredient being paper-thin slices of mutton grilled over a large hot plate by the diners themselves. However, all the other delights of the Peking cuisine were to be savored here as well, including *chiao-tzu*, the small half-moonlike meat dumplings which were the traditional supper of theatregoers, with whose taste in dining I can only say I found myself in complete harmony. Outside the entrance to the restaurant, cooks stood kneading into shape hundreds upon hundreds of the savory dumplings for all the passers-by to see. Those who turned aside to enter were greeted with gusty cries of welcome taken up in relay through the steamy recesses of the kitchen as the diners passed through. When guests departed after their evening, the waiters stood in line to speed them on their way, an acknowledgement that the art of food and eating, like the theatre, was a matter for mutual respect and perception. It was a sentiment those on their way to the Chi-hsiang Theatre would have endorsed as vehemently as they did the performances of their favorite actors.

There is nothing like going to the theatre to learn about theatre, and those I have named were two among many where I grasped at the opportunity to deepen my perceptions during those first days in Peking. The percussive overture called *k'ai ch'ang*, literally "opening the stage," which signalled a performance was about to take place—but on occasion sent the unwary foreign visitor headlong from the theatre—became a familiar sound I learned to tolerate for what would follow.

The Chinese conception of musical form in their theatre was certainly not one that readily accommodated itself to the average untrained Western ear because of the unfamiliar pitch and intonation and especially the sheer volume of sound that to the casual listener often seemed unbearable. The Chinese, of course, would have said exactly the same thing about Western music, for to them on a first hearing our operas and symphonies seemed interminably long and disorganized arrangements of unintelligible sound, lacking the immediacy and brevity of their own forms.

Yet in their theatres the plaintive shrillness of the strings and harsh beat of percussive brass, combined with the powerful cadences of the actors' utterances, presented a grand accumulation of sound which made Peking theatre music an assault upon the senses. In a way this was its theatrical and only function; it had no place as concert music at all, nor was it incidental to the play. Theatre musicians sat among the actors on the stage, where their playing was both aurally and visually integrated with the pacing

Flute player in the stage orchestra

and rhythm of the actors' performance. The musical content was limited and repetitious, but it was precisely these qualities which gave it the strong appeal it had for the ordinary public. Songs, melodies, and versification were easily memorized from a prescribed number of metrical arrangements devised of two principal modes only. The beat was an all-important element rendered by the orchestra leader with hardwood clappers and a small, hard-faced drum. These time-beating instruments defined the rhythmic structure of melodies developed by a type of bowed fiddle called *hu-ch'in*, supported on the seated player's knee and used to accompany the actor's singing and embellish it with a florid, rippling line in which vibrato and glissando effects were

105

given full measure. A large and a small brass gong, together with cymbals, were used for marking entries and exits, accentuating emotional climaxes, and controlling the timing and posturing in dance and combat scenes. It was surely the brass percussion that distracted foreign visitors the most, but far from providing musical anarchy as some were apt to think, these served as a musical control system.

The singing of the actors was a way of expressing human emotions and psychological reactions in an appropriate mood evoked through the variations on a modal theme. Each role category had its specific qualities of pitch, volume, and enunciation; whether the robust tenor of the leading male roles, the extremely high-pitched embellishments of the women's parts, or the thunderous quality of the painted face characters, the particular form of vocal expression was stylized within the patterned relationship of the string and percussion accompaniment. Lines and stanzas were composed in prescribed forms according to a key rhyming system. Euphonic effects were important, as were the emotive effects of pure sound induced by the contrived usage of weeping, laughing, coughing, and so on, each bound by their rhythmic rules of expression. In short, the music of the Peking theatre, simplistic in content and form as it designedly was, functioned as a precisely structured component of the acting forms. It was completely effective for the stage purpose it served and exerted an evocative spell on the playgoers. It was folk music in the more exact meaning of that now much-abused term, firmly ensconced in the consciousness of the ordinary public.

That it was a noisily robust and not essentially subtle form is not in question, and there were many to whom it remained anathema. Among them may be discounted the more critical foreigners, who were under no compulsion to suffer in the theatre anyway. I believe their distaste for theatre music blared out over public address systems and radios in the larger Chinese cities was more justified. It was not only theatre music that offended the hearing ad nauseam but maudlin Western selections — in which Mendelssohn's "Spring Song" and Gounod's "Ave Maria" held pride of place for monotonous frequency — intermingled with the latest yellow music "hits" and stentorian pep talks exhorting citizens to be patriotically thrifty and resist red aggression, all blasting the air. Conviction grew that the ability to transmit noise through space by mechanical means was one of the most dubious gifts conferred on the East by a technological West.

In an era when Western society no longer values quiet, when people consider themselves deprived if they are not sung to, played to, cajoled, informed, preached at, and gabbled at from morning to night on land, or sea, or in the air, it is perhaps presumptuous to speak about the indifference of the Chinese to noise. Yet it did sometimes seem that they had a gregarious capacity for putting up with it equalled by none. This may have had something to do with the communal nature of family life and the close quarters in which so many people lived out their lives in public, so to speak, or it may have been due to the inborn tolerance of their race. Possibly the one begot the other, but it was a characteristic to which Western innovations had added an often questionable magnification.

Peking was little more immune than elsewhere, and the ancient serenity of her streets no proof against the corrosive effects of twentieth-century din so forcible in its many reminders as our stay there came to an end. The days had passed quickly between nights of theatregoing, and it was time to return to Nanking. As we made our farewells to people, we talked confidently of our next visit, of acquaintanceships to be renewed and projects to be developed. Yet somehow it was more good intention than inner conviction, for the hint of things falling apart was already present in the searing anxiety about the future apparent in the conversations of all the Chinese whom we had met. At a farewell dinner given us at the Tung Lai Shun restaurant on our last night, the jovial waiter pouring the warm rice wine in the midst of dining table chatter suddenly became serious and asked if we could not take him to Nanking as our servant — so remote a haven of security it seemed to his eyes.

We went outside early the next morning to take our last look at Peking, since our plane was not due out until late afternoon. The air was cool but the sun bright over the faded persimmon walls and golden roofs of the Imperial palaces that dominated the center of Peking. It was difficult to realize that it was a beleaguered city with a civil war being fought practically on its doorstep. The high walls and towering gates looked eternally the same in their ancient fastness, even though they were draped with the blazoned blue and white slogans of the government. Patriarchs in long blue or grey gowns leisurely took the morning air, carrying the covered cages which held their favorite singing birds. Elderly women teetering on pinched feet stood gossiping outside the grey, one-storied houses lining narrow lanes where secretive walls hid their secluded retreats against a prying world. A squad of soldiers in their unkempt, padded cotton uniforms went by on the double, a surly reminder of present realities. Pedicab drivers, their shaven heads coppered by wind and sun, cruised alongside the curbs, the importunate burr of their voices making it difficult to resist their persistence. We capitulated and engaged two to drive us along to Pei Hai, where the sun sparkled on the waters in a myriad pinpoints of glinting light; the bulbous outline of the great White Dagoba on the hill above, a pseudo Tibetan monument built in the seventeenth century, loomed like some fantastic creation in icing sugar.

As we drove out to the airport that afternoon, the radios in the shops were blaring out the afternoon program. A popular song currently the rage was on the air, assailing the hearing in relays of repetitive sound as our car passed along the bustling streets:

> *Pieh shuo tsai chien, pieh shuo tsai chien,*
> *Tsai hsiang chien shih kuo la to shao nien . . .*

> Do not say goodbye, do not say goodbye,
> Think again of the years that have passed since first we met . . .

It was a prediction.

The untidy sprawl of Nanking jarred on the senses a little after a month of Peking, although the tension created by the threat of war on the very outskirts was less obvious in the Nationalist capital, with an escape route still open thanks to the proximity of the great sophisticated port of Shanghai. Life in Peking had seemed to proceed with a quiet fatalism in spite of student disaffection and chaotic local government. Many intellectuals had appeared resigned to the inevitable, and the tranquil seclusion of the place was somehow reflected in its people.

It was different in Nanking, the seat of a government whose leader continued to assert it had no economic or military problems for the simple reason that he, the all-highest, declared that to be the case. Nanking had its dissidents nevertheless; the summer previously there had been a massive demonstration of students who marched on government buildings in protest against conditions, posting in traditional couplet-style such slogans as "Heaven weeps and the earth sorrows, the people are lean and the officials are fat." The police had been ordered to drive them back and had done so with the sadism for which they had a particular talent. We had students with bandaged heads and bruised faces visiting our library and reading room for days afterwards. The students in Nanking were not as well organized as those in Peking although equally disillusioned; they were too intimidated by the presence among them of the dreaded secret police. We were all disturbed by the case of a girl music student taken from her dormitory at night on political charges and never seen again in the face of unavailing protests. Ever since the 1911 Revolution and the founding of a republic, the Chinese student movement had been a powerful influence in channeling public opinion, and governments were sometimes compelled to give a deferential ear to their vocal opposition, although in this case student protests went unheeded. Tuition and accommodation were free in Chinese universities, but the overcrowded conditions after the war were pitiful in the extreme, and the government subsidies students depended upon for food were inadequate or never paid at all. Thus many of them lived on the verge of starvation, which was the reason for their protests.

In March of 1948, however, there was almost a festive air about Nanking, for the city was seething with the presence of twenty-five hundred delegates elected the previous November and arrived for the inauguration of the First National Assembly in order to elect a new president and vice president. The streets were colorful with the costumes of people from distant border regions and autonomous tribal groups under Chinese jurisdiction. These included the Uighur representatives, Turkic tribespeople from Sinkiang in the far northwestern steppes beyond Tibet. They wore brightly embroidered Moslem skullcaps and broad-striped kaftans in sage, brown, black, and grey over their high leather boots. A few wore their kaftans over Western-style suits and shoes, a visible mingling of past with present that typified the drift of the Asian social tide in a postwar world. The Sinkiang people were skilled performers, with a repertoire embodying song, narrative, and dance drawn from a centuries-old compilation called the *mukam,* or "supreme system." Typical musical instruments were a pear-shaped lute with a very long neck and strings plucked with the fingers; a bowed, stringed instrument the musicologists call a spiked fiddle; a transverse flute; and a round, flat, single-skin drum held in one hand and beaten with the other. Their dances included group pieces, duets, and solos with lively rhythms and melodies, sometimes carried alternately by a single singer and a chorus. The women wore sleeveless, embroidered jackets over blouses and wide trousers, their hair in long braids under their Moslem caps. A solo dancer was often accompanied by concerted handclapping from the group as she advanced with arms raised high in a flamencolike swagger of graceful movement that held the onlooker by its spirited posturing.

At the end of 1947, during diplomatic quarrels between Sinkiang and China and the exchanging of many notes dear to the hearts of fist-shaking politicians everywhere, a troupe of sixty-five Sinkiang dancers were brought to China. This was approved by all of us engaged in the tenuous occupation of cultural relations; it certainly appealed to my apolitical mind. The troupe embarked on a four-month tour of Chinese cities and were given an elaborate public welcome and a fanfare in the press. They were led by Konpalhan, a handsome woman with the bold features of her race — "the flower of the dance," as she was designated by her people and not without reason, as we all agreed after seeing her sense of style and vivacious interpretations. From Nanking the troupe went to Shanghai, where Konpalhan was met by Butterfly Wu, a popular film star who had been the reigning beauty of the Chinese screen before the war. Now she was doing the honors for a visitor who was to become the darling of the press for a few weeks, thereby satisfying the insatiable demands of the illustrated magazines for new cover subjects and political expediency at the same time. Nevertheless, I am grateful for having had that first and last opportunity to see a little-known traditional dance form before political influences began to dominate folk performance throughout China and her autonomous regions.

Although dance had a long history as court entertainment and ritual in the historic past, it remained a neglected public art until the Republican era, apart from the folk dances of rural areas and of course the traditional theatre, a special category all to itself. Dance was the supreme animating element of Peking stage movement, and much of it was traceable to ancient court and ceremonial practices. Broadly speaking, dance on the traditional stage had two main categories: those of a descriptive and spectacular nature involving acrobatics and descriptive mime, and those in the nature of pure gesture sublimated to the voice and movement of the actor. The water sleeves, long, white silk cuffs up to two feet long left open at the seam and attached to the sleeves proper of the Peking actor's robe, admirably emphasized the choreographic importance of gesture. Their controlled manipulation, punctuating the sung rhythms of the actor and stressing emotional climaxes during the play, provided a reminder that garments with long sleeves were once everyday dress in which the movement of the hands stimulated gesture which became dance form.

As for acrobatics, displays were introduced into China from Central Asia in the second century B.C. and became a popular feature of court and public entertainments. There is nothing the Chinese have enjoyed more, and the introduction of acrobatic elements into Peking theatre was indicative of its catering to popular taste.

It was not until the 1920s, however, that wider interests in dance developed, at least in the larger cities where Western-style education for women proceeded apace. Eurythmics, Russian ballet, and the American chorus line all attracted devotees, while ballroom dancing was a permanent attraction in big city life. Many of the large girls' schools in Tientsin, Peking, and Shanghai, several of them run by missionaries, included dancing in their curricula as a part of physical training.

However, while all this activity had created a receptive atmosphere, it could scarcely be called a national dance movement having indigenous sources. Mei Lan-fang had introduced pure dance pieces based on historical sources into the Peking repertoire, and tribal dances were still preserved in many areas with sporadic attempts made to adapt a few of these to the theatre, but there was no systematic study and research being done on such forms at that time. It was not until the war years that anything approaching an indigenous dance movement was initiated. This was through the work of an overseas-born Chinese dancer, Tai Ai-lien, who came from Trinidad in the West Indies and studied ballet in England. She came to China in 1940 and in Chungking formed her own troupe, which traveled around studying local forms; one of their most successful ventures was the adaptation of some Uighur dances from Sinkiang. In 1947 she opened her own school in Shanghai, where I met her briefly before she finally migrated to Peking, having found the Shanghai atmosphere unrewarding for what she wished to do. In 1949 the new government accorded her the recognition given to all important personalities in the arts whose services were required. In 1955 Tai Ailien was appointed principal of the new Peking School of Dance set up with the aid of Russian experts. There she became active both as a teacher and choreographer responsible for the growth of a dance movement which, while it has suffered badly from pseudo-folk treatment and political banality, has provided a new potential for dance development. Certainly there was no comparable movement in dance under the Nanking government, and aside from the traditional theatre, the Sinkiang performance was the only significant event of its kind I remember from those days.

When the meetings of the National Assembly were over, the delegates scattered to their home territories and Nanking returned to normal again. Indeed, it had no doubt remained that way for a majority of its citizens, for whom the machinations of clique politics were of scant interest — with the exception perhaps of newspaper gossip about personalities, and for gossip the Chinese had a particular weakness. Even so, the heated debates at the National Assembly Hall went largely unheeded by a general public for whom the sophistry of their political leaders and the economic insecurity of their day-to-day existence were simply not on the same plane of comprehension.

By virtue of its being the national capital and a university town, Nanking had a polyglot foreign community and a Chinese population drawn from all parts of the nation. It was in many ways a floating population whose people came and went a good deal. This added to the ephemerality of things in a capital already in the twilight of its days, although people relegated such political realities to the backgrounds of their minds in the effort of living for today and trying not to think of tomorrow.

The true Nanking types were the small shopkeepers, traders, market gardeners, farmers, and river people, not to mention the host of pedicab drivers, waiters, and servants of every kind who attended to the needs of Chinese and foreigners alike. The local women were nicknamed Nanching lobo, "Nanking turnips," by the Chinese, their stocky forms and broad faces indicating why. Their standard dress was a blue cotton gown, heavy lisle stock-

Nanching lobo

ings of a pinkish hue, and flat-soled, black cloth shoes with a strap. If the weather was hot or work heavy, gowns were unconcernedly rolled up above the waist to reveal short pants, usually broadly striped, and sturdy gartered thighs. In winter the shoes were replaced by heavy felt slippers or rubber galoshes, the last being almost universal wear for both sexes, while beneath the gown long, Western-style woolen underpants were worn either over stockings or tucked inside them to create a particular kind of crinkled shapelessness. The long, blue or grey cotton gown was virtually a uniform for men also, padded to a bulging thickness in winter. Heavy woolen scarves, stocking caps, and the porkpie-shaped woolen cap with a short peak, reminiscent of those worn by Nepalese mountain guides, completed a style of dress which commended itself more for rough-and-ready practicality than aesthetic considerations. Unheated houses and the damp penetrating chill of the Nanking winter were scarcely conducive to human vanity.

There are other aspects of the Nanking scene to be recalled with that clarity induced by living in another country for any length of time. Such flashes signalled to the senses from the everyday flux of people, places, and events awaken the inner eye with a particular intensity, causing seemingly irrelevant recollections from the past to surface in the mind with a vividness denied to more momentous occasions. A particular landscape, a room, the sound of voices may induce this process of instant recall with special strength, so that small moments of personal living are for me now inextricably fused with the cataclysmic happenings of 1948.

The house in which we had our official quarters in Nanking stood in a fenced plot of ground with a spectacular view of the Purple Mountain that dominated the surrounding countryside. The building was divided into two apartments; ours being on the second floor overlooked a panoramic sweep of land dotted with vegetable plots and the flimsy huts of market gardeners. In the distance the graceful slopes of the mountain on the skyline, as glimpsed through the morning mists or the evening afterglow, left a haunting impression.

As a contrast, the back window of the apartment looked onto the kitchen courtyard below, a scene of clamorous activity and constant bustle in which the shrill chatter of the household servants' wives scrubbing away over their wash tubs, sifting rice, or scolding the children cluttering the courtyard like a brood of ducklings evokes a Chinese quintessence more sharply than any doings of Chiang or Mao. Nanking, for all its unlovely built-up areas, was blessed with a number of beauty spots, especially in the open countryside beyond the city walls. Through the Chung Shan Gate lay the tomb of the first Ming emperor, approached by a long avenue lined on either side with great stone animals and effigies of armed warriors marking the way to the main buildings of the tomb, where the tiled roofs were long gone from the crumbling, persimmon-hued walls. Beyond this memorial to an Imperial past lay the rather pretentious mausoleum of Sun Yat-sen, the acclaimed father figure of the new China, built on a high slope which commanded a magnificent view of wooded country. It was the work of a United States-trained Chinese architect who had studied under the leading American exponent of the "neo-traditional" style and won first prize in a national competition promoted to inspire a design for Sun's tomb. The mausoleum was built with predictable Chinese-styled tile roofing and was reached by terraced flights of wide steps, upon which the weekend crowds liked to linger. The proportions of the tomb maintained an uneasy harmony with the landscape setting, being the legacy of a generation whose mentors stressed period detail at the expense of creative form. Nevertheless, it was a most popular place to take the air and be seen by the world at large. There the army officers, government officials, embassy staffs, and less exalted citizens loved to stroll on weekends and take photographs or be photographed. When the sun shone from a clear sky and the blossoms were out, the whining beggars at the foot of the steps did a fair trade simply because so many people had joined the parade and put the affairs of the world behind them in the sheer pleasure of the moment.

Some distance to the northwest, another road led through the Ho P'ing Gate to the Lotus Lake, a wide irregularly shaped stretch of water covered with a mass of the floating leaves and blossoms which gave it its name. There on summer evenings people hired canopied barges holding anything from four to twenty people, to be poled along by sturdy raucous-voiced women who fought and scrambled like harpies in their attempts to entice would-be passengers to employ their services. Once aboard their craft, however, they became silent figures outlined against the evening sky as they leaned to their long poles, their movements synchronized as though in a dance poised perpetually in time. If the moon was up and good company aboard, so much the better, as one sipped green tea and perhaps listened to the plaintive notes of a flute drifting across the silvered waters from a distant boat.

There was the night when we celebrated my wife's birthday with a merry party consisting of our six Chinese staff members and their wives or husbands. The clear moon cast a shimmering pattern of light across the lake as we were punted along, the boat gliding through the floating carpet of lotus leaves with a gentle swish, our tails trailing in the cool waters. Itinerant salesmen in small boats paddled alongside calling *p'i-chi'u, ch'i-shui, k'e-k'ou k'e-le*, "beer, lemonade, Coca-Cola," for even the Lotus Lake was not immune from the ubiquitous beverage. But the lake was wide and everyday realities were quickly left astern. Soon we moved into quiet backwaters, where toasts were bandied across the low tables placed on the deck to hold our food and rice wine. Invariably on such occasions a member of the group entertained the company by singing some well-known air from the Peking stage repertoire. One of the staff wives turned her back on us and sang facing away from her audience, as was the custom out of courtesy to the guests and as salve to her own modesty. As the last high melancholy note died away in the warm night air, there was an instant in which everyone was caught in the spell of the surroundings before turning to call *hao hao* to the singer. Truly we might have said with the old Chinese poet on that evening, while making due allowance for lyrical inexactitude,

> We drained a hundred jugs of wine.
> A splendid night it was . . .
> In the clear moonlight we were loth to go to bed . . .

Idyllic moments, fated to disappear all too soon.

The summer days passed and with them any hopes that the Chinese government would regain control of either economic or military affairs.

The currency situation had become fantastic, the official rate of exchange bearing absolutely no relation to the one in use. Prices had multiplied forty-five times within the space of a few months, so that when notes were collected from the bank to pay the monthly salaries of the office staff, it required sacks to carry it away — while a small suitcase was required to go shopping in the town. Exchange rates altered hourly, and the first thing anybody did when they were paid was to rush out and convert the wads of paper money into American dollar bills. These were openly for sale throughout the city where money changers carried on their supposedly illegal dealings in broad daylight.

In August, 1948, the government with dramatic fanfare announced their issue of a new currency, the gold yüan. Reportedly backed by a sufficient reserve, this new unit was rated at one yüan to three million of the old currency. In order to safeguard the national budget, the general public were asked to cooperate by handing over all the gold, silver, foreign money, and such assets as jewelry that constituted their only form of savings against the prevailing lunacy of the economic situation. Hoarding, speculation, and black market practices were henceforth forbidden, and Chiang Kai-shek's son was made head of anticorruption operations in Shanghai. Thankful at the long-delayed signs of real action, the public eagerly complied by handing over all their savings, and for a few weeks it almost seemed as though things were on the mend. But when speculation was found still going on at the highest levels and it was seen that the government's plans had no basis in fact, thousands of people realised they had been duped and the public mood was bitter. As a result, the old Chinese silver dollar, *ta t'ou*, made its illegal but open reappearance. Soon everyone was hastily changing their gold yüan notes at streetcorners where men in long gowns stood softly jingling the long pile of heavy silver coins held concealed within their sleeves to attract the attention of would-be buyers, a sound that became as familiar as the chirping of the sparrows in the dusty gutters.

Nothing but bad news came from the war areas, where demoralized government troops suffered defeat after defeat. When in September the provincial capital of Tsinan in Shantung was captured by the communists and Chiang lost eighty thousand fully equipped troops, the mood in Nanking was black indeed. War had now reached the cities, and for the first time the capital seemed threatened. Many people we knew began to talk of moving on; rumors abounded as only rumors can in China, creating an atmosphere of uncertainty. One thing alone seemed positive, the last vestige of faith in the government had been destroyed.

The daily routines continued nevertheless, and the city seemed more crowded than ever with the refugees who began to come in from the northern areas. In Nanking itself there were plenty of people who had nowhere to run away to and nothing to run away with, even had they wanted to do so. There were also those who had no intention of running away — the majority of the students, for example, who awaited the future with a certain expectation. Others waited to see which way the wind blew, for it was still unclear as to whether the communists would march on Peking or Nanking first. Every uncertainty provided a lingering respite, to which the government by remaining in town added its last pretence of normality.

In a perverse way we were busier than ever, with the many students and university people who used our center and library facilities. It was as though we provided some kind of tangible reality upon which people could still depend, a semblance of stability at a time when all else seemed in flux. My evenings were increasingly occupied with arranging film shows, record recitals, lectures, and student meetings. Because of this increased pressure on evening hours and the general situation, my visits to the teahouse theatre soon ceased altogether. Returning from a short visit to Shanghai that fateful autumn, I found that my two actress acquaintances, Miss Wang and Miss Li, had left Nanking for good; it seemed to mark a trend and for me the end of an era. After that my theatregoing was confined to seeing the performances of visiting Shanghai troupes. Conditions in the acting profession had become desperate even for the big names in the stage world. Many performers were at a loss to know what to do, but for most of them there was little choice except to try to carry on. A life on the stage was too precarious at the best of times, yet it is a fact of human nature that even in times of war theatre seems to fulfill a deep-felt need. Speculation about the communists was as prevalent backstage as it was elsewhere; it was rumored that they treated theatre people well and were anxious to use their services. On the other hand, actors were the most traditional of people and hesitant of change. The majority continued to remain fatalistic to the last in the belief that working conditions could scarcely be worse than they were and might conceivably become better. So the theatre world struggled on, and since communication between Nanking and Shanghai remained normal, actors and actresses continued to fulfill tour contracts between the two cities, while those of them who did decide to leave Nanking for good were able to do so by the still efficient rail service with nothing but their consciences to deter them.

One or two of our Chinese acquaintances who decided to disappear from Nanking at that juncture departed in traditional manner by inviting us out to dine. The Chinese have been described as a people most preoccupied with eating, meaning that food accompanies and symbolizes every kind of social and seasonal occasion, including autumn and the parting of friends. These were the apposite gastronomical themes, so to speak, for our host on that particular occasion.

"Crabs, chrysanthemums, wine, a full moon and good friends," was an old saying with which the Chinese expressed full homage to the autumn. A full moon and chrysanthemums were of course special to the September season, and fresh water crabs for which Nanking was known were best eaten then, accompanied by the yellow rice wine of Shaohsing. The friends only had to be chosen, not a difficult matter among the hospitable Chinese.

So it was that one of our earliest Nanking acquaintances invited us to our first crab banquet upon his leaving the capital to live in Hongkong. A characteristic feature of this occasion was the complete informality of the diners in their unrestrained enjoyment of the shellfish. The crabs were served just as they had been boiled, placed on a large dish on the center of the table from where each guest seized one and set about tearing it apart either in the porcelain bowl placed before him or, better still, on the tablecloth itself. There were no concessions to false modesty present, claws being wrenched off and the sharper ones used to extract the more succulent morsels from the armored crevices peculiar to the crab. Shells were cracked adroitly and the contents emptied out with gusto. Then began an uninhibited scooping and sucking, which noisily continued until the last crab was gone and each wine cup emptied. Hot towels were brought, and everyone leaned back in earthy satisfaction as fingers and jowls were wiped with due deliberation around a debris-littered table looking like a beach after a flock of gulls had descended on it. We said our goodbyes with vinous bonhomie under the bright September moonlight — the sorrows of parting, if such they were, softened in characteristic Chinese style.

The moon itself provided the motive for a national festival at that time of the year, celebrated when dusk fell with wine-drinking parties held out of doors for guests to admire the beauty of the moonlight. To commemorate the occasion in the old days, special "mooncakes" containing fruit and spices were baked and placed on the household shrine as well as being offered to neighbors as gifts. The custom persisted, although the "mooncakes" produced by the modern commercial bakeries when we were in China tended to be solidly indigestible for such symbolic delicacies.

The Moon Festival was also regarded as having special marital implications, for women and girls in the past had traditionally offered up their prayers for a suitable husband at that time of year. Autumn therefore was considered a propitious time for marriage, and the events of that uncertain September precipitated a wedding to which we were invited by a family we had known since our arrival in Nanking. The widowed mother of the bridegroom, a determined matriarch of the old school moved by a sense of urgency in the crisis of the times, had decided to put the family affairs in order forthwith and ensure the presence of a new daughter-in-law in her household before moving on. We had seen quite a lot of the bridal pair during our stay; it had always seemed to us that they had only the most academic interest in each other and accepted their union with a kind of fatalistic resignation in the interests of family obligations, from which neither of them seemed capable of withdrawing by their own free will.

They were married in a Western-style church, more because it was fashionable among many middle-class families to favor such a ceremony than from any religious compulsion as the token Christians they were. The reception given after the ceremony was an elaborate affair held in the Nanking International Club and attended by several hundred guests. It was always astonishing to see the number of people invited to even the humblest Chinese wedding. Marriage, far more binding in China than in the West, was the event of a lifetime, a celebration of family solidarity and the homogeneity of the clan; it was the responsibility of parents to celebrate the occasion in the most lavish possible way and not lose face before the community. The consequence was that through the years the average wedding celebration had become an extremely costly obligation that plunged many ordinary people into debt for months to come. The government tried to break people of the habit of overspending in this way by instituting a system of mass weddings. Soon after our arrival in Nanking, eighty couples were married at once by the civil authorities in a single public ceremony intended to set an example in austerity in a time of national crisis. This seemed to be going to the other extreme, and there was something a little incongruous in the sheepish-looking couples lined up in a row with the brides seeming very ill-at-ease in their badly fitting Western bridal outfits rented for the event.

There were other signs to mark autumn's arrival in Nanking for us besides weddings and crab parties. Every day the early morning mists rose below the grey city walls, enveloping the landscape in hazy perspectives reminiscent of Chinese paintings. Through this mist the sun loomed as a great orange disc. Outside every small country dwelling and in every kitchen courtyard in town, lines were suspended to hang rows of long white cabbages limply upside-down, like washing out to dry. After being left for days to shrink and shrivel in the sunlight, they were then pressed down with layers of salt in large earthenware crocks, where they turned into sharp-tasting pickles to be eaten with rice.

Women busy salting their cabbages were a familiar sight in the bright autumn days, marking as it did the rhythmic turn of the seasons and somehow introducing a note of solid reassurance, an avowal of human persistence, in what was rapidly becoming an unreal world. The political situation worsened daily after the fall of Tsinan, and the demoralized government troops suffered one resounding defeat after another. By November there was no one, Chinese or foreign, who had any illusions about the outcome of it all. Nanking's days as the Nationalist capital were quite clearly numbered.

The government was in disorder; it was common talk in the streets that the leaders were preparing to evacuate Nanking. Demands for a negotiated peace with the communists were openly voiced, as were even those for Chiang's resignation. He remained obdurate. Then one day early in November, the Chinese were shocked by the news of the suicide of Ch'en Pu-lei, Chiang's most trusted adviser and long-time confidant. It was officially announced that the criticism of his master and the communists' sweeping advances made him feel that he had outlived his usefulness and impelled him to take his own life. As the Chinese told us the story, Ch'en had called on Chiang to ask him to resign and negotiate a peace with the communists. Chiang, who was reputed to have a fierce temper, flew into such a furious rage that Ch'en went off and wrote him a farewell message before taking an overdose of sleeping pills. Whatever the facts of Ch'en's suicide, the route of his funeral procession lay directly past our house, and for more than an hour we watched the gigantic cavalcade go by. There was limousine after limousine filled with relatives and mourners, followed by cars and trucks bearing huge wreaths and scrolls with laudatory messages of farewell, together with a dozen brass bands scattered at intervals throughout the procession, all playing simultaneously. The most incongruous combinations were heard, including versions of Chopin's "Funeral March" and "Clementine," to name but two contrasting motifs, the whole processional repertoire sounding discordantly off-key to Western ears, while the bandsmen's Ruritanian uniforms and the curlicues of their great brass instruments created the impression of a circus parade instead of a state funeral.

The brass band was presumably a legacy from displays of colonial military pageantry rather than a gift of the missionaries who were among the first teachers of Western music in China. There the use of brass bands for the funeral cortèges of men of substance had become a development unique of its kind. The greater the substance, the more brass bands; three were usual, one at the front, a second in the middle, and a third bringing up the rear of the procession. The Chinese have long been *pasticheurs* in the field of Western music, as evidenced in the heterogeneous compositions which are regarded as creative works in China today, but in the brassy melange of that November funeral, we surely listened to the oddest requiem that ever ushered out a dying regime.

4

THERE WERE OTHER, less bizarre moments of music which come no less quickly to mind from that turbulent era in Nanking. Among my regular office callers was a traditional musician, Liu Pei-mou, who taught at the National Conservatory. Both Chinese and Western-style music were studied at the institution, plans for which had first been promulgated in 1935, although it was not until the years of exile in wartime Chungking that it first came into active being. Like all other professional schools in the postwar years, the conservatory was beset by economic problems and lack of proper teaching facilities.

Liu Pei-mou was an engaging character, a man who spoke good English and French and bubbled over with enthusiasm and intellectual curiosity, to which was added a mischievous sense of humor. In common with the rest of his fellows, he was hard hit by the desperate economic crisis while being skeptical of the politicians. Yet he retained his innate cheerfulness and belief in his music. He was a master of the two-stringed *erh-hu*, a bowed instrument which is played held vertically on the knee of the seated musician and has a plaintive tone mellower in sound than the more strident Peking theatre *hu-ch'in* — with which it was frequently used as secondary accompaniment on stage.

Liu Pei-mou was a talented exponent of what in his case was a family tradition. On his way back from the conservatory, he would often drop in for a chat over the tea which was the perquisite of every Chinese caller. More often than not, he would draw out his *erh-hu* from its blue cotton bag and play for me until the quivering sweetness of its tones resounded through my dusty box of an office, creating moments which transcended the everyday.

In that last autumn before Nanking fell to communist troops, we arranged a public recital by Liu and a fellow musician, Chien Mu-chia, who played the *p'i-p'a* — a graceful pear-shaped, four-stringed lute. This instrument is held vertically on the thigh of the

A stage ghost with the friends of the actors on stage

seated musician, who plucks the strings in rapid repetition to create a rolling sonority of tone punctuated by vibrato stopping and percussive chords. The pear-shaped lute is the most classical of instruments; Buddhist sculptures of the sixth century A.D. confirm its presence in ancient China, and indeed its rippling notes pervade the mind with a sense of distant occasions.

Held in the government's Cultural Hall, our recital was free but by ticket only, and the auditorium was packed. Young and old sat transfixed through the playing of the two traditional musicians entertaining their audience with compositions bearing such titles as "Singing Birds Over the Echoing Mountain," "Moonlight Over the Chinyang River," or "Disarming of the Warrior Emperor." For a brief hour or two, the anxieties and miseries of contemporary existence seemed forgotten by the large gathering, who had retreated into another world where the insistent clamor of a new age became temporarily irrelevant.

Listening to the two Chinese musicians brought to mind a lunchtime concert given by Myra Hess in London's National Gallery after a night of bombing during the Blitz. Never did music sound more precious or awareness of things we stood to lose seem more apparent. Although very different, that Nanking recital also seemed to bring a troubled audience emotional release through music providing a comforting sense of continuity when everything familiar was being threatened.

Liu Pei-mou was heartened by the success of the concert. For him it was a reaffirmation of faith in a disintegrating world before political events overtook a regime that had paid only lip service to the plight of artists, to be replaced by another regime many feared would ransom all artistic expression to dogma.

Although my regular pattern of theatregoing was now completely disrupted by the pressures of the times, there was one performance by a visiting Shanghai troupe I managed to see that stands out clearly in my mind. The fact that such troupes continued to come and go as long as it was possible to do so was significant in itself. It is a fact that the theatres were the last to close their doors before the city fell and the first to open up after the event. Actors were no less anxious within themselves than the rest of the public, but being peripatetic by nature and calling, they more than most were impelled by the irresistible need to survive — which in their case meant getting on the road as long as it was possible to do so.

The program of the visiting Shanghai troupe included a play called *Kuei-fei tsui-chiu*, freely translated as *The Drunken Palace Beauty*. It was a dance piece, although involving a certain amount of singing also; the play was extremely popular with theatregoers, so I was keenly interested to see it for the first time. It offered the kind of virtuoso display the Chinese loved to watch for perfection of technical form and that could only be played by those who had been through the training mill, for the title role was physically demanding. It was an old play with a long history, but Mei Lan-fang had given it a new popularity with his personal interpretation, thereby setting an example emulated by a growing number of very competent young actresses pursuing their stage careers in those days. The actress performing in the play on that occasion was named Ku Cheng-ch'iu. I never saw her on stage again, but she gave what seemed to me then an admirable account of herself. Through the years since I have occasionally wondered what became of all the actresses on the traditional stage of that period. Did some of them leave the theatre forever, to become forgotten names — or did they throw in their lot with the new regime to become equally forgotten in a different sense?

The theme of *The Drunken Palace Beauty* was based on an imagined incident in the daily palace routine of Yang Kuei-fei, the favorite concubine of the T'ang emperor Ming Huang, the tutelary figure of the traditional theatre world. Yang Kuei-fei herself was reputed to be a skilled musician and dancer as well as a noted beauty sharing a common devotion to the arts with her Imperial lover.

By virtue of her privileged position, Kuei-fei became a powerful figure in the sensual and pleasure-loving court of her times, and some of her relatives obtained preference in the palace and rose to influential positions maintained only so long as Kuei-fei remained in favor with the emperor. The Yang family eventually fell from grace through the perfidy of an obscure military adventurer who rose to high rank at court and won the favours of Kuei-fei herself. Taking advantage of his command of a frontier province, the traitor staged a revolt which drove the emperor from his capital. The incensed Imperial troops mutinied as a result and threatened dire reprisals against the palace unless Yang Kuei-fei — whom they considered the source of all the evil — was put to death. In vain the emperor tried to appease her detractors but in the end was compelled to order his favorite to her execution. She was led away and strangled to death before a Buddhist shrine, a deed which became immortalized in Chinese poetry as "the everlasting wrong" and caused Yang Kuei-fei to become canonized as one of the most romantic figures in the Chinese literary pantheon.

The incident upon which the play was based portrayed Yang

Kuei-fei invited to a feast with the emperor in The Pavilion of a Hundred Blossoms. He broke his tryst, however, and instead dined with another concubine in a different part of the palace. Waiting in vain, deserted and forlorn, Yang Kuei-fei began to drink wine alone to forget her troubles and inevitably became intoxicated. The play in fact was a mood study; it required the actor to portray with all the most expressive yet restrained technical means he could muster the successive nuances and climaxes of emotional reaction and change in the behavior of a palace favourite seeking solace for her disappointment, wounded pride, and anger in the wine cup. It was a study in drunkenness, yes, but a drunkenness which was theatrically subordinate to the emotional mood and not the other way around.

The play took an hour to perform and was divided into two scenes. It was essentially a vehicle for solo performance, although there were supernumeraries in the person of two palace eunuchs and ladies in waiting.

In the first scene Yang Kuei-fei, accompanied by the two eunuchs, was portrayed as setting out for the pavilion where she was to join the emperor. Using graceful sleeve and fan movements, she sang to express her happiness as she neared the trysting place. When they arrived at the pavilion, the eunuchs informed Kuei-fei that the emperor had abandoned her that evening. The acting at this point was skillfully contrived to suggest the change to jealousy and then sadness as she ordered the eunuchs to bring the wine. Finally she lost control of herself completely — a state expressed with choreographic delicacy and precision, however — before she was finally assisted off stage by two ladies in waiting, marking the end of the first scene. In the interval before she reappeared, the eunuchs tidied up the pavilion and discussed her plight aloud with each other.

When Kuei-fei came on stage again, she emerged walking backwards flicking her long silk sleeves and staggering a few cunningly unsteady steps. She wore an elaborately spectacular gold and crimson robe with paneled skirts, a tasseled shoulder cape, and a large stiff-jeweled girdle around her waist. On her head she wore the "phoenix crown," an ornate headdress studded with pearl-like decorations resembling tiny mobiles which trembled with every step she took. There followed a display of choreographic sequences in which anger was expressed towards the emperor's empty chair and a mounting suggestion of intoxication climaxed in a celebrated scene when she called for yet more wine. When the eunuch presented the full cup on a tray, the unsteady Kuei-fei moved towards it to bend down and try to drink the wine without lifting the cup. The wine was too warm, however — Chinese wine always being heated before serving — and after expressing her annoyance, she steadied herself with both hands on her waist and finally succeeded in drinking. Taking the cup between her teeth and moving from the waist, she swung her torso backwards and downwards from left to right so that her head practically touched her heels behind her back; then reversing the swing from right to left, she returned to her starting position and replaced the cup on the tray with her mouth. This choreographic feat demanded a strong waist, supple torso, and precision timing and was technically known as the "kite's turn" mastered only in the training school.

The two eunuchs then became alarmed lest she had become too intoxicated and tried to bring her back to her senses by announcing the emperor had arrived. She responded with a drunken mime of welcoming her lover and begging his forgiveness. Suddenly realizing their trickery, she pretended to flirt with the terror-stricken eunuchs and ordered one of them to go and call the emperor back. When the servant refused on the grounds that the emperor's other consort for the night would be jealous and beat him, Yang Kuei-fei smacked his face, then seized his hat and placed it on top of her own headdress while she mimicked a masculine walk. Finally hurling the hat back at its owner, she relapsed into a melancholy soliloquy and was helped away by her ladies in waiting while expressing her hatred at the emperor leaving her to return alone. And so the play ended. It was a typical example of an older style of dance piece, and I look back with satisfaction at having seen it performed when I did. Such plays as this one fell into disfavor when Chiang Ching denounced the traditional stage in a 1968 speech as being dominated by emperors, princes, generals, ministers, scholars, and beauties — by feudal and bourgeois material. Strange that one who so hated emperors and their consorts on the stage should herself have risen to power as the consort of a modern "emperor" no less, only to fall from grace with Mao's departure for her meddling with state affairs. It was curiously in the old-stage tradition and might justifiably have been called a case of the pot calling the kettle black.

I managed to go to the theatre one more time in that period of rising pressures. Again it was to see a visiting troupe from Shanghai performing at the same place, the Chieh Shou T'ang, literally "Birthday Greetings Hall," so named in honor of the Nationalist leader. It was a multi-purpose auditorium in the center of the city where political meetings, concerts, and other events were held in addition to performances by visiting theatrical troupes.

Once more, I saw a play for the first time that was very popular with northern playgoers, *Pa Wang Pieh Chi*, usually translated as *The Emperor's Farewell to His Favorite*, a comparatively modern piece based on an old story about a Chinese warrior-ruler, Hsiang Yü, who lived in the period 232–201 B.C. A courageous fighter but with a hotheaded temperament, he was outwitted by superior strategy in his attempts to seize total power over his rivals and finally trapped into a situation from which there was no retreat, so that he faced surrender or total annihilation. His favorite concubine Yüeh Chi, who never left his side, overheard his battle-weary soldiers at night planning to defect to the other side. Refusing the emperor's offer to let her go also, she first served him with wine before performing his favorite sword dance before him, cutting her throat as she danced out the final movement. Hsiang Yü then took his own life.

A sentimental and melodramatic theme, no doubt, and one to draw the scorn of detractors. Nevertheless, for traditional theatregoers it provided scope for a display of formalized acting styles as they were evinced by two particular role categories, the *ta hua-lien* or "painted face character," that of Hsiang Yü himself, and the *tan* or female role, combining singing, dance, and combat techniques. The juxtaposition of the two roles was not often seen in this way and offered a special attraction for the audience. There was scope for some first-rate duet singing according to Chinese musical standards; moreover, the play concluded with a solo dance using two long swords and performed to the percussive rhythms of a large drum, a visually dramatic sequence that was one of the choreographic favorites of playgoers. Audiences went time and time again to see such plays, just as Western audiences would return to a favorite ballet or opera.

After this there was to be no more theatregoing until the New Year. By early November the Nationalists had lost all Manchuria to the communists, who then embarked on a vast new campaign, the Battle of Huai-Hai, which systematically cut off all strategic communication in central China, opening the way for a direct assault on Nanking and inflicting a crushing defeat on the Nationalist armies.

The government was in disorder, and it was common talk in the streets that evacuation plans were under way. High officials in Nanking began to pack their bags; people at the Ministry of Education who in the past had sometimes seemed to change their posts with alarming rapidity were now not available at all. Important libraries were being packed and art treasures shipped off. The big flight seemed about to begin. Neither Chinese nor foreigners knew with any certainty what would happen when the communists came, but the diplomatic corps had decided to remain until the end in the capital. The customary plans for evacuating families and dependents first if the invading forces proved hostile were promulgated; otherwise the decision of all the embassies to remain was the signal for our work to continue. The Chinese were perhaps a good deal less confident than we were, but the news that our offices were to carry on was of some consolation to our staff. The men were all married with families and had nowhere to go and no job if they did leave, yet it was among the women staff that the greatest confusion prevailed. One awaited the decision of her husband's family to leave and had therefore given notice liable to take effect from hour to hour; another, married to a military officer, expected to be ordered away well before the communists came in. My secretary departed with her husband for his hometown of Canton, the city tipped as the headquarters from which the government was going to operate, and one of my wife's library assistants hastily slipped away to someplace in the country with her two children. But she was back in three weeks, preferring to face the hazards of the city to the boredom of country life. All of which scarcely added to the stability of our existence.

Still, our offices and center were as busy as they had ever been. The library and reading room were thronged from morning to night, while music recitals and film shows were crowded. In a way I suppose it was rather like a drowning man clutching at straws; we provided a seemingly stable point of focus in a world that appeared anything but stable. In addition, admission to our facilities was free, and our building was equipped with lighting and heating of a kind, facilities notably lacking in a majority of Chinese homes by that time. The electricity supply, never very good in Nanking, had become completely unpredictable. In theory we had power every alternate day — in practice, for alternating periods on that day. Acetylene lamps were a boom on the market and became standard equipment in houses, shops, and offices, where their acid glare made everyone look like figures in a fairground. The reason for the power failures was due to lack of coal, the Chinese told us, because the coal-producing areas were in communist hands and any coal that was available was being sold on the black market by corrupt officials. Films were liable to flicker and fade as the soundtrack died away in a hollow gurgling, and record players ran down to an asthmatic stop. As a desperate resort, I sought out the manager of the Nanking Light and Power Company to plead special privilege in view of our efforts on behalf of Nanking citizens. We got our privileges for a period and became so popular that we had to issue tickets for admission to avoid being stampeded. It did not last long, but we made the best of it until we were once more plunged into darkness. Then we went out and bought ourselves a black market generator, which our London office had finally grudgingly allowed was "legitimate expenditure under extraordinary circumstances." The request to "Please forward the receipt for this purchase" was their rather idyllic concept of how Chinese black market operators did business in the back alleys of Nanking.

One of our most constant office visitors was Chang Cheng-shih, a fine arts student in his final year at National Central University. Jim Chang, as he preferred to be known to us, was to all intents and purposes an orphan, for he had become separated from his parents during the great wartime trek across China and had never seen them again. He was a constant borrower from our library, a voracious reader, and a lean, undernourished figure with tousled hair who wore an old G.I. greatcoat with most of its buttons missing and a tattered cotton shirt and trousers, his feet clad in rubber sports shoes whatever the season of the year. He could have passed unnoticed among any group of American university tatterdemalions today, the single difference being that where the modern campus rebels are the product of a trendsetting conformism born of affluence, the appearance of Chang Cheng-shih was indicative only of a desperate lack of resources.

A few days before Christmas, Jim arrived in my office with two of his fellow students, all of them in very low spirits. They told me that overnight and without any warning, their professors had left for Canton, joining in the mad scramble for the planes and trains daily leaving Nanking jammed with those who thought of one thing only, getting themselves out at all costs. This desertion by their teachers was a bitter pill for the students and a distressing symbol of the times. To restore their spirits, I suggested they should organize an exhibition of their paintings in our center, an idea to which they enthusiastically responded. Two days later their show was hung and did not lack for visitors. On the eve of their opening, we held a party in the gallery with soft drinks, cigarettes, pastries, Chinese dumplings, and tea. The students were in good spirits again; they sang folk songs and performed solo dances with the lightheartedness of their kind, as immediate problems were forgotten for a few hours in the satisfaction of something done, a gesture made.

By the time Christmas was upon us, three of our Chinese women staff had departed for Canton with their husbands and families. Peking was reported in a state of siege and communication with our center there was cut off. My office had begun to look like a grain store with the sacks of rice lining the walls. It had been policy for some time to buy in a reserve stock against the eventuality of everyone having to camp out in the building in case of a siege. One or two of the Chinese staff were already sleeping on the premises because of transportation difficulties in the town and the common desire of little groups of colleagues to stay together in the face of the unknown.

However, it became clear from the war news that the communists were going to take Peking first and that Nanking would have another breathing space. People even began to slip back into town again, including the professors of the Fine Arts Department of the National Central University — not that it mattered one way or the other, for little studying was being done at that time; students were too busy organizing themselves for the events to come. Then early in January Chiang Kai-shek made a peace offer to the communists that was immediately rejected, with the result that towards the end of the month the Nationalist leader announced he was going into "retirement" and handed over authority to the vice-president.

When it finally happened, this news of the leader's stepping down stunned the Chinese population at first, and then the exodus began, a steady stream which gained momentum week after week until the final debacle came. Those were strange days preceding the fall of Nanking. Life went on in an outward semblance of everyday familiarity until the very last, but it became difficult to believe that anything was making sense at all, and the only possible thing to do was to abandon oneself to the tide of events. No one even bothered to try to fathom the mad money situation any more; the black market exchange dealers had in effect become an official banking service, to whom everyone automati cally went to convert their mountains of gold yüan notes into illegal Chinese silver dollars or American greenbacks, the rates changing day by day and hour by hour. The shops were full of goods, but the housekeeping bills of the foreign community reached insane proportions. For the local Chinese community, feeding the family became a desperate problem as people stood daily in long lines for rice in short supply, due it was said to the speculations of the dealers rather than the war crisis. Our staff began to feed communally in the office to alleviate a situation in which one black market U.S. dollar sold for 1,800,000 gold yüan. Gasoline was in short supply; the official car and jeep of our organization were drastically rationed for fuel and mileage. I had in any case long since taken to a bicycle as the quickest means of getting to and from our offices. In the town the never more than inadequate municipal bus services had practically ceased to function, and the pedicab reigned supreme as the only reliable form of public transport. Otherwise there remained the horse-drawn victorias which were a leftover from the past in Nanking, all in the last decrepit stages of serviceability and pulled by tired little nags whose bony frames conveyed an impression of spectres from an equine land of the dead.

The pedicab was far and away the most common form of public transport throughout the land in those days, used by everybody and frequently the only means of navigating the tortuous back streets and alleys common to the urban landscape. It was built like an outsized tricycle, with the driver pedaling in front and the passenger seated behind him. The vehicle was fitted with pneumatic tires and rolled along smoothly enough on macadamed roads, but cobbled side streets and earth-surfaced secondary roads could be a test of endurance to jolt the sturdiest anatomy.

Pedicab drivers tended to be ebullient characters, but they were hard worked, underpaid, and had a great deal to put up with from bullying policemen and unreasonable passengers. They were tougher than any Tour de France champions in pedaling stamina, besides being indefatigable hagglers, a necessary occupational qualification in a job where every Chinese passenger was bent on traveling the farthest distance in the town for the most economical price, this being in the natural order of man's affairs. In theory there were set rates for pedicab fares; in practice no Chinese would have engaged a driver without settling on an agreed price first. The pantomime resulting from this preliminary was marked by discursive vigor and gestural accentuation which expressed the inherent theatricality of the Chinese. In life as on the Peking stage, the mundane was invested with a sense of ritual and transmutation of character, during which mild-mannered scholars and gentle young women became as though possessed when scaling down a demanded fare. To say that every pedicab driver was equal to the challenge is to understate a classic example of the irresistible force meeting the immoveable object.

The pedicab drivers lingered on for several years, pursuing their accustomed occupation in the egalitarian environment of Maoist China; they were still much in evidence when we went back in 1956. Today, however, they are reputedly used only as carriers of goods, and adequate public transport services have replaced their former labors.

However, in the last days before the fall of Nanking, the city's pedicab drivers had their brief period of power. They were in constant demand by everyone as the one form of public transport still functioning, and since they were people who had little to lose when the communists came, they basked in a kind of reflected glory. In truth, they became a rather depressed class after 1949, being proclaimed as officially unwanted while being unofficially necessary. Yet in April, 1949, they were being kept on the go; their biggest problem, apart from those that then plagued everybody, was to prevent their vehicles from being stolen from under them by military personnel and others looking for every means possible to flee the city.

Pedicab drivers, by virtue of their trade, knew every quarter of the city; there was nowhere they did not go. They were often particularly knowledgeable about the theatre and what was going on and could always get one to the shows on time. The rows of pedicabs waiting outside the theatre entrances was as characteristic an image of Chinese night life as the lines of hansom cabs outside the London theatres of an earlier era. I relied on the pedicabs a great deal during the final short burst of theatregoing I was able to indulge in, paradoxically enough, that April immediately before the communists crossed the Yangtze and entered the city.

There were two good visiting troupes playing the Nanking theatres then, one at the Nanching Ta Hsi-Yüan, The Great Nanking Playhouse, and the other at Chieh Shou T'ang, The Birthday Greetings Hall described previously. In addition, the first color film of Mei Lan-fang in a play called *Sheng Szu Hen*, with the English title of *Wedding in a Dream*, was being screened at the Ta Hua cinema in the center of the town. These were not inconsiderable offerings in a month when the city was to fall to the communist forces.

At The Great Nanking Playhouse, the troupe was led by Li Wan-ch'un, a well-known Peking actor who was a specialist in fighting roles involving swordsmanship and weapon play. The troupe's principal actress, Wang Ling-yü, was playing in *Breaking Open the Coffin*, an alternate title for the play called *The Butterfly Dream* discussed earlier. It was odd how that piece haunted my theatregoing, for it was also staged by the Shanghai troupe at The Birthday Greeting Hall where an actress called Li Hui-fang played the flirtatious wife of the Taoist metaphysician with tremendous verve and spirit. A few days later, the same troupe staged *The Meeting of Many Heroes*, a collective title for a series of episodes taken from the famous historical novel *The Chronicles of the Three Kingdoms*. The particular episode played on this occasion was one called *Procuring a South East Gale*, a reference to the total destruction by fire of a fleet of war junks carrying the armies of the Prince of Wei across the Yangtze River for a night attack. This defeat was brought about through the schemes of Chou Yü, a young, impulsive adviser to the Duke of Wu, and by Chu-ko Liang, a brilliant strategist with supernatural powers

135

who was adviser to Liu Pei, a military ally of Wu. When the incendiary plot looked as though it would fail at the last moment through winds blowing in the wrong direction to fan the flames, Chu-ko Liang used his magic powers to conjure up a southeast gale which produced the desired results and destroyed the enemy forces.

A certain hidden rivalry between Chou Yü and Chu-ko Liang revealed itself in little incidents which the good actor had to express instantaneously for the onlooker. To take a small but familiar example, both men independently conceived the same plan for attacking the enemy forces. When Chou Yü invited Chu-ko Liang to his headquarters to ask his opinion about destroying the Wei armada, he anticipated the others opinion by suggesting they each write a single Chinese character on the palms of their hands. When the results were displayed, both men had brushed in *huo*, meaning "fire." The gestural nuances and expressive posturing indicating inner psychological reactions which highlighted such theatrically contrived moments as these were eagerly watched for by audiences, for whom the rival strategists were two of the most familiar characters in the San Kuo play cycle.

Chu-ko Liang particularly held a very special place in the affections of theatregoers. Ever since the days when the actress Meng Hsiao-tung had delighted audiences with her interpretation of the famous strategist, he had provided many of the new school of actresses with a favorite role in a trend for male impersonation which became no less an important part of their repertoire than the customary playing of the women's roles. The formalized nature of Chinese acting styles, however, made this form of stage transvestism a somewhat different proposition from more naturalistic sexual portrayal. Audiences relished the piquancy of the transpositional situation and were entertained by the skill and fluency with which actresses achieved the finer points of expression in switching between the male and female roles. In that last April performance, for example, the actress Li Hui-fang, after playing the coquettish widow in *The Butterfly Dream*, made her next stage appearance in *The Meeting of Many Heroes;* there she took not one but two male roles, an astonishing feat of virtuosity, even in a genre where virtuosity was the order of the day. In the first half of the play, she appeared as Lu Su, a conciliatory adviser to the Duke of Wu who acted as a kind of go-between for everybody, while in the second she made her entry as the redoubtable Chu-ko Liang himself. Although both these roles belonged to the same general category, they required many fine distinctions of interpretation; to play them both one after the other in that way was no mean achievement. There were no intervals in Chinese performances; a player had to remain keyed up the whole time, and when as on that occasion an actress had to change costumes and make-up for two different roles between one scene and the next, there was no time for dawdling.

I was immensely attracted by the work of Li Hui-fang, not so much from her ability to play both male and female roles as for her total transcendence of the chemistry of elements, which marks the difference between one who acts and one who appears to be acting while not doing it at all. This was readily apparent on the Chinese stage, where technical competence can be mistaken for fine acting, just as social verisimilitude often is in the West.

Li Hui-fang impressed me so deeply that I asked to be allowed to meet her, and this was soon arranged through the good offices of my Chinese teacher T'ien Shu-hsiu — who came from Peking and was a theatre devotee and invaluable intermediary on occasions such as this. Li Hui-fang proved to be an extremely intelligent and alert young woman, radiating that spirit of indomitability commented on earlier. She had a fiancé in Shanghai who spoke English, she told me, with whom she one day hoped to travel abroad. After one or two backstage meetings, she was so sympathetic towards my theatre research that she offered any help she could give and agreed to come and lunch with us the following week and then pose for me in costume and make-up to enable me to make some detailed drawings at close quarters. To this end she generously offered me several of her costumes not immediately required to take home and study at leisure before she came around. The offer met with disapproving glances from her old termagant of a mother, who sat scowling as a chaperone in one corner of the dressing room and muttered aloud that the foreigner should be asked to pay for the privilege of borrowing the precious costumes — which were of course the actress's personal property. All actors and actresses of repute travelled with their own wardrobes in those days, usually made from the most costly and exquisitely designed materials. It says a great deal for the character of the actress that she instantly and indignantly silenced the old woman, who relapsed still grumbling in her corner, the defender of a tradition which held that everything had its price and the foreigner always paid. Alas, political events put a sudden end to what had seemed an interesting opportunity to learn more in depth about the theatre. All that week rumors had circulated concerning the peace talks going on in Peking between the communists and a representative from the National government in Nanking. An air of crisis hung over the town, and even the theatre audiences were thin that week, an ominous sign. Then on the afternoon of April 21, the communists rejected the Nationalists' peace offer, and Mao ordered his armies to move forward, cross the Yangtze River, and advance on Nanking. The morning of the same day, we learned that the British frigate *Amethyst*, sailing upstream from Shanghai to Nanking on routine duty and carrying provisions, had been fired upon by communist batteries about forty miles from Nanking, inflicting heavy casualties and causing the vessel to run aground. A sister ship, the *Consort*, sent from Nanking where she was on guard duty, was directed to the aid of the stricken *Amethyst* but was in turn heavily attacked and had to turn back with heavy casualties. It was a bad start and there were troubled reactions among the foreign community in Nanking at the news. Conflicting reports of the incident circulated that evening, most people wondering why the *Amethyst* had been ordered to Nanking at such a crucial juncture in the Chinese military situation, but it seemed clear the attack had been deliberate as the stubborn attitude of the communist authorities towards the grounded vessel soon indicated.

That evening the musician Liu Pei-mou and two other Chinese acquaintances had dinner with us. All civilian residents who intended to go had already left Nanking, except for the military and government personnel, and those of us who remained continued to lead as normal a sociable life as possible in the vacuum-like calm of that waiting period. While we were still sitting chatting around the dinner table, a messenger arrived to ask for the return of Li Hui-fang's theatre costumes I had borrowed. She was leaving for Shanghai the next morning, I was told, to prevent their being immobilized in Nanking, and she sent apologies for not being able to keep the promised appointment. Theatre people in Nanking and Shanghai had begun to speculate about the future, for there had been indications from Peking that the authorities were bent on making some far-reaching changes in the entertainment world. In March they had relegated the performing of as many as fifty-five plays popular with the old audiences on the grounds of being licentious, superstitious, feudalistic, or merely farcical. It was too early to know what all this implied for the south as yet, but understandably the one thing that seemed essential for Shanghai actors in the rising crisis was to return to their own territory as quickly as possible, there to face whatever was in store for them. Only a minority of the theatrical profession thought it worth while to follow the government in its flight to Canton.

It would have been far better had I not sent those costumes back, as it turned out; they could have been held in safekeeping for their owner. One of the last senseless acts perpetrated by the departing Nationalist troops was to blow up the buildings of the Central Railway Station, an action serving no useful military purpose, since they left the tracks intact. Later I heard that Li Hui-fang's complete theatrical wardrobe, mislaid by the luggage office personnel in the chaos of events, had been destroyed in the explosion.

The next day the Nationalist troops began pulling out in force, the start of a flight which was to last forty-eight hours, with plane after plane taking off from the airport until all government personnel were evacuated to a man. Trains to Shanghai were still running fairly normally and were less overcrowded by Chinese standards, meaning that people were no longer hanging out of coach windows or clinging to any precarious foothold they could find on the couplings of coaches or even the locomotive itself; the worst of the great railway rush was already over.

Our center was deserted that day, quiet with the kind of stillness that hangs in the atmosphere before a storm. We closed our doors early, the first time we had ever done so. Many shops around us had remained shut all day, an unheard-of occurrence except at the New Year Festival, and their dead frontage offered a touch of desolation to the scene. When the Chinese shopkeeper stopped doing business, the situation had to be critical indeed.

A curfew had been imposed upon the city, but even so we were invited to a dinner party that evening by the Chinese wife of a British Embassy official. The guests included the superintendent of the Central Hospital, one of his pathologists, and the woman curator of the National Museum out near the Chung Shan Gate. We knew them all well and it was a lively party. The curator had been indefatigable in making an apathetic Ministry of Education find funds to complete her building, which at one point had been in danger of remaining unfinished without a roof. Later she had fought tenaciously to prevent government troops being billeted in the museum, the first scientifically equipped institution of its kind.

Conversation at dinner naturally revolved round the central topic of what was going to happen when the communists came. The curator was quietly optimistic; she had managed to keep her museum intact to the bitter end and felt nothing could be worse than the desperate conditions under which people had struggled for so long. The doctors were of the same opinion. Their hospital had been deprived of funds, so-called relief supplies had never reached them, even the electricity to keep a large hospital in running order had been lacking. They had all received printed notices from communist sources, nobody quite knew how, asking all doctors to stay at their posts and promising that their interests would be given priority consideration as being important to a new state. Some people had decided to leave with the government, but a majority had stayed on, the superintendent told us. He himself had been invited to take a public health post in the new government but had declined on the grounds of his responsibilities to a large hospital full of sick people. Yet he thought the new regime could be no worse than the old and there was every prospect of its being better from a medical point of view. It was an opinion one heard expressed by people in so many walks of professional life at that juncture; on that note our party broke up early in deference to the curfew, and we returned home in pedicabs. It was a dark night with no moon. In the far distance dull flashes lit up the sky, and there was the muffled sound of a gun barrage continuing through the night.

We were awakened very early next morning by our agitated Chinese servant, who had for some time resigned himself with philosophic detachment towards the trend of events. He had coined his own portmanteau description for past remembered and presently anticipated national threats with the term "communese." The "communese," he now told us, were reported to have crossed the Yangtse River in force some fifty miles from Nanking and were now heading for the city. In the meantime the city police had quit their posts, leaving the place without law and order. We dressed hastily, and I cycled down to the office by 9 A.M. All was intact, but sure enough there was not a policeman in sight. That slightly comic opera-like uniform—with the high white metal helmet, a kind of caricature of the London bobby's headwear, and the American "doughboy" gaiters—had gone from every traffic control point. Such policemen who were still around had changed into civilian clothes and were hastily commandeering any kind of vehicle in sight to get out of town as fast as they could. Little groups of people stood talking in low voices as they watched from the sidewalks. It was as though the general public were a little stunned with events and were not quite sure what was happening, while the center of the city was thronged with Nationalist rear guard troops abandoning Nanking in frenzied haste.

Our Chinese staff was a little apprehensive, but on the whole things remained remarkably quiet, considering events, and the hordes of looters and rioters it had been feared might roam the city did not materialize. True, some looting had begun but was largely confined to the rice stores and suddenly empty houses of high government officials. Women staggered down the road laughing as they clutched heavy bags of rice—some of which, punctured in the scramble, leaked erratic trails of grain behind the triumphant plunderers. That afternoon there were several explosions, and the Supreme Law Court went up in flames. The vice-president's official residence was sacked, as was that of the city's mayor; there were said to be others, but I have named only personally observed incidents. The rice stores, the law courts, and government residences presented a trinity of targets requiring no profound explanation for singling out during the few hours Nanking was out of control.

Just as curfew began that evening, I received a telephone call from a journalist I knew well on the staff of the *Kiang Nan Wan Pao*, a local evening paper, to say that a Citizens' Protection Committee had been formed to safeguard law and order. He told me also that all Nationalist troops had retreated and the communist forces were expected in the city next day. As we talked the electric power was suddenly switched on, and for the first time in months we had lighting of an intensity such as we had scarcely known. The acetylene gloom was banished, to everyone's relief.

Early next morning I was called to the phone again by my journalist friend, this time to learn that communist forces had entered Nanking at 2 A.M. The Citizens' Protection Committee was headed by Wu Yi-fang, the famous principal of the Christian Ginling Women's College, he continued. If we required any help, he added, the committee's offices were in the Nanking Hotel.

I set off for our office as quickly as possible on my bike, taking a side-street course. The main thoroughfare of the city was lined with curious onlookers staring at the conquering armies marching by. The much thought-about and talked-about communists had arrived at last. At a glance they seemed little different from any other Chinese troops we had seen. They were poorly clothed, poorly shod, and loaded with all kinds of equipment of a most unwarlike nature. Many carried oiled paper umbrellas; some had zinc footbaths strapped to their backs; all of them wore bandoliers of ration millet slung around one shoulder like outsize sausages. Their uniforms were a rather unpleasant yellow-green with no rank badges of any description, only a numbered name-tag stitched above the left breast pocket. They were shod with the eternal blue canvas rubber soled shoes and wore the shapeless soft-peaked cap soon to become a universal fashion among the population at large. It was difficult to believe this was the army that had captured half a continent at a speed surprising even their leaders.

On they went, file after file, looking neither right nor left, trudging beneath the weight of their equipment. On closer scrutiny, they looked physically healthier and tougher than the usual run of Chinese soldiers, since the grimness of their faces was that of determination rather than despair. A squadron of cavalry passed, mounted on the small, shaggy horses of North China, and then the infantry again, American rifles slung over their shoulders or carried in their hands, for this was an army in the field and not the paradeground. There were women marching among them also, their long, straight locks hanging to their shoulders beneath the same unlovely caps as their male comrades. Their weather-beaten peasant faces and sturdy forms, with rifles slung across their shapeless padded tunics, belied every known concept of femininity. They were also a thousand times removed from the gun-wielding ballerinas who were later to dominate the Peking stage.

During the morning a security squad carrying rifles with fixed bayonets came to search our offices, it seemed looking for arms or suspects. They grimaced goodhumoredly at the "No Smoking" notices in the library reading room and, having given us clearance, went off. After that life soon began to settle down to normal routines, and our work in the center was resumed as before. We were not interfered with in any way and resumed almost where we had left off. Almost, but not quite. It became difficult to gain access to many institutions, including National Central University. When I tried to deliver some English medical journals to the superintendent of the Central Hospital as we had customarily done, I was stopped by an armed sentry at the gate, who presented his fixed bayonet squarely at me. However, the communist soldiers who were everywhere seemed well behaved and well disciplined, if taciturn. Being of peasant origin and unfamiliar with city life, they tended to be naive about some things. Cycling home for lunch two days after the communists had arrived, I was stopped by soldiers at a roadblock and made to take a detour. Later we learned there had been an incident at the American Embassy that morning and so the road was closed to traffic. Communist soldiers had entered the embassy and made their way to the ambassador's bedroom, where they were intercepted. There was great consternation, but the two had done no harm to anybody or anything and fears for the implication of the incident seemed to peter out. Later someone told us the two marauders had explained they had never seen an ambassador before and wanted to satisfy their curiosity. Whether apocryphal or not, the explanation was in keeping with the nature of the peasant lads the soldiers were.

We were able to move freely about the town without hindrance, although nobody was allowed to go beyond the limit of the city walls without a permit. A curfew was enforced from 11 P.M. to 5 A.M., but this was as much for our protection as hindrance. Although the communists denied them official recognition, the British and American diplomatic missions had remained in Nanking, while among the other national representatives only the Russians had ostentatiously removed their embassy to Canton. It therefore behooved the communists to keep as orderly a house as possible in Nanking. They faced a huge administrative task, often with relatively inexperienced personnel, and until a civil administration was established, they had to deal with police protection, public utilities, food, health measures, currency, and prices as quickly and efficiently as they could. Considering all the hazards, they did a very practical job in those first months. Nationalist planes flew over several times during the first two or three weeks of communist control, sent on sneak, high-flying bombing raids to try to knock out the electric power plant at Hsia-kuan. There were some casualties among children and civilians, but the attackers failed to achieve their objective — fortunately for us all — in an exercise which at that point seemed only to typify the bankruptcy of a discredited regime.

One of our greatest problems after the "liberation" of Nanking was the lack of funds to purchase food and meet other expenses. The new national currency had not been set up; there were no exchange facilities for foreign currency and no way of getting the black market silver dollars still circulating, since we had no means of buying them. We all began living communally, Chinese and British staff together, on the reserve provisions we had been hoarding against emergencies. But stocks began to run low and we depended on the ingenuity of the household servants to eke out our meals with duck eggs, sesame cakes, and fresh vegetables. It was quite a relief when this state of financial culinary siege ended around mid-May and exchange regulations were promulgated for the new Chinese currency.

Until Shanghai was taken by the communists on May 25, we received no overseas mail or newspapers; cut off from the outside world, we lived in a vacuum within a vacuum, so to speak. Our center was busy daily, and the thrust of our activities was of necessity concentrated there. The library facilities, exhibitions, film shows, and music recitals continued to be popular and well used, with communist uniforms frequently noticeable among our audiences. Even so, we were cut off from many of our university contacts; all kinds of reorganization was afoot in educational institutions, with Soviet friendship and relations providing a dominant theme. It became politic for many academic people not to be seen associating with their former foreign acquaintances, and so they tactfully stayed away.

There were times during that long, hot summer in Nanking

when one became a little wearied by the way some Chinese intellectuals seemed so eager to cast aside mental independence and spurn with almost indecent haste the liberal tradition of academic freedom, of which they had once been considered the bulwarks. There were the few who had always been rigid converts to Marxism, but one felt the majority were liberals with acquired pro-communist sympathies who, although not blind to the shortcomings of communism, saw in it an answer to the desperate problems of their generation. The more charitable interpretation of the parroting of the Communist Party's vehement pro-Soviet propaganda and slanted information was perhaps the insecurity of older intellectuals concerning their own positions under the new regime.

The dog days were lightened, however, when on August 1 we learned that late the night before, the *Amethyst*—held captive for one hundred desperate days—had quietly steamed out past the communist batteries and escaped to Shanghai. It was a feat in the best tradition of adventure stories, but for those of us suffering from the more restrictive practices of communist administration, it seemed also a just answer to political intractability.

Whatever changes were contemplated by Peking in the theatre world, the Nanking authorities at that juncture were too concerned with running the city generally to trouble themselves with such matters as public entertainments. The overall policy seemed rather to be one of tolerance. While so many administrative changes were being enforced on the community, it was possibly considered better to leave its recreations alone, or at least allow the old to continue with the new until cultural policies were more consolidated. Certainly from April, when the communists took over Nanking, until we left in September the theatres continued to stage the old plays as they had always done. The first performance I saw after Nanking fell was in June at the Great Nanking Playhouse, where the main play on the bill was *Jade Screen Mountain*, an old-timer which, significantly enough, had already been placed on the blacklist in Peking. It featured some favorite stage types, an aggressive young hero skilled in sword fighting, a sensuous young wife, and her supportive maid, together with a couple of typical comic characters in the persons of a jovial shopkeeper of wine and a libidinous Buddhist monk.

This play was based on an incident from *Shui Hu Chuan, Tales from the Marshes*, the famous romantic novel which drew its themes from the many legends surrounding the exploits of a band of outlaws who actually existed during the twelfth century. Their feuds against repressive authority inspired a cycle of romanticized tales popularized by the old storytellers and adapted as stage plays to create a gallery of colorful characters who became familiar to every Chinese from childhood.

The action of *Jade Screen Mountain* centered on the measures taken by Shih Hsiu, a skilled fighter with the scimitar, to revenge a sworn companion whose licentious wife was having an affair with a Buddhist monk. Priests and monks were more often than not treated as comic butts on the Peking stage, reflecting a greater Asian tradition from which the spirit of such mockery was derived. It voiced the realization that those who sit on high, even in spiritual authority, are not immune from human failings. Members of religious orders were habitually shown in the white make-up of the clown, and this play was a typical example.

The loyalty of pledged friendship, by which a man shared his pleasures with a boon companion while being faithful to him through thick and thin, was an admired quality in old Chinese society. The unfaithful wife in this play, realizing that her amorous adventures had been discovered, tried to turn her husband against his friend for having made improper advances to her. The discredited Shih Hsiu thereupon vowed that only death would settle this double betrayal of his sworn companion, so the play ended with putting both the secret lovers to the sword. It was a bloody penalty certainly, but murder was always depicted with an almost decorous lack of realism on the Chinese stage, victims being customarily shown as very much alive once the theatrical point was made. A much-anticipated moment in this play came when Shih Hsiu showed himself off to the audience in a dazzling solo demonstration of swordsmanship which fascinated everyone with its stunning precision and feline agility.

One more theatrical event enlivened our last days in Nanking when T'ung Chih-ling, a well-known Peking actress of the old school, arrived with her troupe from the north to give a week's performances at the Grand Theatre, to which we all flocked. This actress was admired for her spirited interpretations and versatility, and she did not let us down on this occasion, playing three different major roles in a play called *The Strange Destiny of*

Yü-ch'iao and Ch'iao-chiao. This piece in itself was only an episode from a much longer play, of which again the previously mentioned *Picking up the Jade Bracelet* was but a single scene.

In the main action of the play, T'ung Chih-ling appeared as Yü-ch'iao, a coquettish maiden; Ch'iao-chiao, a filial daughter of a falsely accused old scholar for whom she went to jail as hostage; and Mama Liu, the wily old marriage go-between. These were three roles which demanded high contrast in expression. Not content with that, the actress also appeared in the demanding title role of *The Drunken Palace Beauty*, which was billed on the same program. It was a quite amazing feat in the best traditions of the new school of Peking actresses, of whom I have said so much, and a fitting note on which to end my theatregoing in Nanking.

Two days later we were on our way to Shanghai to embark on the *General Gordon*, a vessel sent by the American government to evacuate foreign nationals in China. It was undoubtedly one of the most overcrowded ships in maritime history, or so it seemed to those of us who sailed on it. When the communists took Nanking in April, we had been due for a home leave, which events rendered a purely academic matter. However, since the Chinese authorities had indicated our work would be allowed to continue and that we should be allowed to apply for reentry permits to return to our posts, we had been granted exit permits following instructions from London headquarters to proceed on our delayed leave.

Permits were obtained from a bureau set up to deal with foreigners in Nanking. It refused to transact business in English; all communication had to be in Chinese or through an interpreter. This did not make for quick results, and many people became frustrated over delays and obstacles that at times the new bureaucracy seemed to oversee with a certain satisfaction. Considering the general situation, we met with minimum of delay ourselves and were more fortunate in that respect than our colleagues in the American Information Service. We not only received our permits fairly quickly, considering the times, but passed through customs in Shanghai with far less interference than when we had first entered China. Many were not so fortunate, however, and suffered hindrances galore. The summer heat was trying and many people were beginning to suffer from claustrophobic strain. Tempers at times became frayed and pent-up irritation overflowed, but this only made Chinese officials the more impervious. Enduring these weeks required patience on a supreme scale, one quality we had perhaps learned well enough in our relations with the Chinese. As the train pulled out of Nanking station, where the little group of Chinese friends and colleagues seeing us off stood waving until they were lost to view, there was every thought in our minds that we should be returning in a short space of time.

We arrived back in Hongkong from home leave in January, 1950, there to await our reentry permits for Nanking. They never came through, since the Korean War broke out and the Peking government forbade any of us to return to the mainland. In consequence, Hongkong became our base for the next decade. I was attached to our office there for a time and later went to Japan for three years while my wife became the librarian of Hongkong University. However, the early 1950s in Hongkong were more

A Hong Kong amah

fruitful years than might have been supposed for continuing the theatrical interests I had pursued on the mainland.

Hongkong in 1950 was still suggestive of prewar years, with its nineteenth-century colonial-style buildings surrounding the base of the towering Peak as yet unscathed by the rash of high-rise apartments now covering its slopes. The bustling downtown center, with its Edwardian post office, its trams and office buildings, had the atmosphere of a prosperous British provincial city — which the Gloucester shopping arcade, Dairy Farm Tearoom, St. John's Cathedral, and Cricket Club did nothing to dispel. Yet these were only symbols — powerful ones, it is true — but still symbols in a world which, when all was said and done, remained predominantly Chinese.

The indigenous populations of Hongkong and the New Territories — the British-controlled tip of the Chinese mainland lying across the magnificent sweep of the busy harbor — were mostly Cantonese; that is to say, they were from Kwangtung Province in South China. They spoke a completely different dialect from the northern Chinese, with an even more pronounced tonal range and a particular glottal emphasis. Because of the effect this had on idiomatic expression, lyrical meter, and singing style, the Cantonese theatre was a very different proposition from the Peking form, even though it followed basically similar concepts of dramatic technique.

Over the years, however, the Cantonese theatre as a true regional form seemed likely to die out. In Hongkong, due to its proximity to the more mediocre aspects of Western culture, the form had become very debased. In the days when I lived in Hongkong, a typical Cantonese performance was accompanied by an orchestra, in which the saxophone was the principal instrument of song accompaniment. It was joined by a violin and cornet included among the Chinese instruments. Plays were often rehashed from film synopses and cheap novelettes. The sensation of the Cantonese stage in 1950 Hongkong was a play called *The Emperor's Night Sacrifice of His Precious Concubine* or some such title, as I recall. It was about the Ch'ing emperor Kuang Hsü, and an actress named Ch'in Hsiao-li made doubtful theatre history in it by appearing on stage wearing a garishly ornate version of a Manchu court headdress and a flimsy topless shift, her breasts encased in a painted bra. It was almost a striptease act by

149

Chinese standards. It was not surprising, therefore, that serious audiences shunned the Cantonese theatre. Although it did not lack some very talented performers, they seemed to be the victims of a system against which they were powerless. Before the Cultural Revolution devastated the theatrical world in China, there were some very worthwhile efforts to rehabilitate the Cantonese traditional style. There is a move to take up the threads again, it is said, in the climate of current times. Certainly it would serve a desperate need.

Cantonese troupes used to travel far afield in the past — to Shanghai, where there was a large Cantonese colony; to the Straits Settlements; and to San Francisco, which boasted the largest Chinese community beyond the Orient. Occasionally they visited Honolulu and the West Indies. During the days of the gold rush, San Francisco became called "Mountain of Gold," Gum San in Cantonese. When the precious metal was subsequently discovered in Australia, that country was dubbed Sun Gum San, "New Mountain of Gold." In the past when an actor returned from a stint in San Francisco, he became nicknamed Gum San so-and-so and in due course incorporated the nickname in his customary stage name as a mark of professional esteem among his fellows. Actors and actresses who had passed the zenith of their careers in China often went abroad before disappearing from the stage completely, which is one reason why the styles of acting in Malaysia and San Francisco remained more conservative than in novelty-crazy Hongkong.

The Chinese population of Hongkong had substantially changed by 1950, since thousands of refugees from communist China had fled to the colony until the city was crowded to an unheard-of degree. The newcomers included people of different professions and occupations, among them many businessmen from Shanghai. Shanghai people were like the Cantonese in that they spoke their own dialect and were very clannish. They tended to be smart, aggressive, and somewhat ostentatious. Certainly they were very shrewd entrepreneurs. The Cantonese and Shanghai people did not really like each other, but the northerners undoubtedly contributed to new growths in commercial prosperity and private enterprise in Hongkong, where such were considered cardinal virtues.

We caught up with many of our old acquaintances from Nanking, Shanghai, and Peking in this influx until it began to seem the China we had known had been transplanted in microcosm. The Shanghai people were great patrons of the Peking-style theatre, which under their patronage became a little more flamboyant and spectacular — being known as *hai-p'ai,* as contrasted with the *ching-p'ai* of Peking itself. As a result of Shanghai enterprise, the interest of the increased northern population, and the presence of three of China's leading actors in Hongkong, it became possible to set up a regular Saturday afternoon performance of Peking plays at the P'u Ch'ing theatre in Nathan Road, a Cantonese playhouse on the Kowloon side of the harbor. This was far from being the most propitious time for performance, and once a week was little enough for an entertainment that in China had been staged night after night in dozens of different theatres in cities half the size of Hongkong. But it was the only concession that could be wrung from Cantonese theatre managements reluctant to allow northern actors to compete with their own shows and who charged the Peking actors an exorbitant sum for renting the theatre as a result.

During 1950 and 1951 I attended every one of those Saturday performances, which became a cultural oasis for the northern Chinese filling the house each week. Because they were there to satisfy the nostalgia of deprived audiences, the actors ran the gamut of the traditional Peking repertoire; I was able to see a revealing cross section of the best-known plays, several of which I attended two or three times during the course of two years. Through such extensive theatregoing, visits backstage, and the several actors I came to know personally, I was able to extend my knowledge and perception while absorbing some lasting lessons about theatre as an art and discipline. Of the fifty-odd programs still in my possession from that period, it can be confirmed that an average performance consisted of two main plays featuring the leading actors Ma Lien-lang, Chang Chün-ch'iu, and Yü Chen-fei and approximately four shorter pieces played by the supporting actors of the troupe, which was run on traditionally conservative lines. The leader was Chang Chün-ch'iu, who in theatre circles was admired as being one of the *ssu ta ming tan,* the "four younger female impersonators." The Chinese had a passion for classification in the theatre as in most things, so there were previously the "four senior female impersonators" and the four younger. The senior men were Mei Lan-fang, Cheng Yen-ch'iu, Hsun Wei-sheng, and Hsiang Hsiao-yün; the four younger, Chang Chün-ch'iu, Sung Te-chu, Li Shih-fang, and Mao Shih-lai. Li was Mei Lan-fang's star pupil killed in a 1947 air-crash. The two groupings therefore defined a difference in generation and an equivalent high prestige.

Ma Lien-lang was one of the most renowned players of the bearded scholar roles of the day and commanded a wide following. He had been extensively recorded; his voice was to be heard coming over every radio and public address system at all hours of the day or night when I was in China. He was immensely popular with Shanghai audiences, and the Hongkong exiles always crowded the house when Ma Lien-lang was on the stage. He was a product of the famous Fu Lien Cheng, where he had graduated as one of their most brilliant pupils. It was he who first initiated the idea of a Peking troupe in Hongkong, where he had settled at the end of the Japanese war. I was told he was out of favor with the government at the time because he had performed in Japanese-occupied Shanghai. Be that as it may, with the deterioration of the situation on the mainland, he persuaded Chang Chün-ch'iu and Yü Chen-fei to join him in Hongkong. Ma was not an easy person to know, and I never really had a great deal of contact with him beyond a backstage nod. He was said to be very unhappy in Hongkong, heavily in debt, and according to Chinese gossips a smoker of opium. Whatever his personal problems, he was a brilliant actor and my understanding was greatly advanced through being able to see him perform so often.

Yü Chen-fei, the other member of the distinguished trio, played the young hero roles and was one of the most distinguished interpreters of the genre, for which really talented performers were scarce. Yü was a most engaging personality who became a good personal friend and often visited us with his wife. He was a tall, dignified, and as befitting his stage role, very handsome figure, always immaculately dressed in a traditional, long, high-collared Chinese gown. Like many actors, he was quite the dandy. He had a resonant voice and a most infectious laugh and was an extremely sociable person.

Yü Chen-fei was a Soochow man who since childhood had been steeped in *k'un-ch'ü* by his father, a distinguished authority on this dramatic genre. It was a classical lyrical form which had

Yü Chen-fei on stage

153

preceded the more popular Peking style, to which it contributed a great deal of technical procedure and a repertoire of plays. All Peking actors in the old days were trained in this older style first. The principal accompanying instrument was the horizontal bamboo flute, upon which Yü Chen-fei was a most accomplished performer. When he came to our house, he would often play to us after dinner as we sat on the verandah in the warm dusk, the moon rising to throw its shimmer over the waters of the distant harbor. The clear notes of his flute rising and falling in sweet cadences had a high magic on those never-to-be-forgotten evenings.

In addition to his regular weekly performances in Hongkong, Yü Chen-fei gave a number of private performances, often accompanied by his wife who was an enthusiastic amateur performer. Yü himself had begun his stage career as an amateur and was an excellent example of the type of talented person who eventually decided to turn professional and "dive into the sea." Amateur in this sense, however, has a rather different connotation from the way it is often used in the West. From his childhood Yü had been subjected to an intensive training process simply because of the nature of his family background; it was no mere dilettante interest. Many children of Soochow families in the old days were brought up to play, sing, and perform as a normal part of their cultural education if their families were inclined towards theatre, and a great many were in a city that was regarded as the heart of the classical dramatic tradition before the rise of the Peking style. Professional instructors were brought in to tutor children; performances were often given within the households for the delectation of their members, whom it should be remembered in extended families could often be numbered in scores. Yü Chen-fei once told me that he could remember as a small child being rocked to sleep in his mother's arms as she sang tunes from the repertoire as lullabies. During all his professional career, Yü sought to keep the old drama to the fore and worked for its revival, so deeply was it a part of his life.

I first met Chang Chün-ch'iu when I sent him a note complaining that I was unable to obtain tickets for his first performances in Hongkong through the normal channels of the box office. After that he sent a messenger over to the office every Friday with my tickets, and soon I came to know him very well. He was small in stature, gentle-voiced, with large eyes and the complexion of a

White Snake Chang Chün-ch'iu Hongkong 1957

The actor Chang Chün-ch'iu in the play, "The White Snake"

155

baby. His features bore a strong resemblance to his old mother whom I once met backstage. He was exceedingly helpful and co-operative in everything I wanted to do and gave me the free run of the backstage area whenever I wished. He had an unenviable job running a Peking troupe among a predominantly Cantonese community. The financial rewards were meager on the basis of one performance, and as *lao-pan*, the "head of the troupe," he was constantly under pressure from his actors. Theatrical troupes were paid on a cooperative basis, each actor given his portion according to his seniority and rank so that the pickings were very small. I was told by the young principal comic actor of the troupe Wang Te-k'un that he got about HK$ 60 (ten U.S. dollars) for one show, and there was a certain amount of unrest in the troupe from time to time among the junior personnel. For all that, they were a sociable and carefree crowd. There was one glorious occasion when my wife and I had Chang Chün-ch'iu, Yü Chen-fei, and several members of the troupe up to the house for dinner; they were all very relaxed and seemed gratified to be accepted as honored guests and not hired hands. It was a light-hearted, merry evening, during which they entertained us and each other with songs and excerpts from the repertoire. It was always interesting to see how Chinese theatre people lived wholly within the theatre, so to speak, entertaining themselves whenever they got together on any sociable occasion with their own dramatic accomplishments. It was artistic self-sufficiency of a unique kind, due in part perhaps to the way the old-style Chinese actor was taught to make a total gift of himself to his craft.

In December, 1950, I was invited to the wedding of the comic actor Wang Te-k'un. By this time I had almost become an honorary member of the troupe. The ceremony was held in a large restaurant called the Liu Kuo Fan Tien in the Wanchai district of Hongkong. Chinese weddings are not religious consecrations in the sense of Western-style marriages but are civil ceremonies conducted by the family within the family to seal an important mutual contract. In this case, it was the great family of theatre exerting its prerogative. The setting was a large room, at one end a long table set for dinner in foreign style. This had become quite a custom in Hongkong; for one thing, Western meals were more compact and less costly than Chinese wedding banquets with their innumerable dishes, and for another, Western food added a touch of the exotic for those who did not usually eat it, even though they were probably only too glad to get back to Chinese "home cooking" the next day.

The other half of the room was set with chairs before a long table covered with a crimson-embroidered cloth, while on the wall behind hung crimson draperies decorated in gold with the Chinese character *hsi*, signifying an occasion for joy. Two crimson candles stood on the table with a bundle of tapers and gifts in red and gold wrappings. In the far corner was a small table for the signing of the marriage documents, and close by was seated the stage orchestra equipped with drum, wooden clappers, *hu ch'in*, *erh-hu*, gong, and cymbals. All the theatre company were present, with the exception of Chang Chün-ch'iu and Ma Lien-lang, the senior members whose arrival was awaited. Yü Chen-fei was not at this ceremony, since he had yet to join the troupe in Hongkong.

Wang Te-k'un came forward to receive me when I arrived; he was wearing a Western-style business suit and large, crimson rosette in his buttonhole. Then the troupe got down to a little entertainment, each member in turn standing up to sing and act a passage from their personal repertoire with the orchestra accompanying them. Everybody was in good spirits and there was a great deal of banter going on. Wang Te-k'un parodied a Cantonese rendering of a Peking theatre speech as his contribution to the proceedings. Chang Chün-ch'iu presently arrived, dressed in a long, blue silk gown and accompanied by his wife and two personal musicians. Photographs were taken of us all, with a good deal of shuffling and arranging of who stood behind whom. Finally Ma Lien-lang, as the master of ceremonies, made his deliberately late appearance. He was wearing a black silk *ma-kua*, a short waist-length, high-collared tunic, over a long, blue silk gown. The sponsors were thereupon called out one in turn, two of them accompanying Wang Te-k'un to the crimson-draped table, before which stood the master of ceremonies. They were followed by the bride, a rather inconspicuous-looking little woman in a silk *ch'i-p'ao*, the all-purpose garment for both formal and informal occasions, accompanied by her two sponsors. As she walked up to the table, the orchestra provided a rendering of "Here Comes the Bride," causing a good deal of hilarity among the assembled guests. Ma Lien-lang next read the personal histo-

Wang Te-k'un, ch'ou actor

ries of the bride and bridegroom from the papers in his hand. The couple then faced each other, bowed three times, bowed to Ma Lien-lang, then bowed to each sponsor called out by name to make their congratulatory speeches in turn. Finally there was a speech from another presiding member, who introduced me to the guests, and after that photographs and more photographs with the bride looking very embarrassed and downcast as everyone called upon her to smile with scant regard for her shyness. Thus the ceremony ended and Wang Te-k'un escorted me all the way to the street door as I left the company to get on with the wedding banquet.

I came to know Wang Te-k'un very well, and he frequently brought his costumes to our house and posed for me while I made sketches in furtherance of my research. Two other younger members of the troupe I worked with a great deal were Hu Yung-fang, a *wu-sheng* actor, and his sister Hu Hung-yen, a *hua-tan*. They collaborated in my work constantly, and in 1961 I escorted them both to New York at the invitation of a theatre research institute there to work with me on a project with American actors. Hu Hung-yen stayed on in the United States, marrying an interpreter at the United Nations, and later collaborated with me on two separate occasions in a special program I directed for theatre students at the University of Wisconsin — a far cry from Saturday afternoons in the Kowloon theatre.

Those two years spent among the Peking theatre exiles now seem to belong to a distant age in more than one sense. For me they offered an opportunity which could never occur again, but for the actors it was a time of waiting which foreshadowed many changes in their accustomed ways of life. Then early in 1952 I went to Japan and was away from Hongkong for a couple of years. When I returned it was to find the communist authorities had persuaded the actors to return to the mainland. Chang Chün-ch'iu, with his troupe, and Ma Lien-lang were the first to go. However, not everyone went back. Once Chang Chün-ch'iu had made the decision to return, he offered his actors their choice of going with him or staying in Hongkong. Among those who elected to remain were Wang Te-k'un, Hu Yung-fang, and his sister Hu Hung-yen, a trio of young performers with whom I was able to continue my association. Then on March 1, 1955, the Hongkong morning papers carried the news that Yü Chen-fei and his wife had slipped across the border en route for Peking, thus ending a unique interlude in the history of the Chinese theatre.

None of the three talented actors who had brightened the Hongkong scene for so many homesick northerners had truly been at ease in the alien atmosphere of the British colony. Nor had they been able to make Peking theatre a viable financial proposition, either singly or as a group, under the adverse conditions against which they struggled among the indifferent Cantonese community. All of them had run into heavy debt and had a hard time making personal ends meet, much less covering their professional expenses. The Peking authorities provided them with everything they required and paid off all their debts — the one condition being that they never attempt to leave China again. Conditions at that time seemed highly favorable to theatre people on the mainland; to leave Hongkong was like returning home from a foreign country. In China it seemed they were really wanted, and it was not difficult to understand their decision to go back in the euphoria of that period.

5

Six years passed since we left Nanking. All our contacts with mainland Chinese sources were broken off. Letters to friends went unanswered, and official enquiries were ignored. Until Christmas of 1950 a desultory mail had trickled through to Hongkong from one or two people, brief notes containing little more than a few general statements; after that was silence. We stopped trying to keep in touch with people because of the suspicion we might bring upon them.

With the end of the Korean War, it became clear to the outside world that in spite of predictions, the new regime in China was there to stay. The country had a government that had put down corruption to a great extent and instituted social reforms on a large scale. This was the consensus of opinion among the foreign journalists who became the advance guard of a steady flow of officially invited visitors on guided tours. Cultural delegations, labor organizations, schoolteachers, parliamentary groups, and so on began to pass through Hongkong on the great pilgrimage — to return three or four weeks later ready to give their impressions to the world at large. Opinion seemed divided as to whether China was now a new socialist utopia or a police state; it depended on the visitor's sense of proportion. But agreement seemed unanimous on the disappearance of the housefly. It was questionable who was the more naive, the woman scholar impressed because the rattan slippers provided in the railway sleeping cars were never stolen, an observable fact long before the communists took over the railways; or the newspaper correspondent who concluded he was shadowed by armed guards all the way to Peking, when in fact every long-distance train in China had always carried railway police for the welfare of the traveling public, and all police were armed as a matter of course in China — as indeed they are in so many Western countries. This investing of things with a significance they never possessed provoked little confidence in objective reporting. It seemed better to go and see for oneself.

The moment was propitious. A more liberal policy towards the arts was being debated in 1956, as Mao sought greater cooperation from artists, writers, and theatre people, who by this time were stifled and resentful at the party restraints imposed upon them. A campaign launched under the slogan "Let Flowers of Many Kinds Blossom Diverse Schools of Thought Contend," designed to suggest a move towards greater freedom of thought in the arts and literature, was getting under way. I sent a letter through the China Travel Service to the Ministry of Foreign Affairs in Peking, asking permission to visit China in a private and personal capacity in order to meet with Mei Lan-fang and other actors as well as to see what was going on in the theatre world. Within four weeks time my wife and I were sitting in the waiting room of the Shumchun station across the Chinese border, ready to board the train for Canton, our entry formalities having been completed. As China did not observe Hongkong's British summer time, in stepping over the border we had stepped back an hour; while waiting for the train, we were served a simple lunch and entertained with music over the station's public address system. There was singing by massed choirs, by then very popular in new China, selections from the repertoire of the Peking actor Ma Lien-lang, and what sounded suspiciously like a "yellow music" piece from the other side of the border.

We were the only passengers in the first-class coach reserved for foreigners, and the green plush seating had the faded look of a colonial past. The only other occupants were the attendant and a railway policeman whose white, high-collared tunic, navy trousers, and squat peaked cap added a distinctly Russian note to his appearance. The loudspeaker system on the train was raucously loud in admonishing passengers what and what not to do on their journey. Then there was more choral singing. During a blessed interval of silence, we observed the coach attendant, swatter in hand, vigorously pursuing a single fly on its erratic way down the coach, presumably a stowaway from Hongkong threatening to embarrass us all.

Through the windows could be seen the interminable rice fields stretching away for mile after mile, patterned with the stooping figures of the toiling villagers, here and there a boy astride a water buffalo to break the monotony of the scene. The political slogans painted on the sides of some new, ugly red brick building rising above the grey conglomeration of a village, or the banners and posters which blazoned every station with the messages of Mao, were indicative of the times. Otherwise we saw nothing very different at that distance from the China we had always known.

We arrived at Canton promptly and were met by a polite China Travel Service representative who escorted us to the Ai Kuan Hotel, where we were to be left to our own devices until boarding the midnight train, on which they had booked a sleeper for us. The hotel, a high building towering over the Pearl River waterfront, was a gloomy place built we were told by Japanese aggressors and Chinese capitalist traitors during the war and now reserved for foreign guests. The interior indicated that capitalist taste, like its Marxist counterpart, was no better than it ought to be in terms of architectural design.

We washed and set off to stroll round the town a little before dinner. It was a hot, humid afternoon and the sidewalks were

The railway station policeman

crowded in a familiar way, but Canton at that juncture had little appeal to the eye. The streets, need it be said, were clean and well swept, but roads and sidewalks were in poor shape and most buildings seemed in shabby need of paint and renovation. In the muddy ooze at Shameen, some children catching frogs paused to fix upon us the long, curious, and unrelenting stare of their kind. Walking back along the waterfront, we passed a group of grinning coolies who turned to call "hello"; and one of them cried out, "English." It was the first and only time we were to be acknowledged publicly as anything but Russian during our stay in new China.

On the quayside little groups of people stood talking in the warm night air, which echoed to the constant clack-clack of wooden clogs on the roadway. As we reached the hotel, the high cadence of a bamboo flute was heard in a drift of sound for a moment above the sirens of the chugging river craft. In the Ai Kuan's tawdry dining room, we were served an excellent Cantonese dinner, the fried rice famous in that province, chicken with melon, fried shrimp balls, egg and spinach soup. Curiously enough, we seemed to be the only ones among our fellow travelers tempted by the local fare. The rest of them, for the most part burly Russians and their wives, dined upon cucumber and tomato salad, ham, sweet pastries, bottled beer, and the odd glass of brandy. It was a pattern we were often to notice on our journeys; whenever we came across Russians, whether in restaurants or railway dining cars, they never called voluntarily for Chinese food. It did not even seem to be a question of, "Well, I like Chinese food but it doesn't like me" so much as sheer, rugged peasant resistance to the unorthodox.

As we drove to the station, the streets were as dark as in a wartime city; it was a relief to leave the outer gloom and board the train where the familiar four-berthed compartment had a welcoming air. Our travel companions were two middle-aged Chinese, Mr. and Mrs. Huang, who nodded to us a little nervously, wondering perhaps if we were the Russians we also had surmised our fellow passengers might be. They were already preparing for bed, and with the customary scuffling and shuffling out of garments, we quickly followed their example. In no time at all, we were drifting into sleep, lulled by the monotonous sound of the wheels below as the train rattled on into the heart of China.

We rose at 6:30 A.M. for the mad scramble at the two toilets.

But our compartment attendant was most helpful and brought bucket and water to the compartment. We were able to complete our ablutions in comparative ease, our companions having gone to the dining car, where we shortly followed them. There the attendants were setting out baskets of lichees on a corner table, resulting in an immediate rush to buy them, with everyone for themselves and no attempt at lining up. Most of the customers seemed to be young people who entered yawning and puffy-eyed, the early morning unloveliness of the human race not enhanced by the sloppy caps on the back of women's pigtailed heads, the general untidiness of dress, and an almost calculated uncouthness of behavior. Breakfast that morning was not a shining example of the new social virtues. The meal itself consisted of ham and eggs indifferently cooked, faintly scorched sour rye bread, and abominable coffee—no worse than many another railway meal in the past but certainly no better. After that when the train made stops, we purchased food from the platform vendors, whose white caps and surgical masks became recognizable as the new trademark of all catering services, and shared our picnics with the Huangs. Our fellow travelers were on their way to

Railway station refreshment stall

visit their son in Peking, they told us, and both were as curious and apprehensive as any foreigners.

At Henshan a group of Russians left the train to stretch their legs and buy oranges on the platform. Behind the station barrier the waiting crowd stared their fill. One bystander with the face of a lohan seemed petrified with astonishment until he began to grin and point, whereupon he was promptly moved on by the station policeman. The Soviet comrades, no less than the rest of us outsiders, were a source of visual entertainment. Everything changes; nothing changes.

We arrived at Wuchang at 5 A.M.; there we left our train, since we had to cross the wide sweep of the Yangtze River by ferry to make our Peking connection at Hankow on the other side. The great bridge which has now done away with the need for this cumbersome change was then still under construction. As the Peking train did not leave until 11 P.M., we had the whole day in Hankow before us. After a bath and breakfast in a hotel, to which clung the aura of old "China hand" days, the young man from the China Travel Service responsible for our itinerary straightway escorted us to see the bridge, which had become the pride of the nation.

The enthusiastic official taking us around the site first showed us the plans in the workers' common room, where we sipped tea and listened to a lengthy technical account of the engineering process. This got a little above our very untechnical heads, although there was nothing difficult to understand about the bridge we were taken to view from a raised bamboo platform overlooking the river. The eight piers to support the great spans were already built and straddled the wide stretch of water where tall-sailed junks tacked in the wind. From our side of the river girders and supports had begun to reach out into space, while on the banks far below hundreds of workers created a human avalanche of activity as they surged backwards and forward, up and down, in a continuous turmoil of movement and sound.

We left the site in an atmosphere of cordial goodwill and considerable admiration for what was obviously an engineering feat of some magnitude, a testimony to replacing empty talk with accomplished fact. Driving back along the muddy road from the site, surrounded by canteens, bathhouses, shops, and hoardings plastered with slogans and pictures of model workers engaged on the bridge, a new housing complex under construction was pointed out to us. The ugly red brick blocks were obviously a different proposition from the hovels that had passed for workers' dwellings in the past. But I wondered why social progress had to be partnered by unrelieved drabness. It was a question I was to ask myself frequently in the days to come.

From the bridge we were taken to see the Soviet exhibition housed in a pillared palace that had taken four months to build, we were told, and contained displays of nearly everything pertaining to the daily life of industrialized society. It was an astonishing manifestation of contemporary productiveness with a nineteenth-century air, as expressed in the vast canvases depicting revolutionary scenes, heroes from Russian history, and tractor-filled idylls displayed in the art galleries on the second floor. Serious young Chinese women guides armed with wooden pointers left no minute detail of the illustrative panorama unexplored or unexplained — such passionate earnestness there was, such voluble patter. Around us the crowds jostled and peered, and we ourselves became part of the exhibit as the whispering sightseers, gazes fixed on our English clothes, manifest their anxiety to let all and sundry know that we had been recognized as Soviet citizens.

Watching the foreigners on the train

167

After that we were ready for lunch, having early that morning stipulated it should be a Chinese one. This decision had visibly perturbed our Mr. Liu of the Travel Service. Now convinced that he had mistaken our intentions, he told us lunch would be waiting at the hotel. When we insisted we did not wish to eat the dull Western fare provided there, he was perplexed and became very worried indeed when again we demanded a Chinese meal. The suspicion crossed our minds that there must be a security regulation against foreigners eating in the town, but this he hotly denied. After reassuring himself once more as to our wishes, he stopped before a restaurant and asked us to wait while he went in. He returned all smiles, and we entered a shabby, tumbledown interior, where as we had hopefully anticipated, the food was very good indeed — a fact equally acknowledged by our reluctant guide. The place was full of workers, technicians of some kind, who nudged each other and commented about us quite openly. They all wore the ubiquitous cap and had been drinking wine, a sign of new trends indeed at that time of day. I asked Mr. Liu if foreigners were unwelcome in the town. He explained that foreigners were not unwelcome but that they never came into the town, at least to eat. Hankow was no country village, but an important transit center on the traditional pilgrim's way to Peking. It was a city of some size, albeit a rather ugly one, yet it apparently provoked little curiosity on the part of Russians. This was only one of many indications we were to receive that as the first private visitors, we did not conform to the book of rules for official welcome of foreign guests. Of the hundreds who had visited the new China at that time, not one had paid his own way and there was a difference.

"Yours will be a pioneering job," they had told me when I first went to China; returning after all those years, it seemed I was still a pioneer. I was to find this was a disadvantage when trying to break down the resistance of those schooled to believe that for foreigners everything was to be done in the most lavish way. If you were not being entertained by the Chinese government, and very few visitors in those days were not, then some foreign organization was obviously taking care of matters. To give our hosts their due, once they had grasped the idea of a private traveler, they did their best to help but not before some strain was put upon our very unofficial purse.

When we got aboard the Peking train that night, we found the Huangs from Hongkong sharing our compartment once more, and we greeted each other like long-lost friends as we settled in. The coach in which we had been allotted berths was a brand new one in which everything shone, from the newly varnished woodwork to the thermos flask standing against a potted plant on the little window table. Even the attendants themselves seemed new, for this was a crack train bound for the capital of China. We were up at six the next morning, wakened by the music of the loudspeakers at the station where we stopped. The attendants were already assiduously swabbing down the corridors, cleaning, and polishing until it seemed the train itself was far more spick-and-span than its passengers, whose slovenly clothes and behavior intruded everywhere. People's dress was for me the most significant visible reminder that the Chinese revolution had drawn its strength from the village in subjugating the city. The army that conquered China had largely come from the peasant population, and the civilian administrative cadres who took over from the army were originally peasants who had been specially trained and politically indoctrinated. The natural suspicion and contempt for city decadence of the peasant was symbolically expressed in the brusque behavior and sloppy dress transmitted by the political vanguard to the nation at large. Traveling by train

The Comrade

revealed this transformation in microcosm, particularly in the dining cars. There young men in crumpled slacks and tunics of unisexual cut, wearing soft peak caps seemingly never removed at any time, ate hearty meals while slumped over tables as they effectively demonstrated the cult of social gracelessness peculiar to a class of young people one presumed to be the Communist Party's children.

The following morning we reached Anyang at breakfast time and got down on the platform to stretch our legs. A number of passengers were doing their morning exercises to music coming over the loudspeakers. *I, erh, san,* "one, two, three"; a fat army officer who kept his military cap on could not touch his toes and whirled his arms like flails. People were buying the whole cooked chickens which seemed to be a specialty on the food vendors' wagons there. The Huangs purchased one and later shared it with us in the compartment, dissecting the tender flesh with a penknife—the kind of picnic that is remembered through the years long after more elaborate feasts have been forgotten. Soon long extracts from the Peking theatre repertoire were heard over

Morning exercises, 7 A.M. Anyang station

the clamor of the train's loudspeakers, to which we had all been constantly submitted since leaving Canton. Our impending arrival in the capital was also evident in the increased bustle among the passengers, who were quite noisy in the dining car that evening with a good deal of beer and brandy being drunk in celebration. We had a farewell meal with the Huangs, who called for a bottle of the fiery local wine displayed on the dining car tables, and we toasted our travels together.

We arrived in Peking at 10 p.m. and were met by two China Travel Service representatives — one of whom, Miss Wu, announced herself as our guide during our stay. We drove through a Peking submerged in half-darkness in which the remembered forms of buildings and street vistas slid away into the shadows as the C.T.S. car took us to our hotel, a new tall building in the old Legation Quarter. We were shown to our room on the fifth floor, comfortably furnished with its own small bathroom, and weary from our long journey, we slept soundly.

Up early the next morning, we found that our window overlooked a stretch of the old city wall with the grey vista of Peking beyond. Directly below were some drab brick buildings near which two students were ostentatiously doing exercises on parallel bars in the street. One began to feel that physical exercise as an aid to national fitness was also becoming a social cult. We went down — or rather up — to breakfast, for the vast dining room was on the sixth floor, where we were shown to a table by one of the waitresses. They were all dressed in black with bunched sleeves, white aprons, and collars, which created a curiously dated appearance reminiscent of Lyons teashop "nippies" in London of the 1920s. Breakfast was a multi-national affair with the Russians predominant; we had to persuade our waitress that we only wanted toast, fruit and coffee — not cereals, porridge, fish, bacon and eggs, sweet pastries, brandy and beer, which seemed to be the fare set before many of the guests. Labor heroes possibly, I surmised, rewarded by a vacation in China.

Breakfast over, we went down and called two pedicabs to take us to the C.T.S. office. The drivers, named Yang and Tung according to the license plates on their vehicles, which were in a ruinous state, wanted to wait outside the office for us. "*Mei yu shih*," "business is bad," said Yang mournfully, so we left them there while we had a conference with Miss Wu. She was a pleasant girl from Shanghai, very young, very new to her job, and understandably not very knowledgeable about the theatrical world of Peking. As private travelers who knew their way around in China, we caused a problem since we were not covered by the rules and regulations for looking after foreign visitors. In those days the latter were assumed to travel only in officially sponsored parties. We constituted a precedent and the travel specialists were at a loss how to deal with such a deviation from conformity.

However, I was in China for a specific professional purpose at some cost to myself. I was anxious to ensure that my requests were being dealt with at higher levels and that we should not be fobbed off with routine tourist trips, for which I had little stomach at the best of times. I told them so as politely as I could. Miss Wu assured me that my requests had gone forward and that first they were trying to arrange a meeting with Mei Lan-fang.

Two days later she arrived at the hotel at breakfast time to say they were hoping to confirm a meeting with Mei that afternoon and that she would notify me later. She also brought our residence forms to be signed. These asked for a personal history since the age of twelve, among other things, and whether one had ever committed any crime — I wondered who answered such a question in the affirmative. At 12:30 Miss Wu rang to say I was to meet Mei Lan-fang at the old Peking Club at 2 P.M. We called for her and set off in pedicabs for the club, where we were met by the secretary of the All China Drama Association, a bespectacled, solemn-faced woman in the customary drab uniform of her kind. She never smiled and insisted on addressing us in Chinese through Miss Wu, who passed on the secretary's message of welcome delivered in a flat, monotonous tone and sounding as though it had been said a score of times, which doubtless it had. It was based on the "bridge of culture" theme and sounded very corny, as Americans would say.

The door opened and Mei Lan-fang entered, followed by his secretary Hsü Lai-yuän. He came straight over to meet me, waving aside the All China Dramatic Association woman who had immediately stepped forward to take charge. Instead, she had to remain silent on a chair in a corner for the rest of the interview. The great actor was dressed in a neat Western-style suit, his secretary in a dark blue Sun Yat-sen uniform of the kind worn by officials before 1949. At the time of this meeting, Mei was sixty-three. He was a small man, rounder in the face and a little plumper than of old, but he had no grey hairs and seemed in excellent physical shape. He left the impression of a frank and outgoing personality, extremely modest, as the truly talented so often are, but with great strength of character. He had a most easy manner, and after shaking hands he began talking right away, saying he had heard about me from Yü Chen-fei. I had a letter for Mei from a great friend of ours in Hongkong, John Grose, which I handed to him. His voice became wistful as he exclaimed, "Ah, a dear friend of twenty years ago." John Grose was a Hongkong businessman, the son of an English merchant who had gone out to Shanghai in the nineteenth century and taken a "temporary" Chinese wife, as was the custom in those days. When the merchant finally returned to England, he made provisions for the education of his son, whom the mother took to Hongkong where he grew up completely bilingual. The boy became a man who moved easily between two worlds; he was sophisticated, cultured, a true connoisseur of Chinese food, and had a dry sense of humor. He was also a passionate lover of the Chinese theatre and one of Mei Lan-fang's sponsors when the actor first performed in Hongkong. That was in 1922 and the two men had become good friends.

On the outbreak of the Sino-Japanese War in 1937, Mei moved to Hongkong and appeared on stage there with his troupe in May, 1938. After that he continued to live quietly in the British colony, awaiting the turn of events. He spent a lot of his time with a small group of special friends, including John Grose, who often spoke feelingly of those days which drew Mei and himself together in a spirit of camaraderie. When the Japanese captured Hongkong in 1941, the invaders tried to persuade Mei to give a public performance, but he steadfastly refused to do so. Then one day he came to say goodbye to John, who once described it to me as a very emotional occasion. Mei had been ordered to Canton by the Japanese and suspected they again wanted him to perform. Since he intended to refuse, he feared that he might not be allowed to return and had therefore brought his expensive camera for his friend to sell and thus provide some aid for the Mei family. John later bartered it for two sacks of rice. As it turned out, the actor's premonitions proved groundless; he was asked to do nothing worse than attend a Japanese national occasion in Canton, where he was informed that on his return he would be repatriated to Shanghai with his family. This indeed proved the case; Mei and his family were returned by special plane to Shanghai, where he lived in seclusion until the end of the war. Although the Japanese hoped he would relent once he returned home, they never troubled him again. During his stay in Hongkong, Mei had grown a moustache as a symbol of his professional withdrawal and did not shave it off until V.J. Day, surely one of the more unusual manifestations of patriotism.

Mei and John Grose never saw each other again after the actor returned to Shanghai, so that the letter I delivered doubtless brought memories flooding back for Mei. He asked me about John, with whom we had dined the day before leaving for Peking, and he seemed touched by the immediacy of the contact. He told me he was busy preparing to go to Japan, and I said that we had heard about the proposed trip in Hongkong and had all hoped to meet with him there en route. He seemed pleased with the idea but added that he did not know how "they" would arrange his schedule for him. Soon after I got back to Hongkong, he did in fact arrive by train at the Hongkong border on the way to Japan. John Grose wrote to the authorities beforehand asking if we might have a meeting with the great actor, but this was categorically refused. Mei was allowed to chat only with the press upon his arrival. When he returned from Japan two months later, he was rushed over the border immediately for Peking, so a rare opportunity for his friends and admirers was lost forever.

We talked about theatre in the new China, and Mei praised the improved conditions of theatre people and the experiments that were taking place. He himself had been a great experimenter in his time, the focus for many innovations in the old theatre, including his support for actresses of which I spoke earlier. He gave much credit where credit seemed due but was by no means uncritical, although his remarks were tempered with native tact. I told him that I was to visit the theatre training school the next day, and he expressed approval yet warned that the students were not perfect. In his brief comments I sensed the judgement of the master of a tradition holding perfection to be a supreme goal that standards were not being maintained because of the new politically biased methods of student training.

I spoke about the films being done of him and expressed disappointment that a more thorough attempt had not been made to record the technical aspects of his art and methods of training in complete detail — a true documentary of a disappearing art, in other words, instead of colorful spectacle dependent on the clichés of the technicolor cameras. He agreed with my criticisms and said that he personally considered the film an unsuitable medium for Peking stage methods. Here he began to make some of his points by using his most expressive hands to illustrate the importance of gestural forms on the stage, with respect to spatial relationships and the ineffectiveness of the film medium in encompassing their particular subtleties. I wished then that a film camera could have recorded that spontaneous demonstration.

At the time of this meeting, the first two volumes of Mei's memoirs *My Forty Years on the Stage* had recently been published. They had been compiled with the help of his amanuensis Hsü Lai-yüän, who had traveled around with Mei while taking the notes. I had the ambitious plan in those days of making a detailed translation of the memoirs which would be extensively annotated and illustrated, thus providing a unique record in English of the Peking actor's world. One of my purposes in returning to China was to get Mei's approval for the idea and ask if he would agree to correspond with me and answer queries. He and Hsü willingly assented and Mei emphasized that he would do all he could to help. However, though I sent my first inquiries later in a letter from Hongkong, together with an old photograph of theatre people upon which I wanted his opinion, he did not reply — and my photograph was not returned. Presumably he never received the letter, or if he did was prevented by circumstances from replying. The political climate was changing once more, and difficult times lay ahead for the old theatre community, not excluding Mei himself. I did not attempt to write again; it was probably ingenuous of me ever to have thought the idea possible, that such freedom of exchange would be condoned by the stubborn attitudes continuing to prevail in China. I abandoned my plan, since the chances of implementing it at that time seemed increasingly remote and without Mei's collaboration it no longer had point. As it turned out, his memoirs were never completed due to his untimely death.

The hour allotted for my interview passed all too quickly, and it was time for Mei to go. He insisted on our riding with him in his car, an old-fashioned-looking black limousine, the windows of which were concealed by small lace curtains. His driver dropped us off at our hotel, and we said our goodbyes conscious of a unique and historic encounter.

That evening a messenger came around to the hotel bringing a signed copy of Mei's memoirs and two tickets for *The Fifteen Strings of Cash*, an old play then being restaged to great acclaim from theatre circles in Peking. Mei had spoken about it at our meeting and said I should see it.

At eight o'clock the next morning, Miss Wu called for us in a taxi to go to the dramatic training school where a visit to classes had been arranged. We were met outside the school, a large, severe, grey barrackslike building and shown upstairs into the typical institutional reception room: lace antimacassars on the armchairs, thermos flasks of hot water, lidded tea mugs on the glass topped side tables, plus the inevitable portrait of Mao decorating the bare walls. The principal, Liu Chung-ch'iu, came in and we were introduced. He had a thick Central China accent, wore his hair parted in the middle, and looked as well as sounded somewhat out of place as the director of a Peking theatrical organization. He was a political administrator, I guessed, rather than a theatre man. I was told the school was founded in 1950, that it was co-educational, and that the training period was seven years. The first class had therefore not yet graduated. In addition to the traditional Peking style, the school also trained personnel for *p'ing-chü* and *Hupeh pang-tzu*, two north regional folk forms, the principal told us. Students were given a general education concurrently with their professional training, and everyone had to attend a daily session of political instruction, he added. In answer to my further questions, he explained that the old system of training boys to play women's roles had definitely been discontinued; the students were taught roles according to their sex only. A student began specialized training for particular roles in the fourth year, and as in the past classes started in the early morning at 6 A.M. with practice in singing and acrobatic training. This was followed by learning play texts and scene rehearsals; the afternoons were devoted exclusively to general education and political instruction, the evenings to practice and recapitulation. Peking theatre training had always imposed a backbreaking

schedule, but I did wonder what had to give with Marxist school-
ing now imposed upon everything else. I asked the principal if
the students were able to carry such a heavy schedule. He simply
replied in his impassive manner that the school aimed to produce
good actors to serve the Chinese people — which as so often in
new China was no answer at all. I then asked him about plays in
relating students to theatre history, using the example of *Ssu
Lang Visits His Mother*, which had been removed from the repertoire yet was associated in people's minds with the actor T'an
Hsin-p'ei, an important figure in the history of the Peking
theatre. The principal said they explained to students that T'an
Hsin-p'ei was a good actor, but the play was not good and therefore there was no need to emulate him. Again that oblique begging of the question, which one soon learned to anticipate but
found no way of countering in the new order. The principal on
this occasion was either being deliberately obtuse or else was
completely out of touch with what was going on in the theatre
world. Three days later we were to attend a performance of *Ssu
Lang Visits His Mother*, the first since the "liberation," we were
told. It was staged in the Yin Lo T'ang, a covered open-air theatre
in the Chung Shan Park before an audience of twenty-five hundred. The role of the Princess was played by Chang Chün-ch'iu.

Having reached an impasse with asking questions obviously in
the category of those not to be answered, we set off to visit the
classes — with periodic breaks of ten minutes, when the students
did the now apparently fashionable physical training. Both boys
and girls wore flat-soled Chinese shoes and loose-fitting, blue
cotton training costumes. In addition, some of the boys sported
American-style baseball caps whose functional purpose was
never made clear to me. I assumed they were a dress item for the
benefit of foreign visitors. In the first classroom we visited,
fourth-year boys were working at the bar, practicing leg movements for the bearded scholar roles. The standards of physical
accomplishment seemed very uneven. The leader of the line was
professionally agile, with his feet kicked above his head each
time as required, but others had attained less accurate degrees of
physical control, and a few were simply inadequate and would
never have been allowed to continue by the old training standards. There seemed to be no direct coaxing, scolding, or exhor-
tation going on between the teachers and their pupils; whether

177

that was for the visitor's benefit I could not say, but everything seemed a little colorless and even mechanical. Each time we entered a classroom and each time we left, there was a burst of staccato clapping from the students, stopping everything they were doing to indulge in this new-style greeting, presumably copied from the Russians. It all seemed a little forced and artificial and I personally found it tiresome, not to say time-wasting, since one was supposed to return the applause, which then could become unending while the students did their duty to those they doubtless assumed were yet another curious pair of Soviet visitors.

Next came two girls' classes, in the first of which a group was practicing sleeve movements in rehearsal tunics equipped for the purpose; they were walking in file while pointing in unison as they went through a routine of coordinating graceful hand gestures with the manipulation of the long, white silk water sleeves. These were especially important in the women's roles, particularly those portraying loyal wives, filial daughters, and women in distress or defiance. For such stage interpretations as these, the water sleeves became expressive aids for depicting emotional moods like sorrow, fear, and anger. Chinese stage costume had its earliest origins in the robes and skirts worn for court song and dance entertainments, so that its primary function was to facilitate graceful movement and decorative forms. It is understandable, therefore, how the water sleeves became so important an accessory of theatre costumes. Sleeve techniques were only mastered through the long practice and training which all theatre students received, and a truly expressive control of them in performance marked the difference between a good and an indifferent actor or actress.

The second girls' class was engaged in the vigorous gymnastics that were a central feature of Chinese dramatic training. The group was busy practicing bends, twists, running, and turning, basic techniques which would stand them in good stead in the more energetic amazon roles. Nearby a class of small boys in the first year were doing handsprings and turning cartwheels, their bodies already as flexible as eels at the start of an arduous process designed to condition the actor's total being to a pitch of instantaneous response at whatever level demanded of him.

Next door a smaller classroom contained a trio of senior students rehearsing a scene from a play, one among the scores which students would master completely by the end of their training period. Each student had to become thoroughly familiar with the principal roles of the genre in which he specialized. Plays were literally absorbed through the mind, memory, and body, and most trained actors in the past could take over roles other than their own at a minute's notice in case of a stage emergency, so familiar were they with the entire content and form of the repertoire. In the smaller touring troupes, this was often a case of necessity, for Chinese acting companies had to be self-sufficient. Sometimes on a special occasion like the Chinese New Year season, a well-known actor might switch from his customary roles just for the sheer novelty of it to amuse the audience. For example, I once saw Chang Chün-ch'iu in Hongkong appear in a young hero part instead of his customary role as a female impersonator, a divertissement which tickled the holiday crowd. In contrast to this, one Saturday afternoon when a painted face actor failed to turn up for the performance, the comic actor Wang Te-k'un took over and saved the situation. This was not an easy feat at such short notice but again was an indication of the resourcefulness bred in the Chinese actor.

From acting we passed to a music class, where a stage orchestra in the new style was being conducted by a teacher. It was very different from the traditional theatre ensemble, excluding as it did the *hu-ch'in*, the standby of the old Peking stage. This instrument grouping consisted of *erh-hu*, flute, dulcimer, an ancient harmonic instrument called the *sheng*, small cymbals, and three large new string instruments functioning rather like cellos and bass, together with a drum to make up the combination. It represented a current trend to create a new musical style with an emphasis on Western-style harmony and modulation and to adapt traditional instruments or create new ones to suit that purpose.

Among the purely technical but deeply consequential changes imposed in the early days after 1949 was the removal of the stage musicians from their hallowed place on the open stage — first to a position in the wings, where they could not be seen by the audience, and finally to an orchestra pit in front of the stage in Western style. This marked the triumph of a reform long a bone of contention among those who called for artistic reforms to accord more with Western ideas. They objected to the musicians being on the stage; first, because the volume of sound was distracting for the audience, and second, because they considered the custom was nothing more than a conservative pandering to outmoded traditions. This was well enough in disciplinary intent, but it chose to ignore the innate aesthetic nature of a style of performance in which the musicians, both visually and aurally, were essentially a component of the acting. It was undoubtedly true that before 1949 general discipline and behavior in the traditional theatre had reached a low ebb, even by Chinese standards of let well alone, although the apathy and sloppiness were probably as much a reflection of the rapidly deteriorating national morale as to the careless abuse of old traditions. After 1949 the authorities did excellent work in encouraging better standards of conduct and discipline, from which playgoers benefited. But improving conditions for the audience and the smooth running of performances, vital though these were, was a somewhat different thing from transforming the basic aesthetics of a performing style. The Peking theatre performance, with its emphasis on spatial dimension and disregard for naturalism, was concerned with a pattern of imagery to which the stage music provided an immediacy of relationship. The introduction of an orchestra pit and the curtained, picture-frame stage transformed Chinese theatrical performance into Western-scale spectacle, including the new heavy emphasis on lighting and scenic effect with which the Chinese have since become preoccupied.

I felt the orchestral pit neutralized the former theatrical function of the stage orchestra by making it more incidental in musical purpose. Indeed, at times the playing bore a resemblance to the oriental mood music we once associated with the cinema, since reformers not only removed the orchestra from the stage but altered the nature of the music itself by imposing a Westernized gloss. To do this, traditional instruments had been modified to provide greater volume and sonority and, above all, to attain a Western-emulated harmony. In their modern music as in their theatre, the Chinese seemed handicapped by an inadequate substantive knowledge of Western principles, a too-heavy reliance on Russian-style social realism, and a failure to explore their own traditional forms for new musical needs rather than transforming them for ideological purposes. These at least were my conclusions from what I saw and heard.

Under the new policies of Mao's wife, the theatre musicians

were returned to the stage in the shape of a full-scale, Western-style symphony orchestra followed by an even more curious ensemble with a grand piano accompanying the actors and assisted by four traditional instruments — namely gong, cymbals, time-beating drum with clappers, and the *hu-ch'in*. This change in musical reasoning was justified with the slogan, "Make the past serve the present and foreign things serve China," the results of which scarcely justified to the Western ear the high claims made for it.

Although matters had not advanced to this extreme point when I toured the new theatre school, the embryo-stage musicians were obviously designed to be exponents of the new hybridism. They were even playing from Western-style scores, a far remove from the old-style theatre musicians who knew their repertoire by heart.

After watching a group practicing their combat routines in the shape of violent tumbling and fighting with swords, we ended our classroom tour by listening to a group of girls practicing singing as they acted out a climactic scene — while in an opposite corner, five students sat around an elderly instructor reciting passages of dialogue in repetition. We left the school amid a positive barrage of handclapping and were escorted to the door by the principal, who had arranged for the school's official car to take us back to our hotel. This was much to the relief of Miss Wu, our official China Travel Service escort who was sometimes a little worried by our unorthodox methods of getting around.

We invited her back to lunch with us at our hotel and there learned a little about her own life. She was one of a family of eight, she told us, and had joined the State Travel Service after graduation. Young and still a little inexperienced, she seemed slightly homesick for her home city of Shanghai, or so we sensed. Peking was her first assignment, and she said employees were customarily posted away from their home area. She was paid 50 yüan a month, worth about twenty U.S. dollars. She told us she paid 1 yüan a month for rent at her official hostel. In the canteen there, breakfast cost her 4 fen; lunch and dinner 8–12 fen — 1 yüan being the equivalent of 10 mao or 100 fen. And the rice was better than that at the Hsin Ch'ao Hotel where we were lunching, she added with a smile. Thus was the cost of living for one of her class and occupation in the halcyon days before the Cultural Revolution.

The next morning we had to be off early to attend the special performance at the new T'ien Ch'iao hsi-ch'ang, a theatre outside the Ch'ien Men Gate, for which Mei Lan-fang had sent us tickets. The performance began at 9 A.M. in order to allow theatre people to see for themselves the new play *Fifteen Strings of Cash*, which had created a furor as a model example of an old and forgotten drama revived and adapted for contemporary audiences. The theatre was a new, Western-style auditorium with a curtained proscenium stage and a wide orchestra pit in front. We had two excellent seats, to which we were hustled by a brusquely rude young woman, a kind that seemed not uncommon in the new China, and the curtain went up precisely on time with a silent audience already seated in place. Was this combination of phenomena perhaps due to the presence of bullying woman ushers, I wondered.

The play we were about to see had long disappeared from the knowledge of northern playgoers and we were told had been seen only rarely in its home territory of Soochow. This 1956 revival was a pruned version that had been staged by the Chekiang K'un-ch'u Dramatic Troupe in the original Soochow dialect and created an overnight sensation. Pruned though it was, the play ran for three and three-quarter hours, with two long intervals in the Western manner when the audience went outside to smoke — that being forbidden in the auditorium, another startling but sensible innovation.

For those who did not speak the Soochow dialect, and they were the majority present, the printed text of the dialogue was projected on a screen at the side of the proscenium. It says a great deal for the quality of the acting that the play had achieved success with audiences everywhere although the dialect was unfamiliar. The new version also pleased officialdom because it provided justification of their latest slogan, "Weed out the old and let the new emerge." In point of fact, it was the old emerging rather than the new which gave this play its aura, in particular the performance of a veteran Soochow actor, Wang Ch'uang-sung, who played the villain of the piece nicknamed Lou the Rat. Wang gave one of the most compelling displays of pure acting I have seen anywhere. What worried me was the new trend of introducing realistic scenic elements and stage properties that betrayed the self-sufficiency of the acting and added unnecessary visual distractions. This was a weakness that became increasingly obvious in the new methods which never seemed able to let well alone; in other words, to know what to leave out, a paramount virtue in the old theatre aesthetic.

The play began with a bibulous pork butcher returning home with a borrowed fifteen strings to start up his bankrupt business again. In his cups, he teased his stepdaughter by pretending he had procured the money by selling her as a serving girl to grace the dowry of a bride-to-be. The terrified girl waited until the butcher had fallen into a drunken sleep, then fled the house to take shelter with a distant aunt. Later Lou the Rat, rogue and gambler, passed by and, finding the door ajar and lights still burning, stealthily crept into the butcher's house to see what he could find. Discovering the drunkard fast asleep with the fifteen strings of cash partly visible beneath his pillow, he tried to filch the money but only succeeded in waking his intended victim. A fierce struggle took place; in the heat of the fight, Lou the Rat seized the nearest weapon and felled his opponent with a meat chopper.

Next morning the neighbors discovered the butcher's corpse with his stepdaughter nowhere to be found. Lou the Rat had by then joined the group and set about allaying suspicion by insinuating that the girl had a lover and that the two had killed the pork butcher and decamped with his money. The watch was called out and a search ordered. The girl was discovered traveling along the highway with a merchant's apprentice sent to buy goods in the town where her aunt lived, to which he had offered to guide the runaway. Unfortunately for the apprentice — and by one of those curious coincidences so common to the theatre — his purchase money was found to total exactly fifteen strings of cash. The couple were immediately arrested and thrown into jail. An obtuse circuit judge thereupon sentenced them to death, citing justification as follows:

> The proverb runs, "To catch a thief first take him with his loot.
> To call a woman a deceiver first catch her with her lover."

In desperation, the accused couple appealed to the local Prefect ordered to carry out their sentence. Moved by their passionate pleas, he obtained reluctant permission from the Provincial Governor to conduct his own investigation of the crime. Disguised as a fortuneteller, he tracked down Lou the Rat hiding in a country temple and there extracted a confession. The murderer was brought to trial, and the innocent pair set free with recompense for the wrong done them.

The scene in the temple was a memorable one, with the actor Wang Ch'uang-suns excelling himself in portraying a guilty man passing through a mounting series of emotional crises in which suspicion, wonderment, and relief were in turn subdued by blank terror in being found out. It was consummately done; attention was held throughout by the lucidity and rhythmic balance of Wang's brilliant acting.

Some limitations notwithstanding, I thought the *Fifteen Strings of Cash* justified the praise given it. True, it drew upon the elements of romantic melodrama which were the basis for so many Chinese plays, always open to the charge of literary triteness. But the acting was superbly done, and this was essentially the gist of the matter for Chinese tastes. Although the play was not entirely free from a certain synthetic glitter, due in part to the production methods which prevailed in China, nevertheless I felt that if this play represented the worst excesses of reforms in the traditional theatre, there were good grounds for optimism. Alas, the deluge was still to come.

During one of the intervals in the play, our seat row emptied and suddenly I saw Chang Chün-ch'iu sitting at the far end. Almost simultaneously he glanced in my direction and came straight over to greet us. He was wearing "liberation dress," the high-collared, military-style tunic, trousers, and inevitable cap — but all smartly tailored in dove-grey baratheit cloth. It was interesting to see how the actors retained their dandyism in those days by defying the sloppy conformism of political dress on its own level, as it were.

It was a warm, friendly reunion and Chang promised that he would send around tickets to our hotel for his performance of *Ssu Lang Visits His Mother.* My questions to the principal of the training school were finally answered. This was one of those coincidental meetings that almost seem prearranged. I had intended to try to contact Chang Chün-ch'iu but had little knowledge of his whereabouts or how he stood with the authorities. Very well, it seemed, for his troupe was at that time accounted one of the leading city companies. So there it was, all nicely arranged without my having to do anything but go to the theatre — thanks to the hospitality of Mei Lan-fang and the helpfulness of the Bureau for Cultural Relations and their intermediary the China Travel Service.

The next day a meeting had been arranged for me with T'ien Han, President of the China Union of Dramatists. He was a figurehead of the modern drama movement in China. Playwright, critic, teacher, film script writer, and left wing sympathizer, T'ien Han, like many of his contemporaries, had first studied in Japan. He later was a member of the Creation Society, an influential literary group active until 1929 when it was banned by the Nationalist government. His first plays were published in the Society's journal. He left the Society to teach and then opened his own school, which closed because of financial problems. But out of it grew the South China Society, which became a pioneer force in the early modern theatre movement under T'ien Han's leadership. Through this group he started a "small stage" movement, which was a rudimentary attempt to form a repertory system for students to learn through practice. For a time the group traveled a circuit performing their plays, but the government closed them down for good in 1930. The following year T'ien Han joined the new League of Left Wing Dramatists and became increasingly occupied with revolutionary themes in his writing while also engaging in musical-library work for a prominent film company. When Shanghai was attacked in 1932, the League of Left Wing Dramatists became too vocal in their anti-Japanese propaganda for the Nationalist government's liking and several members were arrested, including T'ien Han. Nevertheless, during the war he held high posts in the Nationalist government's cultural and propaganda affairs departments, one of his functions being to organize touring Peking drama troupes in the northwestern provinces. He also experimented with revising old plays for modern audiences, his best-known adaptation being *The White Snake*. For this he was strongly criticized by many who averred he had done nothing to improve the original. After the war he returned to Shanghai to teach but moved to Hongkong until 1948, when he joined the communists in Manchuria. After 1949 he emerged as a central figure in formulating the new government's cultural policies and held a number of high posts. He also wrote costume plays with historical figures as their heroes. However, in 1966 he fell afoul of the Cultural Revolution and was viciously denounced with all the political rancor of the period.

At the time I met T'ien Han, he was still high in office. We were invited for afternoon tea to his house, a gracious old Peking-style dwelling entered through a courtyard. I naturally looked forward to meeting a man whose name was so prominent in modern Chinese cultural history and had led such a colorful career in the theatre. T'ien Han received us most graciously. He was dressed in a Western-style suit, wore glasses, and had his grey hair short cropped. He looked and sounded like my idea of the typical Chinese "authority" on something or other, as of course he very definitely was. He spoke English and when he relapsed into Chinese it was larded with "che ko, che ko, che ko," a conversational interpolation rather like the "ok, so . . ." which strews the talk of many American intellectuals — or the "don't you know" which provides a recurrent pause in the discussions of British university types. We talked at some length about the play *Fifteen Strings of Cash* — at least T'ien Han did, for like many "authorities," I believe, he was accustomed to the sound of his own voice. He explained that *Shih Wu T'iao*, the older version of the play, had too complicated a story and used too many archaic expressions for a modern audience. Therefore, a new company like the Chekiang troupe had to compromise between the old and new, resulting in only half a *k'un-ch'ü* play in the true sense. I spoke about the acting and said I still thought modern Chinese theatre had a great deal to learn from an actor like Wan Ch'uang-sung. He agreed with that but launched into a long explanation of the ideals of the modern Chinese theatre in relation to building the new socialist society. It sounded rather like the official handouts until he got on to the theme of theatre education and the better production of Western-style drama, subjects upon which he spoke out of a long experience and where perhaps his greatest contributions had been made in the past. Our conversation was interrupted by Mrs. Han bringing in tea, cakes, and fruit, over which old photograph albums of traditional performances and performers were brought out and studied during our tea. There were dozens of pictures; with typical Chinese hospitality, a number of them were offered to me to keep and take away. I have them still, the only evidence of an interesting encounter with an extrovert personality who held the stage for more than fifty years as a pioneer in China's emerging new culture.

The day after the visit to T'ien Han, I had an early morning caller in the person of one of Chang Chün-ch'iu's stagehands bringing our tickets for the performance that evening and an invitation to lunch with the actor and his wife. The wheel had come full circle, for it was the same messenger who used to bring my tickets across the harbor in Hongkong for the Saturday afternoon performance at the P'u Ch'ing theatre each week. We chatted and I asked how he liked his new environment. He was enthusiastic, saying they were immeasurably better off than in Hongkong where they had lived from hand-to-mouth. He promised to come for me after the performance to take me backstage.

We could not accept Chang Chün-ch'iu's lunch invitation, as it turned out, because I had just been informed that I had an appointment at the Peking Film Studios at 1:30 P.M. with Ch'eng Yen-ch'iu, the Peking actor who was being filmed in one of the plays he had made famous, *Huang-shan lei, Tears in the Wilderness.* Ch'eng was one of the "big four" female impersonators, in his heyday rivalling Mei Lan-fang in popularity.

Ch'eng's great contribution in the eyes of the theatre fans was a very individual style of singing characterized by a soft, undulating, haunting quality that was greatly admired, particularly by women theatregoers — among whom he had an ardent following. His most successful plays were written especially for him, and his acting in these was noted for his distinctive and delicately expressive use of the water sleeves. In 1932 Ch'eng visited Europe to study Western theatre and opera as a prelude to his becoming head of the co-educational Chinese Theatre Training Academy. The school was compelled to close in 1937 with the outbreak of the Sino-Japanese War, and Ch'eng himself was prevented from taking his troupe to Paris where he had been invited to perform. In 1942 he sold all his theatrical costumes and refused to perform on the stage, supporting himself by farming. He returned to the theatre after the war but made relatively few appearances. When the communists came to power, he was encouraged to take an active part in affairs again and was kept very busy with teaching a younger generation until his death in 1968. Ch'eng Yen-ch'iu had also been a great friend of John Grose in Hongkong, from whom I was carrying a letter for the actor.

It was a long and dusty pedicab drive to the film studios. Our conscientious Miss Wu, slightly flustered at being unfamiliar with the district, doubtless wondered what new theatrical pranks

I was leading her into this time. We arrived at the wrong gate and had to be redirected by a group of loafing pedicab drivers whose broad Peking dialect sounded as though their mouths were full of toffee. However, we finally discovered the entrance where we were expected and led through some barrackslike buildings, past a large bronze statuary group of generously muscled workers, and into the by now too-familiar reception room with plush chairs and Mao's larger-than-life portrait on the wall. A young member of the office staff came in and chatted with us; tea was brought with fruit and, of all things, plates of liqueur chocolates. Finally we were led down to the studio where shooting was to begin. *Tears in the Wilderness* had been one of Ch'eng's popular stage plays, and the film was being made as a record of his theatrical art under the direction of Wu Tsu-kuang, the writer and dramatic critic. I found myself sitting next to Hou Hsi-jui, once one of the most famous painted face actors in the Peking theatre but by then retired from the stage, a toothless old man chainsmoking cigarettes down to the stub end. He had been asked to take part in the film, he told me. It was his first one and he seemed a little anxious about it. His normal speaking manner held that hoarseness common with retired actors after the years of heavy strain put upon the vocal chords. At times his voice seemed almost a croaky whisper, but when he was finally called out to take the stage, his speech became a tornado of sound—thus did the old actor retain his powers. They were doing a retake which involved Ch'eng Yen-ch'iu rushing on stage, flinging himself down on one knee, throwing his right arm above his head with the long water sleeve hanging free, and then sustaining a gentle quivering motion with both sleeves. It was a very typical stage posture symbolizing great agitation of the mind and an extremely graceful example of choreographic form when performed by the master actor. However, I was a little taken aback by the size of Ch'eng Yen-ch'iu, whom I had never seen previously. He was a tall man, nearly six feet like many of pure Manchu descent, which he was, although according to the records he had always been a most elegant performer. I had been told he had grown very stout in middle age, an unfortunate handicap for one playing the fragile matron and daughters of the Peking repertoire; despite this, I had not been prepared for the reality. Ch'eng seemed at that moment of entry enormous; it was not so much a question of fat as girth—

he was so broad — and that combined with his natural height created a bulk that at first was most visually distracting. He was still extraordinarily light and graceful in his movements, and his voice remained sweet and true, but he was obviously long past his zenith as a stage performer. It says a great deal about the old aesthetic standards of the Chinese that they were prepared to make a film about a great actor in decline in order to record the essence of the acting process itself, while overlooking a physical deficiency to which no Western mind could have remained indifferent in an equivalent situation.

They shot the scene twice, and then Ch'eng Yen-ch'iu came out in everyday dress. We were introduced and a photograph was taken of us together before we returned to the reception room accompanied by the director Wu Tsu-kuang. I handed Ch'eng the letter I was carrying from John Grose, and after reading it he remarked with the same wistful note I had sensed in Mei Lan-fang's voice that it was thirty years since he and John had seen each other. That was a long time indeed, in terms of the changes that had taken place and the frustrations Ch'eng himself had suffered in his professional life. He had a soft, almost inaudible voice in ordinary conversation and the looks of the *bon viveur* he was, according to what others had told me, being endowed with what Chinese call "the capacity of the ocean," *hai liang.* He asked questions about John and we talked about filming. Wu Tsu-kuang said it was a policy to make some film records of the older stage artists and that to be able to do one of Ch'eng Yen-ch'iu was a rare opportunity — although the actor himself seemed to find it something of a strain, which was hardly surprising. Like Mei, he remarked that "they had wanted it," which presumably meant that pressures were put upon the actors. I never saw a copy of the film nor do I know if one exists, but presumably no others were made of Ch'eng, since he died two years later. He seemed a friendly, good-natured personality and a man of integrity. He was very apologetic for not being able to entertain us in proper fashion as friends of an old friend, because his time was so pressured with the daily film making. We promised to take his special greetings to John, to whom he wrote a letter concerning our visit. The studio sent us back in the official car accompanied by Ch'eng, whom we dropped off at the narrow Peking *hu-t'ung,* or "lane," where his residence lay. There we said a final goodbye to one who

seemed a lonely figure from a vanished world of theatre. His untimely death preceded that of Mei Lan-fang by three years, but at
least he was spared the worst excesses thrust upon his artistic
contemporaries during the Cultural Revolution. The traditional
theatre came under particularly heavy criticism, and many of the
most celebrated performers were vilified in the press for their
"feudalistic" attitudes. Mao's wife, a former actress who never
made the grade, is said to have vented her personal spite on the
traditional theatre when she gained political power. Be that as it
may, the older actors fell upon hard times as a result of her cultural policies.

That evening we went on to see Chang Chün-ch'iu's troupe
perform *Ssu Lang Visits His Mother*, the first revival it was said
since the "liberation." The theatre, the Yin Lo T'ang situated in the
Chung Shan Park, was a large open-air structure covered by a
roof supported on pillars and seating more than two thousand
people. The stage had a rectangular, curtained proscenium with
an orchestra pit below it. The house was filled to capacity; the
audience, perhaps not surprisingly, looked much like the old-
style gatherings with plenty of greybeards and grandmas among
the crowd, all chatting, smoking, and nibbling their dried melon
seeds.

There were three layers of stage curtains — grey, dark green,
and pale blue — used for the scene changes, and the old property
man of former times was no longer in evidence. If a chair had to
be moved in the course of performance, it was done by one of the
supernumerary players, *lung-t'ao*, who represented attendants,
soldiers, and so on. Their pacing had been sharpened from the
old days and they wore new costumes, as did the cast in general;
there appeared to be a tendency to simplify patterns and use bold
single colors. There was a concession to the new realism in the
scene where Ssu Lang returned from his midnight visit; painted
scenery was used to represent the city gate instead of the old
blue-and-white brick patterned curtain suspended on two bamboo poles. A rather more trite example of this kind of thing was
seen in the short piece *Shuang Li K'uei, The Two Li K'uei*, which
preceded the main play.

Li K'uei was a character from the cycle of plays based on the
novel *Tales from the Marshes*, and the role was one for a painted
face actor whose bravura style was far removed from any sug-

gestion of realism. Yet the property chair that in the past had always been considered a symbol for a mountain now had a small scenic representation of a mountain propped in front of it. It was this kind of thing that I found so unnecessary. The business of the theatre is with the image of reality and not with reality itself, and this was certainly a precept which the Chinese have always honored in their theatre. Drinking too deeply at the Russian well has led that precept astray. In their concern for new levels of competence in using the Western proscenium-style stage and technical gadgetry, I feel the Chinese have begun to mistake sterile realism for valid new expression and by doing so are in danger of losing their own theatrical integrity in the process. They will have to find their way back.

Apart from details like those mentioned, my general impression of the *Ssu Lang* performance was that the content of the play remained more or less the same. The pace and timing were brisked up a little, since the orchestra of course sat in the pit below the front stage. The audience seemed to accept the play in a light-hearted spirit and the actors too; it obviously went over well as performed by the Third Municipal Peking Drama Troupe with Chang Chün-ch'iu in the role of the Princess.

True to his word, Chang's assistant came to take me backstage after the show. Chang Chün-ch'iu greeted us through his make-up and while he removed it asked about people in Hongkong, including Wang Te-k'un, his former troupe member who by then was having a hard time economically. He asked me to convey to Wang an offer to help the latter get back to China. Chang Chün-ch'iu had changed not at all and seemed to be firmly established as the leader of Peking's premier municipal troupes. All present spoke of the improved conditions they now worked under, and the backstage area in which we talked bore no comparison with the muddle they had been faced with in Hongkong. There the whole company had shared one large untidy room, with only makeshift screens to partition off dressing areas. Whatever questions remained in one's mind, there had obviously been a tremendous drive to improve production conditions for the better welfare of the actors and stage personnel. In this, I supposed men like T'ien Han and his colleagues had been able to help. There was every indication that common sense had prevailed and a true concern existed for practical working conditions in the arts at last.

Before we said goodnight to them all, Chang Chün-ch'iu asked us to lunch with him the next day. I left the theatre gratified at the genuine warmth which had persisted from the Hongkong days. As we drove back to the hotel, our two pedicab drivers pedaled abreast of each other, their shaven polls glistening in the bright moonlight as they chatted away about *Ssu Lang Visits His Mother* and whether it had come to stay, passing from that to the private lives of actors, including Chang Chün-ch'iu himself, upon which they seemed authorities. After all, the old Peking pedicab drivers spent a great deal of time around the theatres; few could be better qualified as the peripatetic bearers of backstage titbits catering to that universal human pastime, gossip. As to the pedicab drivers' surmises about *Ssu Lang Visits His Mother*, the records show that after its revival the play was performed at intervals, the last time in Peking as far as I know being August, 1962. In June, 1957, just a little more than a year after that opening performance we saw, a special meeting of the Actors Union was convened in Shanghai for a discussion, "Why do audiences like this play?" Apparently they discovered that audiences did like it, which would not have surprised our Peking pedicab drivers. As a result of the deliberations, a new script of the piece was issued in November, 1957, in an edition of forty thousand copies. It was interesting from two points of view: first, it showed the variations that can exist in a single play through the interpretations of different actors; and second, it provided changes considered necessary by the committee printed as footnotes to the original text, which remained unchanged. The general form of the play was the same, except that the original thirteen scenes had been broken down into six, a concession to the new method of staging with the use of curtains. The alterations were largely stylistic in providing what the committee considered better sounds for singing, smoother enunciation, and such technical improvements. Therefore, in theory the text would have differed from a "standard" 1938 version, the one used by the old actor T'an Hsin-p'ei who first made the play famous. But since there were at least two other scripts in use before 1949 which also varied in the ways discussed here, it could be interpreted that the 1957 version, in spite of the proposed alterations and minor changes, was in fact just another variation of a hallowed process. The audiences liked the play.

But the actors were not going to be allowed to get away with that, authorities decided. In 1963 my former Chinese teacher, T'ien Shu-hsiu, sent me a translation of an article she had read in a Peking newspaper entitled "On the Origin of *Ssu Lang Visits His Mother.*" It was a sarcastic attack, in which the writer enumerated the supposed artistic and dramatic qualities of the play before contemptuously rejecting them on ideological grounds. "Many good-hearted comrades," he concluded, "are reluctant to give up *Ssu Lang Visits His Mother.* They consider it a piece of art which has attained perfection. They favor rearranging the play . . . the play simply does not have a basic ideology which justifies re-arrangement." All in all, the article showed scant sympathy for the play's obvious popularity and only seemed intended to destroy that which had resisted its detractors until then.

The day after the *Ssu Lang* performance, we lunched with Chang Chün-ch'iu at a restaurant called Hung-pin lou in Li T'ieh-kuai Street, known as the site of Mei Lan-fang's birthplace. Chang's assistant was waiting to greet us at the door of the restaurant, where he paid off our pedicabs and escorted us inside. The restaurant had formerly been an old Peking-style mansion. We were led through several courtyards to the private dining room, where we were received by Chang and his wife, whom we had met before in Hongkong. We sat and drank tea first; Chang Chün-ch'iu told me he had also invited Ma Tse-tsang, the talented Hongkong Cantonese actor, but other engagements had prevented his acceptance. Ma was at that time in China with his former wife Hung Hsien-nu, an equally gifted Cantonese actress. The two were there at the invitation of the authorities to discuss reforms of the debased Cantonese theatre. As events turned out, we were to meet them both in Shanghai later.

It was a relaxed and most enjoyable lunch party in the quiet ambience of that old Peking house. They asked about my work in theatre and future plans; Chang said that the next time we came back, he would ask us to stay in his home, where I could work as I wished — a golden invitation but far beyond the dreams of realization in the light of future events. For lunch we drank Chinese-made, Western-style wine and Chinese brewed beer, both of which were very popular in new China at that time, as we had observed in the railway dining cars. The "four dishes," the equivalent of our hors d'oeuvres, served with the luncheon also seemed somewhat Westernized.

We said our goodbyes in that atmosphere of well-being and affinity with one's fellowmen that Chinese hospitality so cunningly induces and set off in two pedicabs bound for a shop near the Ch'ien Men, since I wanted to buy some authentic swords for *t'ai chi* practice. I had inquired at lunchtime about possibilities, and our pedicab drivers had been directed where to go. The shop was in an old-fashioned quarter of the town where foreigners presumably no longer ventured, for as we got down from our pedicabs to enter the place, we were immediately surrounded by a swarm of small children who gathered around with whispered exclamations and penetrating stares. These reached proportionate intensity with the swelling of their ranks. The dark interior of the shop was crowded with knives, axes, swords, and domestic hardware of every kind; as the polite shopkeeper brought out several blades for my inspection, the mass of curious little faces at the door fanned out and broke from the pressure of more and more children pushing from behind to gaze their fill also. Soon there seemed to be as many children in the shop as there were outside, until the exasperated shopkeeper turned and, with a magnificent gesture that appeared to enfold a score of the grinning urchins within the span of his arms, swept them to the door with the gentle admonition, "Small comrades, you had better leave." With that I hurriedly paid for my swords, and we made for our pedicabs before the tide of curiosity was on the rise again.

The next theatrical event on my engagement list was of a rather different kind, a performance of a new play by Ts'ao Yü, a writer who before the war had been regarded as China's brightest hope for the future of a modern-style theatre that was socially concerned and objectively presented.

Ts'ao Yü studied Western literature and drama at Peking University. He made his youthful reputation with a play called *Thunderstorm*, which was published in a literary quarterly in 1934 and staged by a Shanghai university dramatic club in 1935. It had its first impact on a wider public when it was put on by the China Travelling Dramatic Troupe in 1936 and became an overnight success. T'ang, the leader and founder of this troupe, was an actor who had been to Europe and felt that if a modern theatre was going to compete with the old-style theatre on a box office level, there would have to be a new approach to performance. He gathered a number of dedicated people around him, and they worked on a cooperative basis whereby members received no pay but were provided with basic board and lodging. If a production sold out, every member received a maximum bonus of one dollar. If a play incurred a loss, they received nothing. Any profits were plowed back to buy costumes and better technical equipment. The members of the company were united by a common dedication, and this early repertory system provided training for several promising stage artists, including Pai Yang, who later left her successful theatre career to become one of China's best-known film stars. It was she who played in *Thunderstorm*, which became a record-breaking performance. The China Travelling Dramatic Troupe ceased its activities with the outbreak of war in 1937, but during its day it was probably one of the more productive theatrical experiments of its period. Dedicated to putting good modern theatre on a self-supporting basis, it was marked by a professional approach relatively free of intellectual preciousness or political prejudice. It was the first attempt to create a repertory theatre that would become part of the nation's cultural life, with no strings attached beyond insistence on good professional standards of acting.

Without this invigorating force, Ts'ao Yü might have remained a playwright of the printed page. His *Thunderstorm* was a long, four-act play with a prologue and epilogue. The action took place within twenty-four hours and was theatrically emphasized by the physical menace of a gathering storm. The theme concerned the revelation of a complex pattern of adultery within a wealthy industrialist's family, whose spiritual destruction was used as a symbol for the disintegration of the old middle-class society. By Western standards the play was far too long and drew upon theatrical devices that were, to say the least, a little shopsoiled. However, Ts'ao Yü had a sense of tragedy and, derivative though he was, portrayed characters whose psychological motives were credible to Chinese audiences — while his absorption of Western methods was marked by a degree of dramatic understanding lacking in his predecessors. His failing, a common one in modern Chinese theatre, was to be discursive at the expense of the continuity of stage action. Nothing he wrote after *Thunderstorm* made the same public impact; his major work was produced within six years, and the war years were unproductive for him. He visited the United States in 1946, but this had no particular effect on his still fallow writing. In 1949 he was among the majority of prominent figures in the arts and literature who supported the new government's cultural policies. He was given certain administrative posts but remained silent until 1956, when his new play *Bright Skies* was given its premiere. It turned out to be a dull exercise in anti-American propaganda, a lampoon of the old Peking Union Medical College purporting to show the ruthless and criminal methods of the American medical administration. It also portrayed attempts of the Communist Party to reeducate the Chinese medical staff, who were at first resistant but eventually responsive when the "Resist America, Aid Korea" struggle began. Central to the theme was the fact that the former American dean of the college had murdered a Chinese worker's wife to get her bones as pathological specimens. The play was staged in the Peking People's Art Theatre, which was miles from our hotel. Unfortunately, the desk receptionist misdirected our pedicab drivers, who made the most valiant efforts to get us there on time when they discovered the error — it being a new theatre with which they were not familiar. We arrived there at 7:40; the play started at 7:30 and finished at 11:00, so we had plenty of time to catch up with developments. The ushers let us in without demur, provided we sat at the back until the first interval, but I noticed all the way through the performance people were creeping in late. I suspected business was not too brisk, since discipline was relaxed in this way and I was not surprised, for it was a tedious play to sit through. I felt less guilty at my boredom when I noticed several people around me nodding off. It was a curiously mixed audience that included some of what I imagine were the "bright young set," if such a term could be applied. A young man in a smart tweed jacket sat with his arm around his girl companion in the row in front, where there was also a young fellow wearing a particularly sporty version of the ubiquitous cap.

The play itself was heavily realistic both in sets and costume, which showed an unmistakeable Russian influence; the plot as a whole was long-winded and marked by bathos and lack of dramatic tension, with such maudlin tableaux as two young pioneers amusing the sick, including the blind hero of all heroes from the Korean War. The acting was forced and unnatural when it attempted to depict foreign manners, and the diction was very poor — the actors dropped their voices or talked away from the audience so that it was often impossible to hear them. It was a curious thing that although in their traditional theatre the Chinese paid such attention to voice training and vocal projection, they gave these little attention in their modern theatre. It was a dull, disappointing evening that to my mind shattered any lingering hopes of the creative regeneration of a playwright once considered so promising by the Chinese.

Ts'ao Yü had become head of the Central Drama Institute, one among several of the new institutions I visited during my stay. It was established in 1950 through a merger of the drama school of the communist North China University and the old Academy of Dramatic Art at Nanking. At its inception students were given a year's basic training, at the end of which half of them were posted to an itinerant propaganda drama corps, the other half being retained for further advanced training. The second group after graduation were then posted to the propaganda organization as superintending cadres. Matters seemed rather flexible, for at the end of 1952 over a hundred students were graduated prior to completing their full course of study, presumably in answer to political needs. A special course for training directors was set up in 1954 with some thirty members from regional propaganda drama corps enrolled for training.

When I visited the institute, I was told the prime function of the school was to train actors, directors, and designers for modern theatre. They ran a four-year course for actors and another for designers, while the directing course was said to be five years — although whether this was a theoretical statement or not I was not quite clear, since the first directing course was given for one and a half years. According to the syllabus as it was explained to me, the actor trainees studied dramatic theory and dialogue — by which they meant voice, I presumed — as well as literature, foreign languages, music, Chinese traditional drama, and Marxist-Leninism. It sounded an ambitious program to me, which somehow did not seem to be borne out by the work I saw going on during an admittedly brief visit. They told me two hundred students were enrolled and much of the teaching was being done by Russian instructors who did a three-year tour before returning to their own country to be replaced by new people.

197

Sure enough, in the first rehearsal room I visited, a Soviet teacher was making notes on his Russian script as he watched the students perform a modern play called *Her Friends*. It sounded a highly polemical piece, and the participants appeared ill-at-ease in the roles. Their movements were stiff and forced, and their diction even in the classroom was often inaudible; they dropped their voices the whole time. In short, there was little sense of real theatre in what they did.

In the next room another group of students, again with a Russian instructor, were rehearsing a scene from *Fifteen Strings of Cash*, adapted as a modern costume piece. Here the difference clearly showed; the play was something they instinctively understood and their indigenous sense of mime and gesture came through. It was alive and less forced, more natural than the other; the actors were being Chinese. From the rehearsal rooms I visited two design classes, a first-year group drawing from plaster casts and a more advanced one drawing from a live model. They were ranged in a semi-circle at their easels around the plaster cast or the model; as one went around each group, there was the curious sense of looking at the same drawing only in slightly different perspective imposed by the student's viewpoint, so identical was the style of execution and standard of accomplishment. Their drawings were highly photographic, done in black lead pencil with all the highlights stippled in. They might have been the product of any Western art school at the turn of the century. There was not the slightest indication of even a glance at their own splendid traditions of draftsmanship, with its vibrant line and sense of movement. So too with the rooms of costume designs after Bakst and the model stage sets, which evidenced the most niggling kinds of realism. They were dull, orthodox, and conforming to the most plebian standards and color sense with not a glimpse of a Chinese imagination breaking in anywhere.

I ended my tour in the "experimental" theatre of the institute, where a directing student was lecturing his class on Stanislavsky prior to rehearsing some scenes with his actors. The exercise seemed to be largely discursive, and of the acting I saw none. I left feeling disappointed. It had only been a short visit, too short to make sweeping generalizations, I suppose. Had it been possible to spend several weeks in observation, doubtless some gold among the dross would have been revealed in the shape of discernible talent, although no amount of observation could have dispelled the sterility imposed by political conformism which imbued everything that was going on.

I wished I could have described to them a true incident told to me by a friend in our embassy. I would have said, "Look, here is a true example of socialist realism. Go away and act a play based on this theme." It concerned a foreign husband and a Chinese wife with a daughter whom they both adored, although they themselves did not get on very well and lived apart. The advent of a communist regime reconciled them because of their child, and they applied for exit permits to leave China. In the meantime the young communists had exerted their influence on the child, who finally denounced both her parents and said she did not want to leave. But the authorities compelled the parents to leave on the grounds that they had asked to go and would not allow the girl to leave because she wanted to stay; the parents lost their daughter and gained an incompatible exile.

The friend who told me that story was also responsible for our meeting with a young Chinese couple who provided an insight into a different kind of human situation, one that nevertheless touched upon the complexities and tensions below the surface of peoples' lives in the ferment of the new China. Embassy people had become quite restricted in their contacts with ordinary Chinese people outside the internal activities of a diplomatic body that was only granted recognition as a "mission."

In this particular case the personal contact had been deliberately sought by a young man with a cultivated background who rejected the political control of people's personal relationships and sought an intellectual lifeline to the world of foreign culture and social intercourse. Looking back on the phenomenon now, it seems hardly possible that he was not eventually denounced and made to suffer for his temerity but we never heard what became of him, since the lines of communication later became broken. And it would have been foolhardy to have mentioned such a subject in writing, even had there been someone to ask.

We met the young couple in question at a dinner our embassy friends arranged in a small, obscure restaurant near Ch'ien Men, reached by a rickety flight of steep steps leading to a ramshackle room with whitewashed walls. There we ate a rough-and-ready but excellently cooked meal of sour sweet pork, chicken, and prawns with yellow rice and drank wine served in large cups. We had the place to ourselves. The young couple were well dressed, the wife in a smart *ch'i p'ao*, the traditional tight-fitting Chinese woman's gown that as an accepted form of everyday dress was in process of disappearing from the social scene completely. The husband was a modern actor who, as it turned out, had been in the cast of the Ts'ao Yü play we had seen. He came of a good literary family apparently, and both he and his wife spoke excellent English. He was a graduate of Pei Ta University and had studied under the poet William Empson, he told us. He added that he had taken up acting as his war job when the Korean conflict had broken out and people like himself could offer themselves for propaganda recruitment. He described how recruits had been given several months training by rehearsing a single play only. This included everyone being compelled to study social conditions and undergo actual experiences in relation to the piece, as well as doing hours of political research to understand the background and times to which it related, the period of the Korean War. In answer to my question, he agreed that all this was done at the expense of any intensive training in the craft of acting. He also explained that the company to which he was posted performed mostly in the Peking area but that a second company was attached to the army and therefore toured a great deal. His own company staged four or five plays a year; business was not very brisk at that juncture, he added, confirming what I had suspected at the performance of *Bright Skies.* The decline in box office receipts he attributed to the fact that workers' unions were no longer buying blocks of tickets outright for giving away to their members. This he considered could be a good thing for the theatre because when people have to pay for tickets, they dislike being preached at. It was a brief but revealing encounter. If the young couple did not talk a great deal at the dinner table, they remained perfectly natural and there was nothing furtive about their responses. Certainly they could hardly be called a typical example of "the people," but they represented the tip of an intellectual iceberg that caused Mao eventually to launch his most destructive campaign against artists and intellectuals who revealed themselves as "enemies of the people" by their inability to conform intellectually and artistically with the Party line. The people: how empty the word began to sound in China. I wondered where any man

200

obtains the prerogative to be their sole arbiter and the censor of all the rest.

Our funds were getting low, and it was time to move on to Shanghai. We did not try to say any goodbyes because we realized people would be too busy, a euphemism used by everybody in a new way. It was not merely because people worked long hours — they certainly did that — but those we met seemed preoccupied within themselves. Younger people particularly gave the impression of being scarcely aware of a world outside Peking and certainly not beyond China, while an older generation — and this applied particularly to former university acquaintances we saw — made it clear by their evasiveness that they did not wish to hear about such things anyway.

"People here are too busy to write letters," one Chinese acquaintance told me. I had complained that since 1950 we had stopped writing letters to China as a futile exercise, since they were consistently ignored. The obvious conclusion was that people did not write because they were afraid or forbidden to do so, and one did not want to embarrass them. Being too busy seemed an inadequate explanation, but it was constantly advanced. No, said another friend, people did not write because they were frightened or forbidden but because there were too many things to explain about the new China. As time passed these became more numerous, and so one never wrote. It was a new angle and plausible to a point. Certainly it was not easy to explain a social upheaval of such magnitude to those far removed from it. There were too many pressures on everyone involved in such a gigantic eruption. Yet this scarcely altered the fact that it would have been satisfying to know one's friends were still there to do any explaining. Human nature is frail and needs assurance, even when revolutions are afoot.

The express for Shanghai left Peking at 5 P.M. This time the inevitable had happened, and we found we were sharing our compartment with two Russian travelers, although they were very different from the general run of their countrymen we had encountered so far. The elder of them, with his imperial beard, meerschaum pipe, and poplin summer suit, looked like a character straight out of Chekhov, while in contrast his companion was burly with close-cropped hair. They seemed a little nonplused at first, but we eventually settled down to each other's presence.

The two Russians seemed to be technical specialists, judging by the diagrams they later pored over, and were accompanied by Russian-speaking interpreters, a couple of girls who were in a compartment further down the coach and appeared occasionally to chat with their guests. Both girls were young, with the inevitable twin-plaited pigtails; one wore slacks, shirt, and heavy boots, the other a printed cotton dress, striped ankle socks, and clumsy shoes. They giggled a good deal but resolutely refused to acknowledge our presence by so much as a nod, a question, or a smile for the whole of the journey. Since both Russians and Chinese obviously did not understand English, we knew no Russian, and the interpreters ignored our Chinese, it was a rather curious journey. We were obviously an enigma to everybody; at one point we overheard the two interpreters chatting among themselves as to what we could possibly be in a world of Soviet hegemony. Finally with obvious relief at finding an acceptable solution to the threat we offered comradely conformity, they designated us East Germans.

The two Russians were in fact punctiliously courteous to my wife as far as they could be with our lack of communication. Doubtless had we continued further with them, the ice which was just beginning to thaw would have melted further, in spite of the priggish pair of young Marxists who were their interpreters. We were breaking our journey at Nanking for two days to catch a glimpse of our former haunts and look up any old acquaintances who might still be there. The train arrived in mid-morning at Pukow on the northern bank of the Yangtze, the southern terminus of the old Tientsiu-Pukow railway, and there our coaches were shunted in three portions onto a train ferry which took us to Nanking on the opposite side. As we crossed the vast sweep of the Yangtze, its shining surface looked more like a great sheet of yellow linoleum than water, so dense was its silted flow. And in the distance across the river was glimpsed the silhouette of the Purple Mountain. We detrained at the Nanking station with our luggage, and the last we saw of our Russians was the pair of them strolling up and down the platform sucking ice cream lollipops as they gave us almost affable nods of farewell.

For once the Travel Service seemed to have broken down; there was no one to meet us. We went to the stationmaster's office. After much telephoning, he conjured up a young woman who professed to know nothing about anything and directed us to a small station wagon through a staring crowd that gazed and gazed again at what they apparently thought were two apparitions from another world. As we drove off through the streets, it was like stepping back into yesterday, so familiar was the setting — including the blue cotton-clad "Nanching lobos" crossing the road with their polished redwood nightsoil buckets gripped in one hand. We had been booked a room in what was formerly the Nanking International Club, now a guest house. Although the reception desk seemed not to expect us, we were given an exceedingly comfortable room overlooking the hotel grounds, where bands of yellow-robed Buddhist priests were wandering around — a special delegation from Tibet, we were told. This was three years before the Chinese invaded that country.

Then two young men from the China Travel Service appeared to greet us whom we eventually nicknamed Box and Cox. At first they told us the letter from Peking announcing our visit had not arrived, which accounted for the muddle. This was later changed to claiming the letter had arrived but said we were due in Nanking a day later. We deemed it better not to query these discrepancies for the sake of the honor of the Travel Service and our own peace of mind. Our guides then informed us that none of the people we had asked to see were in Nanking anymore except Wu Yi-fang, the former president of Ginling Women's College, who had invited us to have tea with her at 4:30 next day. Otherwise we were free to go our ways. Nevertheless, it took a little time to convince them that we should not require their services aside from our travel arrangements. It seemed hard for the pair to believe that we were capable of surviving alone in a city we had known long before they did, judging by their accents, which were certainly not local. However, we finally managed to convince them that we were well able to get on a bus by ourselves, eat Chinese food, and in general did not need them to hold our hands.

Since all our old acquaintances had gone, we confined ourselves to looking around Nanking, which as far as one could see had not changed at all. It was like awakening from sleep and saying, "Oh I dreamed we had left Nanking." True, the streets and lanes were cleaner and free from garbage, the new public buses bearing the Skoda trademark were more efficient and comfortable than the rattletraps of the past — but the pedicabs were still there, like their Peking counterparts in the last stages of disintegration; even the *ma-ch'e*, the sorry horse-drawn victorias, remained on the streets. Above it all the Purple Mountain loomed from its dozen different viewpoints across the crazy architectural conglomeration we had always perceived as Nanking.

After dinner on that first evening, we took a bus down to Hsin Chieh K'ou, the city's center where Sun Yat-sen continued to look down from his pedestal in frock-coated isolation, although the pedestal had become an ornate, canopied structure now dwarfing the figure of the patriot himself. There was a new National Department Store on the corner, but little else was different. We strolled along to our old offices and there was the familiar frontage; they had not even bothered to paint out the faded Chinese characters for The British Council for Cultural Relations. Ying-kuo wen-hua wei-yuan hui remained painted across the top of the main windows, a ghostly reminder to set the thoughts wandering down a dozen different byways. The next morning we took pedicabs and explored familiar streets, including Hunan-lu where we had once lived. Our former residence was still reached by the same narrow lane and past the same smelly ditch, but the garden was an overgrown wilderness with sprouting weeds two feet high, and the house itself crumbling to decay. This was fit testimony to the orgy of postwar jerrybuilding in the Nationalist capital but a melancholy reminder all the same. That afternoon we kept our appointment with Wu Yi-fang, being graciously received by her in her home and served afternoon tea in English style. Wu Yi-fang was one of the most distinguished figures in the Chinese educational field, whom we had known well in the past as president of the famous Ginling Women's College, where she had ruled since 1928, the first woman to hold such a presidency in China. At the time of our meeting, she was commissioner of education for Kiangsu Province.

Wu Yi-fang was the daughter of a Ch'ing dynasty official and had a long and distinguished educational background both in China and the United States. She became converted to Christianity in 1918 and thereafter took a leading part in Christian affairs throughout China as well as serving the government in advisory ways. She was the only woman in the Chinese delegation to the United Nations at San Francisco in 1945.

Wu Yi-fang was a most capable administrator, a woman of great determination and strength of character who constantly fought on behalf of Chinese women and their place in the professional world. She headed the Citizens' Protection Committee when the communists entered Nanking and insisted on remaining there in spite of many who urged her to leave China at the time.

When we met her again, she seemed not to have changed at all and was still the same dignified, precise, and rather contained personality. She was the only one of our former academic acquaintances we met on that visit who spoke quite freely of her former friends and colleagues, asked questions about the outside world, and expressed interest in what we ourselves were doing. She spoke very highly of the new educational methods and said the greatest difficulty was the lack of students to take up teaching, causing a shortage in the profession. Her former responsibility, Ginling College, had become merged as the Normal College of what had become the new University of Nanking. It was a rational encounter and a cordial one. Whether beneath that calm and slightly severe personality there were hidden doubts was impossible to say. For a brief and fleeting moment during our conversation, I had the sense of someone who had gone through a difficult period and been allowed to make her peace with the regime, but I may have been wrong. One had become attuned in those days to searching every nuance of expression in the attempt to see beneath the constant assertions that on occasion smacked of political hagiolatry, and at times it was possible to read too much into Chinese behavior as a result.

After saying goodbye to Wu Yi-fang, I ordered our pedicabs to drive down to Fu Tzu-miao — to see in a spirit of nostalgia what had become of the old theatre quarter where I spent so much time in the past. We arrived at the narrow, cobbled entry to the quarter without mishap, only to be surrounded immediately by a mob of excited children materializing, it appeared, out of thin air. Our drivers were brought to a complete stop by sheer weight of numbers as we were surrounded on every side by the swelling ranks of happily grinning girls and boys, large and small, clapping their hands in time to a steady chant of *su-lien jen, su-lien jen,* "Soviet people!" The blockade was complete; the numbers grew and grew until any attempt at moving forward was out of the question. Time was passing, our drivers decided to beat a retreat, and we turned for home with the cries and handclapping growing fainter in the distance. It was perhaps as good a symbol as any of a new age.

On our last day in Nanking, we had our obliging hotel waiter make us a picnic lunch and took it out to the Lotus Lake. There we found the boats were hired by the hour at a fixed rate. The boatwomen had become quiet people who took their turn by rota, instead of the shouting harpies who had once pushed and bargained to fix the highest price and the ultra highest if you were a foreigner. Such were the minutiae of social discipline which impressed one in the new China.

We climbed aboard our canopied barge and were poled slowly away from the shore. The quiet air was at first disturbed by the harsh din of recorded popular music mingled with the raucous tones of an announcer from some kind of pleasure ground on one of the lake's small islands, but we steadily drew away from it towards a distant bridge through which the Purple Mountain was seen cloud-shadowed in the distance. Once under the bridge we drifted into the remoter part of the lake, where the lotus leaves clustered thickly on the surface of the water and the horizon was bounded by the grey line of the old city wall. A fish plopped here and there, and diamond gobbets of water rolled across the spreading lotus leaves slowly turned aside by our nosing prow. The sun shone brightly and we ate our sandwiches in an unbroken quiet between the lake and the skies, except for the sharp cry of a water bird squattering among the lotus leaves and the soft ripple of the water past our anchored boat.

We left Nanking the next morning at a very early hour, but the saffron-robed priests were already strolling or meditating in the hotel grounds, their garments clasped tightly around them. They had been there when we came and added a last echo to the mind's refrain: everything changes, nothing changes. The Shanghai train was crowded, and we were in one of those saloon coaches where everybody sat in fours with a small table between them. There were many army officers in our coach, including a young one who sat opposite us. Hearing us speak Chinese to the coach attendant, he invited us to join a game of cards which had begun at the table behind him and was attracting considerable attention from a circle of onlookers. Among them was a loud-voiced Shanghai type who could easily have passed as one of Tu Yueh-sheng's henchmen in the past with his close-cropped bullet head and "liberation" suiting in a natty, broad pin-striped serge that would not have disgraced his stocky form in the bad old days. We declined the game of cards, since neither of us knew a thing about them but thanked the officer for his friendly gesture. Further down the line we stopped at a station where people got out to buy small baskets of *p'i-p'a*, an apricotlike fruit. Somebody across the aisle offered us one, and the young officer leaned over and asked us, "Do you have *p'i-p'a* in Moscow, comrades?" I replied that we were from England, not Russia. The young officer looked startled and sat back with a rather subdued "Oh, English people." There was a noticeable silence, where a few moments ago chattiness had prevailed. It was not so much a question of unfriendliness to the English as people being suddenly thrown off balance with no precedent to set them back. Two English persons traveling unaccompanied on a Chinese train in 1956 was something for which they had no directives. For the remainder of the journey to Shanghai, we were discreetly but effectively omitted from the ongoing conversations as though we had never been there.

The Travel Service representative who met us at Shanghai was efficient to a degree; in no time at all he had our travel permits stamped by the station authorities and we were whisked off in a car to our hotel, the former Cathay Mansions. It encompassed a tall block of former luxury apartments in the French quarter, where the aura of old China-hand days hung over the somber mock Gothic of our eighth-floor suite. Our travel escort told us that the secretary of the China Dramatists Union would be returning with him at 3:30 P.M. to escort us to Yü Chen-fei's apartment and went off, leaving us to lunch in the hotel.

The secretary of the Union, Mr. Lu, turned out to be a pleasant young man, and we soon arrived at Yü Chen-fei's home, also in the old French quarter. The actor and his wife were waiting there and seemed delighted to see us, as indeed we were them, for Yü Chen-fei was a very close friend from the past. It was a happy reunion, although tinged with sadness, as it turned out. Mrs. Yü was not very well and suffering from "bronchitis," she told us, adding that she had got up especially from her sickbed that day to meet us for the important occasion. It was indeed that for us all because soon after we returned to Hongkong I received a letter from Yü Chen-fei telling us that unhappily his wife was dead of the cancer from which she was in fact suffering at the time.

Yü Chen-fei looked his usual immaculate self in his very dapper *chieh fang i-fu*, "liberation suit," smartly tailored in dove-grey barathea cloth similar to that worn by the actors in Peking. We sat and chatted around a glass-topped table, under which were displayed photographs of Yü with Mei Lan-fang in a film of *The White Snake* they had recently made. He brought out a poster I had once designed for a special performance he had given in Hongkong and showed it to Mr. Lu, the Union Secretary. I was touched to see how much he valued it as a souvenir. We toasted each other in the Czech cacao liqueur and apricot brandy Mrs. Yü brought out, after which Mr. Lu got up to go, saying that he would leave us to chat since we were old friends and promising to send around two tickets to our hotel for a special Shaohsing performance that evening.

From what Yü Chen-fei said, he had been principally concerned with making films with Mei Lan-fang and teaching since his return. Mei and Yü had been close colleagues for many years, and their joint four-days' *k'un-ch'ü* performance in Shanghai after the Japanese defeat in 1945 was a happy augury for the theatre world that the integrity of the old standards had been maintained. It was Mei who had been an instrumental factor in persuading Yü Chen-fei to return to Shanghai, for Yü had resisted going back longer than his other colleagues, being somewhat hesitant about the consequences and his bad standing with the authorities for having left China in the first place. Mrs. Yü told me that their fears had been groundless, since the communists had treated them well. They were provided their apartment by the government and Yü Chen-fei was paid a regular stipend whether he was acting or not. He was, however, strictly forbidden to leave the country on any pretext, and they were not allowed to change their apartment for one of their own choosing. She did add that a few months before they would never have been left alone to talk with us as they were doing then; that seemed a matter of great satisfaction which I did not attempt to dispel by pointing out that a few months before we would never have been allowed into China anyway. The readiness to see only the positive, while pushing aside matters suggesting an iron control of human liberty that ran far below the surface aspects of Chinese life, was

208

Yü Chen-fei, the celebrated hsiao-sheng actor and friend of the author

understandable to some extent, if disquieting to our Western convictions.

Two years before Yü Chen-fei's return to China, a new school to train young actors and actresses in *k'un-ch'ü* had been founded in a modest way and he was now associated with it. While we were chatting the phone rang to say the school was expecting us, so off we all went to pay a visit. I gathered the school was not normally in session on that particular day, but some of the stuents had been brought back since there were visitors. In addition to *k'un-ch'ü*, Shaohsing drama was taught there as being the principal "folk drama" of the area.

The students were in their second year but obviously too inexperienced as yet to show us anything very exciting. There was one class of girls giving a group demonstration of *hsiao-sheng*, "young hero," movements in Shaohsing style, while in the other class all boys were doing the same thing in *k'un-ch'ü* style. The girls seemed better than the boys at that particular juncture, I thought, but they were possibly all tired at being dragged back to show their paces. The school building itself was a rather ramshackle Western-style house far out in the suburbs.

Out of such modest beginnings an ambitious new group, the Shanghai City School of Peking and *K'un-ch'ü* Drama, was set up in 1960 with Yü Chen-fei as the president and artistic director of the Shanghai Youth Peking Drama Troupe—with which he travelled to Hongkong in 1962 for a month's run. By this time I was in the United States, but I heard the young actors were enthusiastically received and Yü Chen-fei himself was rapturously welcomed on his return by old friends.

After leaving the school, we took Yü Chen-fei and his wife back to their apartment and said goodbye after being asked to meet them for lunch the next day. We then hurried back to the hotel for a hasty meal before going on to the theatre. It had turned quite cold, and there was a kind of sea fret blowing up from the waterfront, creating a ghostly effect in the darkened streets. They were still busy but with people intent on a purpose, it seemed, whether hastening to a meeting, the theatre, or merely making for home. There were no night prowlers, no pleasure-seekers surging beneath the dazzle of the arc lights, no sounds of laughter or raised voices; people were subdued and even the streetcorner vendors of cigarettes, noodles, and bean curd seemed to conduct their business in a low key. That the communist authorities had done an amazing job of reform in a city whose streets had once been the kingdom of the depraved was indisputable, yet it seemed a pity that in casting out evil they left joylessness behind. The Shaohsing performance was at the old Lyceum Theatre where I had seen the last performance by Mei Lan-fang in 1948; its Western-style auditorium had remained much the same except for being considerably better kept than it had been on that occasion. I have spoken of the Shaohsing drama before. It was a regional style very popular in the Shanghai area that from its earliest origins as a simple rural entertainment underwent many changes. In the course of centuries, it was transformed into a theatrical form performed entirely by women. It became noted for its lachrymal repertoire, the splendor of its costumes, and the excellence of its women performers, who caught the fancy of audiences long appreciative of the finer points of sexual metamorphosis in a dramatic context. It was a very popular entertainment among middle-class women theatregoers, who were not averse to a "good cry" in their theatre and loved the costumed spectacle.

In 1942 there were some new patterns of performance established by a very talented actress, Yüan Hsueh-fen, under whose direction modern scenery and lighting were introduced and individual writers and directors were invited to work for her theatre, which had always tended to be more realistic than the traditional Peking style — upon which it drew quite freely for many of its approaches. They began staging plays that, although set in a historic past, criticized present-day social problems and injustices by implication. This was a well-tried device in China, understood by all, and when aimed at Mao Tse-tung himself in the play *The Dismissal of Hai Jui* by Wu Han staged in 1961, raised a storm of events which finally led to the excesses of Mao's Cultural Revolution.

When the communists took over Shanghai, the Shaohsing troupes were reorganized and passed through a period of "proletarian" drama. Eventually a new company called the Shanghai Experimental Shaohsing Group was formed, led by Yüan Hsueh-fen, and it was this troupe we saw. One of their plays was a Shaohsing version of a popular new Peking drama in traditional style called *Women Generals of the Yang Family*. The theme concerned the patriotic Yang family, four generations of which fought against foreign invaders and were all killed in battle, leaving twelve widows. When opinion at court then became divided as to whether they should continue resistance or not, the aged great-grandmother of the Yangs volunteered to lead the fight against the enemy; with the help of the other women of the family, she drove out the invaders. The play had the advantage of satisfying current patriotic sentiments and at the same time providing some colorful and vigorous stage action in traditional vein, although Yüan Hsueh-fen did not take part herself. She incidentally gained distinction in the 1950s for her performance as the heroine in the film *Liang Shan-po and Chu Ying-t'ai* based on a Shaohsing theme, which won considerable international acclaim and was perhaps the first truly successful attempt to translate a traditional style of Chinese drama into film terms. This may have been due to the more realistic nature of the Shaohsing acting style itself.

The productions that we saw were well staged and skillfully co-ordinated. They had the "new look" certainly with their Westernized stage sets, music, and immaculate costumes. But I must admit I found something a little synthetic in the new production methods, and Shaohsing drama was not a form that had the strongest appeal for me. What I did admire was the utter devotion and intensity of those actresses to their craft. The vibrancy and energy of their individual performances, together with the complete involvement evident in every move that they made or sound they uttered, was justification enough for not missing that occasion.

The next day Yü Chen-fei and his wife called to take us to lunch. We were to catch a train at 3 P.M. because we were making a stop overnight at Hangchow on our way to Canton and with funds now getting perilously low, we had to be on our way. It was an interesting lunch party, held in a well-known restaurant which was packed. We sat at a large, round table in the center of a room which we shared with two other parties. Gone was the private room for one's special guests of the old days; now everybody shared their parties together. Besides Yü Chen-fei and his wife, there were present Mr. Lu of the Chinese Dramatists Union; a pupil of Yü Chen-fei; a silent young man who looked after all the practical details, the dogsbody that every leading actor seemed to have; and Fu Shih-ta, a bohemian painter we had known in former days who had been calling on us when the Yü's arrived at our hotel and so was included in the party. He was the last person I had expected to see, for he was an individualist belonging to no particular school or style who had always gone his own free way. Curiously enough, he seemed to have managed to survive without any drastic changes in his way of life. Whether events eventually overtook him in his freedom I do not know; he told us that he had never written to many of his English friends because letters were opened, and English people always asked lots of questions about other people they had known in China, he added wryly. Finally we were joined by Ma Shih-tseng, the veteran Hongkong actor, and his former wife Hung Hsien-nu, both of them leading figures on the Cantonese stage. They had been invited to China to further a new plan of reform for the traditional Cantonese theatre now sunk into such low repute in Hongkong. *The Runaway Maid*, a revised play based on a traditional script, had just been given a successful premiere in Peking with Ma Shih-tseng and Hung Hsien-nu in the leading roles. She had been studying *hsiao-sheng* techniques with Yü Chen-fei in connection with her part in the play. They were in process of making a film of it before returning to Canton. The traditional Cantonese theatre had common roots with the Peking style, but the singing conventions and acting forms were less rigid than in the northern theatre, and the natural voice was used instead of the Peking-style falsetto. In addition, many local southern folk tunes had been incorporated in the Cantonese texts, while the structures of dialogue and recitative were influenced by the different range of tones in Cantonese — six instead of four, as in Peking dialect. In short, the individual quality of the traditional Cantonese theatre owed everything to its musical-vocal elements, and it was these that Ma Shih-tseng and Hung Hsien-nu had been working to restore in response to the saxophone-dominated wailing of the Hongkong form. I eventually saw the film they made, and it certainly justified the claims made for a new dignity in Cantonese performance. An incident in the play called for the heroine to be disguised as a young scholar; it was in order to perfect her style for this that Hung Hsien-nu had studied *hsiao-sheng* techniques with Yü Chen-fei, and his influence on the actress's performance was clearly visible.

Both Ma Shih-tseng and Hung Hsien-nu spoke fluent Peking dialect and some English, so they added sparkle to the luncheon party. Looking back on it now, the event was a unique encounter in bringing together three such prominent yet different personalities of the Chinese theatre, an occasion to have made stagedoor fans turn green with envy.

Ma Shih-tseng looked the complete Hongkong dandy with his jaunty Panama hat, spotless Palm Beach suit, and shining gold wrist watch. He had long been the idol of the Hongkong stage and was regarded as a brilliant and versatile actor — too versatile, some thought, in meeting the commercial demands of the Hongkong stage and the hotchpotch tastes of the city's playgoers. That he had been brought back to China in order to help restore the old-style Cantonese drama to some of its former glory was nevertheless a measure of his high standing as an actor.

Hung Hsien-nu was informally dressed in slacks and blouse; she was small with an extremely vivacious personality and most expressive eyes. Born in the Portuguese colony of Macao, she first went on the stage when she was fifteen. Ma Shih-tseng had seen her and, taking an interest in her work, subsequently encouraged her development as an actress. She was extremely popular with the public and after the war worked a great deal in films. Among them all *The Runaway Maid* probably did most justice to her delicacy and grace as a traditional performer.

Soon it was time for us to leave. Ma Shih-tseng and Hung Hsien-nu offered to drive us back to our hotel in their car, and Yü Chen-fei insisted on coming with us. We said farewell to the others at the restaurant and bade the Cantonese actor and his wife goodbye at the entrance to the hotel, where our efficient Travel Service man was waiting for us. The four of us got to the station just in time and scrambled aboard the very crowded train with our luggage, a seat having been found for us. In no time at all, we were pulling out of the station. Yü Chen-fei stood waving until he was lost to view, a warm and somehow moving farewell to the theatre people with whom we had passed so many rewarding hours.

We were to make an overnight stop at Hangchow on our way out of China while the opportunity existed to catch a glimpse of the West Lake again, since we did not know if we should ever get back that way. One of the most hackneyed proverbs in the Chinese vocabulary runs, "Heaven above, Hangchow and Soochow below." In fact, Hangchow turned out to be the least heavenly experience of the whole trip. We arrived at 3 P.M. to find no one was meeting our train. All travel arrangements were made in advance between the various city offices, and we depended on being met to know where we were to stay. The officials were in general quite efficient; until then only those in Nanking had missed their cue. It had grown very hot and we were a little emotionally drained after Shanghai. A helpful station attendant went off to search and returned with a surly-looking character who seemed utterly and openly indifferent to our presence yet whom the attendant assured us was our man. We set off to his curt beckoning, he keeping well in front of us to avoid contamination until we had completed passport formalities. By then he grudgingly allowed his name was Lu. He led us to our hotel, a rather ugly, vast new building on the far side of the lake. Our room was hot, unventilated, with no view, obviously one of the worst in the hotel. We began to realize we had been singled out for a little petty obstructionism. After thirty minutes arguing, we persuaded the room boy to find us a cooler, less expensive room and went to confirm with the reception desk where a large sign in Russian, Chinese, French, and English proclaimed "information." But the sign itself was the nearest to any information we could get; there was not a soul to be found. The impression had grown during our stay that all hotels were staffed by very young people and if they were good, they were very good — but if they were bad, they were like a lot of sulky adolescents.

We found the dining room, cheap brown stain on its floors, a stage at one end draped with a garish, green silk curtain, and full of bamboo chairs and tables. It looked like a second-rate hotel in an English seaside resort at the end of the season. We were served cold chicken salad and beer, but at least the waiter was on speaking terms with his guests. At a nearby table there was a party of Russians drinking a great deal of wine followed by tipsy speeches of comradeship relayed by two Chinese translators for several of their compatriots in the party. Otherwise we were the only diners in a place conspicuously empty of guests. Next morning we were up early, somewhat dismayed that our short trip to Hangchow had become so disappointing. The surly Lu appeared and began to badger us about hiring a car, an interpreter, and a boat on the lake. We let him order the latter, since that was what we were mainly there for. It had become quite obvious that Hangchow was no place for "do-it-yourself" visitors to expect willing cooperation; they evidently were viewed as threats to the professionals. The boatwoman was hired; we took some sandwiches and set off in a pleasant little craft with a table in the center, at which we sat facing each other. Soon we were far out on the glassy surface of the tranquil lake set between cypress-studded hills, the obnoxious Mr. Lu well forgotten in the sublimity of our surroundings and the great calm of the sky and water between which we seemed to float gently in a void. We landed on a small island studded with pavilions laid out with the elegance and symmetry favored by the ancients who understandably had once made the glorious lake their haunt of pleasure. Returning to our boat, we sailed on, remote from everything, with only dragonflies skimming the lake's surface to break the sense of infinite tranquility and relaxation.

We stayed out on the lake three hours and then returned to pack and wait for Lu, scheduled to appear at 5 P.M. but predictably conspicuous by his absence. We were about to set off for the station ourselves in desperation when he sauntered in, calling out to the reception desk to make sure we had been charged for two nights' stay. He then proceeded to ensure that we were double-charged for everything else when he presented the bills for our general expenses. It took far more of our dwindling cash than we had bargained for, and because of Lu's tardiness we were late at the station. Since the passport office and waiting rooms were closed, we had difficulty getting our documents stamped. Fortunately the train was late and it was with few regrets that we climbed aboard. "Heaven above, Hangchow and the deplorable Lu below," would have seemed an apter version of the proverb at that particular moment.

But Hangchow was soon forgotten on the train. The attendants were courtesy personified, and we were sharing our sleeping compartment with two most affable Chinese travelers. They left the train for their destination in the small hours, and from then on we had the luxury of the compartment to ourselves all the way to Canton. We were the only two foreigners on the train, and the dining car people were worried because they had not been warned and were carrying nothing to suit Western tastes. When we told them we preferred Chinese food anyway, they were all smiles and came to our compartment and consulted us with the menu before every mealtime as though it were for the Emperor himself. Not a very appropriate simile for a Marxist state, perhaps, but it was also China. When we entered the dining car for breakfast the first morning, there sitting at a table near us was the young officer on the Shanghai train who had asked about the availability of *p'i-p'a* in Moscow. He jumped up immediately, came over, and shook hands while making an affable query as to our welfare. Everybody smiled and harmony was restored to the universe. The day turned hot as we raced towards the damp heat of the south. Outside paddy fields stretched away on either side of the train, interminable patchworks of symmetrical cultivation with not an inch of ground wasted. Even the narrow pathways between the rice plots were planted with beans. Heavy raindrops beat against the carriage windows, and lightning flashed across a countryside shrouded with the driving torrents of a storm. Then the sun appeared again, and a long line of black ducks was visible waddling slowly along a narrow path between the rice fields, where straw-hatted men and women bent to their unceasing labors knee-deep in the squares of wetness. A group of peasants clambered up a grassy slope, bearing a large red coffin suspended from a pole supported on the shoulders of

Peasant funeral, Hunan Province, viewed from the train

two people, behind whom a third member clashing cymbals led a small group of mourners. Earth to earth.

We arrived at Canton promptly at 7:30 A.M. The train crew brought us their criticism book to sign. We could only give them praise; we all shook hands and our journey was done. We were met by Miss Ho of the Travel Service and a friend of past days, a university professor whom we had notified of our arrival, since we had failed to contact him at the beginning of our trip. They had a car and drove us to the Ai Kuan Hotel, from where we had first set out on a journey which now seemed years ago.

We had a shower and changed, then went to lunch with our friend in an old-style galleried restaurant with a courtyard in the center. It was designated Food Week in Canton, and the court-yard was devoted to an exhibition that consisted of glass cases containing varnished wooden models of different kinds of local food, rather like the displays one saw outside small eating places and railway station buffets in Japan. In the center of the court-yard among all the glass cases stood a model of an extraordinar-ily ornate, five-tiered, Western-style wedding cake, with an ear-nest young woman explaining the contents to a staring group. We were shown into a private room off one of the galleries. The lunch was in *yam-cha* style; that is to say, waiters and waitresses came round bearing trays containing individual portions of dif-ferent delicacies from which the diner made his selection. Can-tonese *yam-cha* is a unique meal of its kind, very popular among both Chinese and foreign customers and with good cause. In spite of Food Week, the *yam-cha* on that occasion was a little dull. We had the opportunity to say so at the end of the meal when the waiter brought around his criticism book for our com-ments, but that would have been discourteous to our host and was not of very great concern in any case. Had it been Hang-chow, it might have been a different matter, but we never saw a sign of a criticism book there.

Our host seemed a little ill-at-ease in the way we had noticed when meeting another university acquaintance in Peking and put up the same nervous defence of anything that bordered on criti-cism. He was a man we had known very well in the past, first met on the ship sailing to China. A scholar of some repute, he was fa-miliar with Western ways and had studied in both America and England; in Nanking he had been a constant visitor to our house.

Yet he did not seem interested in what we had been doing all this time or what we had seen in China. When questioned, he was reluctant in reply. He justified political indoctrination of students, asserted that they could get any Western books whenever they wanted—although the evidence from all we had seen in China was to the contrary; he even rejected our accounts of people's behavior at Hangchow, condoning it by saying it must have been something in our manner. Occasionally there were flashes of his former self, and for old times' sake he was obviously doing his best. But there was something ambivalent in his behavior, whether it was asserting that everything was now unconditionally for the best in their new society or resorting to the by-then familiar argument that everybody was too busy getting on with their work and therefore had no time for anything else. We tried to persuade him to have dinner with us that evening after driving back to his campus, but he pleaded that he had a meeting and had to see a student within the hour. He walked back to the car with us and we said goodbye. He added that he had been happy to meet us again, but everything in his manner suggested he was relieved to see us go.

We returned to our hotel, where our efficient Miss Ho arrived to tell us that all our travel arrangements were in order for the next day—the hotel would awaken us at 5:30 A.M. and she would be around to take us to the station. We decided to have an early night; our money was all spent and the one desire now was to be on our way. A sudden shower spattered against the window and ceased as quickly as it had begun. The moon came up high over the river, and the hooting of ships' sirens haunted the restless half-sleeping, half-waking which precedes the traveler's early morning start.

True to her word, Miss Ho met us on the dot and had us seated on the train half an hour before departure, where she said her goodbye as precisely and punctiliously as everything else she did. The train soon filled with the noisy, loud-voiced Cantonese in their pajama suits and black pongee loaded with baskets and bundles as they returned from family visits, everyone talking at the top of their voice without pause or hindrance. Already the atmosphere was quite different from our traveling in the rest of China, as amid the babel of voices the train drew out of the station and we were on our way back to the outside world.

219

Before we arrived at Shumchum, all tickets were collected and the railway policeman and conductors began counting the number of passengers head by head, a process laboriously completed before anyone was allowed off the train. When the train came to a stop, we sat until the surging crowd had been disgorged and then stepped down to meet the last of our long series of couriers, waiting for us on the platform. We were taken to the waiting room where we had begun our travels and filled in all the necessary forms before moving forward to baggage inspection. While in Peking I had bought some old costumes quite cheaply, including a silk dragon robe of the kind high officials used to send as tribute to the palace. It was rather worn but quite a rare costume, for which I paid the equivalent of forty U.S. dollars; I wanted it as a museum piece, nothing more. The new communist ruling was that no one was allowed to take anything out of China over one hundred years old, and the robe was certainly more than that. I placed it in the bottom of my suitcase and decided to trust to chance. If the robe was impounded, so much the worse; if not, all to the good. Soon I was next in the line, and the customs officer beckoned me to open the case in which the robe was packed and began to turn over the contents. He seized upon the copy of Mei Lan-fang's book the actor had presented to me in Peking. Seeing the inscription on the fly-leaf, he turned to me with a face transformed. "You know Mei Lan-fang, comrade?" he inquired. I assured him that I did. Expressing his admiration of the famous actor, he carefully replaced the volume, closed the lid of my suitcase, and smilingly waved me on.

INDEX

DESIGNED BY ED FRANK
COMPOSED BY METRICOMP, GRUNDY CENTER, IOWA
MANUFACTURED BY EDWARDS BROTHERS, INC.,
ANN ARBOR, MICHIGAN
TEXT AND DISPLAY LINES ARE SET IN PALATINO

Ⓦ

Library of Congress Cataloging in Publication Data
Scott, A. C. (Adolphe Clarence), 1909–
Actors are madmen.
Includes index.
1. Theater — China — History — 20th century.
2. Chinese drama — 20th century — History and
criticism. 3. China — Description and travel —
1901–1948. I. Title.
PN2874.S36   792'.0951   81-70013
ISBN 0-299-08860-X   AACR2